Democratizing Finance

The Real Utopias Project

Series editor: Erik Olin Wright

The Real Utopias Project embraces a tension between dreams and practice. It is founded on the belief that what is pragmatically possible is not fixed independently of our imaginations, but is itself shaped by our visions. The fulfillment of such a belief involves "real utopias"—utopian ideals grounded in the real potentials for redesigning social institutions.

In its attempt at sustaining and deepening serious discussion of radical alternatives to existing social practices, the Real Utopias Project examines various basic institutions—property rights and the market, secondary associations, the family, the welfare state, among others—and focuses on specific proposals for their fundamental redesign. The books in the series are the result of workshop conferences, at which groups of scholars respond to provocative manuscripts.

Democratizing Finance

Restructuring Credit to Transform Society

Fred Block and Robert Hockett

with contributions by
Robert Hockett, Fred Block,
William H. Simon, David Woodruff,
Michael A. McCarthy, Sarah Quinn,
Mark Igra, Selen Güler,
Mary Mellor, Lenore Palladino

and a preface by
Erik Olin Wright

Edited and introduced by
Fred Block

VERSO
London • New York

First published by Verso 2022
Collection © Verso 2022
Contributions © Contributors 2022

All rights reserved

The moral rights of the editor and authors have been asserted

1 3 5 7 9 10 8 6 4 2

Verso
UK: 6 Meard Street, London W1F 0EG
US: 20 Jay Street, Suite 1010, Brooklyn, NY 11201
versobooks.com

Verso is the imprint of New Left Books

ISBN-13: 978-1-83976-267-3
ISBN-13: 978-1-83976-268-0 (UK EBK)
ISBN-13: 978-1-83976-269-7 (US EBK)

British Library Cataloguing in Publication Data
A catalogue record for this book is available from the British Library

Library of Congress Control Number: 2021948551

Typeset in Sabon by MJ&N Gavan, Truro, Cornwall
Printed and bound by CPI Group (UK) Ltd, Croydon CR0 4YY

Contents

Preface: The Real Utopias Project, *Erik Olin Wright* — vii
Acknowledgments — x
Introduction: The Meaning of Financial
   Democratization, *Fred Block* — 1

I. Anchor Essays
1. Finance without Financiers, *Robert Hockett* — 23
2. Financial Democratization and the Transition to
   Socialism, *Fred Block* — 80

II. The Politics of Financial Reform
3. Economic Democracy and Enterprise Form in
   Finance, *William H. Simon* — 119
4. To Democratize Finance, Democratize Central
   Banking, *David M. Woodruff* — 138
5. Three Modes of Democratic Participation in Finance,
   Michael A. McCarthy — 159

III. Alternative Financial Visions
6. "A Modern Financial Tool Kit": Lessons from
   Adolf A. Berle for a More Democratic Financial
   System, *Sarah Quinn, Mark Igra, and Selen Güler* — 189
7. Democratizing Finance or Democratizing Money?
   Mary Mellor — 223
8. Democratizing Investment, *Lenore Palladino* — 244

Concluding Observations, *Fred Block* — 268
Notes — 276
Name Index — 311

Preface

The Real Utopias Project

Erik Olin Wright

The current era is characterized by two widely held feelings among people living in the developed capitalist world and much of the rest of the world as well. On the one hand capitalism seems exhausted, incapable of generating widespread prosperity and security; stagnation, crisis, deepening inequality, and precariousness are the new norms. On the other hand, despite this, capitalism seems triumphant, an implacable force of nature; there is no alternative. This dismal diagnosis both of the world as it is and of the world as it might be underwrites a politics of despair rather than hope.

This is the context in which elaborating coherent alternatives to capitalism becomes ever more urgent. The Real Utopias Project was begun in the early 1990s in response to this challenge. The general idea of the project is to explore alternatives to existing institutions of domination and inequality. These alternatives (1) embody our deepest aspirations for a just and humane world—thus "utopia," and (2) can to a greater or lesser extent be built in the world as it is, prefiguring the world as it could be, and moving us in that direction, thus "real." The objective is to formulate visions for radical alternatives embodying the emancipatory values of democracy, equality, and solidarity that also specify realistic steps for solving existing problems.

PREFACE

Finance poses a particularly sharp challenge to the idea of "real utopia." Proposals for real utopias are different from simple ameliorative reforms that just try to improve conditions of life in the world as it is; real utopias try to begin the task of transcending the existing structures of domination and inequality by building pieces of an emancipatory alternative in a world that could be within the spaces where this is possible in the world as it is. The question for finance, then, is this: *what institutional designs for a more democratic and egalitarian financial system can be instituted in the present that plausibly prefigure a radically democratic economy beyond capitalism?* This book in the Real Utopias Project is an attempt to grapple with this problem.

Criticism by political progressives of the financial systems of capitalist economies are familiar: the system disproportionately benefits the rich and powerful and contributes to growing inequality within contemporary capitalist societies; existing financial systems misallocate investments toward speculation and away from projects that would broadly benefit society as a whole; financial institutions, especially those controlling vast amounts of capital, expose large numbers of people to risks not of their choosing; and the dynamics of financial markets concentrate power in the hands of the wealthy, thus more broadly undermining democracy. This is powerful criticism.

What critics on the left generally lack is a comparable understanding of the sorts of changes in financial institutions that would best advance emancipatory values. To be sure, there are many solid ameliorative proposals for financial reforms that would significantly improve things within capitalist systems. What is lacking are systematic discussions of institutional design by radical critics of capitalism whose visions are not simply to make capitalism work better, but to transcend capitalism. Progressive critics of capitalism have much to say about transforming power relations within firms (e.g., worker cooperatives or stakeholder boards of directors), redesigning the system of income distribution (e.g., unconditional basic income), democratizing democracy (e.g., participatory budgeting or sortation assemblies), new forms of post-market productive cooperation (e.g.,

Preface

peer-to-peer collaborative production), and many other aspects of economic and political institutions. But about finance, there is generally little beyond standard views of the need for strong regulation and breaking up banks that are "too big to fail."

Democratizing Finance is an attempt to push progressive discussion of finance in new directions by exploring the real utopian idea that it is possible to do more than simply use the power of the state to regulate capitalist finance in ways that dampen its most harmful effects. New institutional designs for finance can point beyond capitalism itself.

Acknowledgments

Erik Olin Wright passed away in January of 2019. However, this volume is a result of his meticulous work over an extended period of time. Wright hosted an informal workshop in Madison, Wisconsin, in May of 2016 where Robert Hockett and Fred Block presented earlier versions of the anchor papers that appear in this volume. Both authors were given extensive feedback and instructions to complete improved versions by the spring of 2017. Those drafts were then circulated to ten potential commentators, who were invited to a more formal conference held in Madison in July 2018. Erik's preface to this volume is taken from the invitation he wrote to invite participants to that conference. By the time of the conference, however, Erik had been diagnosed with acute myeloid leukemia, and he was only able to join us remotely for some welcoming remarks. However, Erik continued to provide input until his death.

As with previous volumes in the Real Utopias Project, we are grateful to the Wisconsin Alumni Research Foundation and the Anonymous Fund of the University of Wisconsin for supporting the conference that led to this volume. We are also grateful to the staff of what is now the Havens Wright Center for Social Justice at the University of Wisconsin for help with the logistics of the workshop and the conference.

Earlier versions of a number of the papers included in this volume were published in a special issue of *Politics & Society*, copyright Sage Publications, Inc., 2019, and are reproduced here with permission. They are:

Acknowledgments

Chapter 1, Robert Hockett, "Finance without Financiers," *Politics & Society* 47, 4 (December 2019), 491–527.

Chapter 2, Fred Block, "Financial Democratization and the Transition to Socialism," ibid., 529–56.

Chapter 3, William H. Simon, "Economic Democracy and Enterprise Form in Finance," ibid., 557–71.

Chapter 4, David M. Woodruff, "To Democratize Finance, Democratize Central Banking," ibid., 593–610.

Chapter 5, Michael A. McCarthy, "Three Modes of Democratic Participation in Finance," ibid., 611–33.

Chapter 7, Mary Mellor, "Democratizing Finance or Democratizing Money?", ibid., 635–50.

Chapter 8, Lenore Palladino, "Democratizing Investment," ibid., 573–91.

Introduction

The Meaning of Financial Democratization

Fred Block

This book intervenes in a long-standing debate about how finance should be organized and how credit should be allocated among different people and different projects. Deep conflicts over the organization of banking, finance, and access to credit have a very long history. The Catholic Church banned the practice of charging interest on loans for centuries, and a similar prohibition is still maintained by many Islamic authorities. In those places where modern economic growth took off in the nineteenth and twentieth centuries, hostility toward and distrust of bankers and moneylenders was common and intense. Images of nefarious bankers with octopus-like tentacles were used by both those on the political left and anti-Semitic movements on the right. This hostility reached a crescendo during the Great Depression of the 1930s when bankers and financiers were blamed for the miseries of mass unemployment, hunger, and mass evictions.[1]

In the crucible of the 1930s and 1940s, debates about restructuring the financial system were particularly broad ranging and intense. Moreover, politicians of many different viewpoints carried out significant restructuring of national financial institutions. There was also a broad consensus that the restoration of the international gold standard after World War I had contributed to the severity of the Great Depression.[2] So during World War II, Franklin Roosevelt and Winston Churchill recognized that a reform of the global financial system was an urgent necessity in planning for the postwar period. They set in motion the process that led to the Bretton Woods Conference, which created the International Monetary Fund and the World Bank.

The new financial arrangements that were cobbled together both at the national and the global level helped establish a framework for thirty years of relatively stable economic growth in the United States, Western Europe, and Japan. The reforms and regulations imposed in the 1930s and 1940s were largely successful in curbing the excesses of speculative activity that had fed the stock market crash in 1929. However, the unfortunate consequence of this success was that those previously intense debates about the organization of banking and finance either disappeared or moved to the margins of politics.

The great irony is that these successes effectively lulled people to sleep; the politics of finance ceased to be an urgent political issue. This made it possible for financial interests to dismantle the reforms and regulations that had kept speculative activity in check. Step by step, starting in the 1970s, and accelerating in each successive decade, US policymakers embarked on a process of financialization of the US economy and the global economy.[3] Financial activity as a share of the total economy and as a share of profits began a dramatic rise. Most spectacularly, the total nominal value of derivatives, including bets on the future direction of interest rates, reached $640 trillion by 2019.

We know now, however, that this process of financialization dramatically increased the fragility of the global economy. This was painfully demonstrated by the severity of the 2008–2009 global financial crisis and the prolonged process of recovery.[4] The fact is that the global financial system has teetered on the edge of complete collapse twice in just twelve years.

Introduction

The first crisis

The first crisis began in 2008 right after a prolonged increase in the price of US residential housing had come to an abrupt end. Wall Street firms had met strong demand by investors—both in the US and abroad—for safe bonds by packaging US mortgages into collateralized mortgage obligations.[5] However, as the quantity of new prime or high-quality mortgages began to fall, the firms began to package together subprime loans, most of which were going to black and brown homeowners. Many of these loans had initial low "teaser" interest rates that would reset to substantially higher rates over time or after a late payment. Salespeople fanned out through black and brown neighborhoods to offer homeowners the opportunity to refinance their houses at seemingly attractive interest rates. The deals were sometimes sweetened with an initial cash payment to the homeowner since rising home prices had increased the value of homes in these neighborhoods. This predatory and racist lending was a profitable business as long as housing prices were rising. When a family could no longer keep up payments on the loan, the house could be sold at a profit to another family that could be signed up for yet another subprime loan.

Transforming subprime mortgages into AAA bonds depended on the cooperation of the bond rating agencies. Cooperation was forthcoming because the agencies were being paid by the same investment banks that were packaging these securities. If firms issuing the ratings were too fussy about the worthiness of a particular offering, they risked losing their business to a competitor. Meanwhile, banking regulators around the world relied on these private, for-profit, credit rating agencies as they assessed the balance sheets of financial institutions. In short, they outsourced their work to private firms that could easily be corrupted.

In some cities and some states, the authorities tried to clamp down on this expansion of predatory lending that targeted the same minority neighborhoods that had earlier been victimized by banks that refused to lend on any terms. However, the mortgage industry was successful in getting federal authorities to insist that the regulation of mortgage lending was exclusively a federal prerogative. Meanwhile, the leadership at the Federal Reserve Bank ignored warnings that the rise in home prices and the big expansion in mortgage lending was an unsustainable and dangerous bubble.

In 2007, the long rise in residential housing prices came to an end and prices began to decline. The impact was felt immediately by both prime and subprime borrowers, many of whom now owed more on their mortgages than their houses were worth. But it was default rates on subprime mortgages that rose most quickly. Those default rates were far in excess of the worst case the financial engineers had planned for. The consequence was that the value of those AAA bonds based on subprime mortgages fell precipitously, so the assets that banks and other financial institutions were holding as safe and reliable investments were transformed overnight into toxic sludge that nobody would purchase at any price. Moreover, the uncertainty, especially over rising default rates, cast a shadow on all of the mortgage-based bonds.

As the banking crisis grew, the US authorities sought to contain it by discretely rescuing some of the failing financial entities. However, when negotiations to rescue Lehman Brothers broke down in September 2008, its bankruptcy set in motion a general panic. Many firms were directly impacted because Lehman owed them money, but others around the world were forced to look more closely at their balance sheets. When they made the appropriate adjustment for the declining value of their mortgage bond portfolios, their liabilities now exceeded their assets. In both cases, the result was the same: financial firms needed to halt any new lending and husband the resources they had in hand.

An almost instantaneous halt in new credits caused the global economy to seize up. Financing of exports and imports was no longer available, so global trade dropped sharply. Firms, both big and small, lost their access to new credit and started limiting their outlays. They responded by reducing the number of people they employed, and with rising unemployment, consumer demand began to slide. The global economy was in free fall.

Introduction

Rescuing the global economy from free fall required heroic measures. The US Congress passed a $700 billion package in October 2008 to rescue the banks by helping them remove the toxic sludge of mortgage bonds from their balance sheets. Less visibly, the Federal Reserve Bank opened its spigots to lend vast amounts to financial institutions around the world. Through one window alone, the Term Auction Facility, the Fed made loans of $3.8 trillion, the majority of which went to foreign banks.[6]

Moreover, governments around the world also enacted tax cuts and emergency spending programs to get the global economy restarted. The Obama administration's American Recovery and Reinvestment Act designated $831 billion to revive the economy. The Chinese stimulus bill promised to spend $586 billion over two years, and similarly large initiatives occurred in Europe. In addition, the International Monetary Fund distributed $250 billion worth of special drawing rights (SDRs) to member nations in the fall of 2009. This was the first use of SDRs since 1981. This distribution augmented each nation's international currency reserves, so that governments could pursue stimulus without the standard worries of depleting their reserves.

Together, these efforts were successful in restarting the global economy. But the pain continued through the recovery, as it took years for elevated levels of unemployment to come down. In a number of countries, borrowers still had to cope with high levels of mortgage debt taken on before the crisis, although the US was unique in that it suffered an annual rate of more than a million homes foreclosed every year from 2007 through 2015.

The response to the global financial crisis followed a familiar pattern. No matter how recklessly they had loaned or invested funds, banks were rescued, while ordinary citizens ended up paying the bills. Moreover, there were even deeper levels of injustice. Banks and other financial institutions had been the leaders of the parade toward ever-higher compensation for top executives. Hedge funds, for example, were the first to report that some of their top managers earned more than a billion dollars per year.

Just as the world was beginning to recover from the global financial crisis, the European debt crisis erupted in 2010.

Portugal, Ireland, Italy, Greece, Spain, and Cyprus had relied heavily on foreign capital both to finance government deficits and for private borrowing, including mortgage lending. German and French banks were on the other end of many of these deals and their solvency would again be problematic if these investments turned bad. So the institutions of the European Community launched rescue efforts that provided public funds in exchange for governments pursuing aggressive austerity efforts. The rescues provided disproportionate benefits to the German and French banks, which were able to reduce their exposure to these countries. However, austerity measures led to high levels of unemployment as well as forced cuts in government spending in Spain, Italy, and Greece.

A second looming crisis

Another near financial crisis occurred in early 2020 as the spread of the COVID-19 virus disrupted financial markets. As one nation after another required people to stay at home and socially distance, there were sudden drops in employment, economic output, and international trade. Many nations quickly took emergency action to maintain employment and consumer purchasing power. However, the danger was acute that these protective measures could be overwhelmed by another meltdown in the tightly coupled global financial system.

Such a meltdown was narrowly averted in March of 2020. Wealthy investors from around the world have invested at least $2.5 trillion in US-based hedge funds that often pursue risky and unconventional investment strategies to produce higher rates of return. One such strategy is to make highly leveraged bets on the future of interest rates, making use of funds borrowed in the repo market. (This is an institution set up to allow banks and other financial institutions to borrow from each other over the short term using Treasury bonds as collateral through repurchase agreements. However, as Robert Hockett shows in his contribution to this volume, since multiple parties can borrow on the same bonds, the amount of credit creation is virtually unlimited.) But as financial markets were rocked by the pandemic, interest rates suddenly moved in the wrong direction and these hedge funds faced huge losses.[7]

The collapse of a number of large hedge funds could easily have set off the same kind of chain reaction as the Lehman Brothers bankruptcy did in 2008. Since hedge funds borrowed billions from big banks, those banks would suddenly have holes in their balance sheet and would have to suspend new lending, creating new shocks for an already vulnerable global economy. This time, however, the Federal Reserve recognized the danger and stepped in with huge purchases of government bonds. This pushed interest rates in the anticipated direction and saved the hedge funds from disaster. While the Dodd-Frank legislation was supposed to put an end to government bailouts, the Fed quietly bailed out the high-risk and lightly regulated hedge fund industry.

While the Fed's actions were successful in March of 2020, the risks of another financial chain reaction are considerable. Corporate debt levels reached a record high of $13.5 trillion globally at the end of 2019.[8] The longer the pandemic lasts, the greater the chance that defaults on those debts will mount. Actions by governments and central banks might be able to cushion the impact of such defaults on the financial system, but the authorities could be overwhelmed by the magnitude of the problem and constrained by the amount of emergency lending they had previously undertaken.

Beyond instability

The threat posed by global financial instability is reason enough to revive the debates over the organization of finance that were widespread in the 1930s and 1940s. However, there are two other factors driving a return of financial reform proposals. First, there is the looming threat of a global climate catastrophe caused by continuing use of fossil fuels. Finance, both nationally and globally, has been heavily implicated in the petroleum economy, supporting exploration, pipelines, and shipping, and sustaining the world's major oil-producing states. Moreover, existing financial institutions have been extremely reluctant to redirect capital flows to support renewable energy and conservation initiatives.

It follows that the calls around the world by activists and some politicians for a "Green New Deal" must be understood as projects of fundamental financial reform. The goal is to create barriers to the flow of capital into the fossil fuel economy, while simultaneously creating channels through which financial investments will flow to clean energy, retrofitting of existing structures, and energy conservation. Different advocates have different strategies for achieving these dual objectives, but there is a broad consensus that the climate crisis cannot be addressed without substantial restructuring of finance both within countries and globally.

Finally, the COVID-19 pandemic has demonstrated that investment patterns around the world have neglected pressing human needs. Many societies have shortchanged the funding of the public health system with the consequence that the pandemic has put a severe strain on existing medical resources. The world's poor people are often crowded into inadequate housing that makes effective social distancing impossible. In the United States, when schools moved from in-person to online, two previously hidden inequalities could no longer be ignored: millions of children depend on meals provided in schools to get enough to eat, and many also lack the hardware or the internet connection needed to take advantage of remote instruction.

Moreover, in the United States, the heavy toll of the disease in black, brown, and Native American communities has also focused public attention on the extreme inequalities in the distribution of wealth.[9] The legacies of slavery, dispossession, and racial apartheid are reflected in the different accumulation of wealth across ethnic lines. So when the police murder of George Floyd in Minneapolis in May of 2020 produced a vast upsurge in protests, the demands of the protesters were not confined to defunding the police and reforming the criminal justice system. There were calls for fundamental financial reform that would

Introduction

reverse the disparities in wealth between white families and black, brown, and Native American families.[10]

The combination of financial instability and unmet needs has led to the return of ideas about financial restructuring that were absent from US politics for several generations. In cities across the country, activists have been agitating for the creation of public banks that would allocate credit more equitably, following the model of North Dakota's long-established public bank.[11] Support has also grown for reviving postal banking, which would make banking services available to millions of poor people who currently need to rely on the extortionate practices of payday lenders.[12] As discussed in subsequent chapters, there are now many other proposals circulating for significant financial reform.

In the European Community, the struggle against COVID-19 also placed financial reform on the historical agenda. During the eurozone debt crisis from 2009 to 2012, the European authorities rescued the weak economies of Portugal, Italy, Spain, and Greece, but each of these nations was required to accept a period of painful austerity. Greece's austerity was particularly severe since the country required very substantial debt relief. However, when the pandemic hit some of these same countries particularly hard, there was little appetite for more austerity. Such a response was seen as needlessly cruel and likely to victimize the very people who had suffered most in the pandemic.

Instead, the European Community took the first timid steps toward a major financial reform—the mutualization of debt across the community. An agreement was reached that the European Community would float bonds and make funds available to member states, with roughly half distributed as grants and the other half distributed as low-interest loans. This was widely seen as a turning point in which the more prosperous countries of Northern Europe were recognizing their responsibility to assist the less prosperous people of Southern Europe in their struggles with COVID-19. To be sure, it remains uncertain as to whether this is simply a response to an acute crisis or whether it foretells a higher level of mutual obligations within the European Community.

At the global level as well, the pandemic has generated calls for significant financial reform. Developing nations have been particularly hard-hit by the simultaneous shocks of slowing global trade and the steep costs of keeping the virus in check. In April, the Group of Twenty announced a plan that would relieve seventy-six of the world's poorest countries of paying some $20 billion on both private and official debt. But demands for bolder action that would provide even larger debt relief to an expanded group of countries have been widespread. The governor of the Bank of China called in July 2020 for a very large, perhaps $500 billion, allocation of special drawing rights through the International Monetary Fund. The special drawing rights are added to national currency reserves, and they buffer nations from a worsening balance of payments. A comparable issue of SDRs—worth $250 billion—was made in 2009 as a way to counter the severity of the global downturn.

A wide range of different ideas is now circulating about measures to reform or transform the organization of finance, including the nationalization of the largest private banks; the creation of new public sector banks at the national, regional, and global level; and a stricter regulatory regime for existing banks. At the global level, there have been calls for replacing the dollar with an internationally created reserve currency and establishing a global financial transaction tax to reduce speculative capital movements.

In evaluating these and other reform ideas, there are two distinct issues. The first is adequacy: Is the reform likely to make a significant difference in terms of the dysfunctionality of the current financial system? Will it reduce the instability created by the unrelenting search for high returns in the current system? Will it improve the way that capital is allocated? Will it reduce the huge inequalities of income and power that are built into the current financial system? Will it prove durable as a reform or will it quickly be reabsorbed or neutralized? The second issue is feasibility: Is the proposed reform something that could actually be adopted and implemented without some kind of revolutionary upheaval? Is it imaginable that the opposition of financial interests could be overcome by assembling a large enough coalition in support of the measure? Is it likely that such a coalition could be sustained long enough for the reform to make a real difference?

There are, of course, no definitive answers to questions of effectiveness and feasibility since how things will unfold in the future is unknowable. And yet, social movements and political parties have to adopt strategies to respond to institutions that are producing destructive results. For movements or parties to invest resources in reform strategies that are either inadequate or infeasible can be extremely costly. Opportunities to enact major reforms are rare, indeed, so pursuing a flawed reform strategy can be catastrophic.

The only way to handle this problem is for these movements or parties to encourage a vigorous process of debate and discussion through which the relative strengths and weaknesses of different financial reform strategies are examined. While these discussions of different reform ideas have already begun, the purpose of this book is to sharpen the terms of this debate. We do this by centering the discussion on the democratization of the financial system. Our view is that any reform proposal that does not work to redistribute power away from existing institutions will be ineffective.

The history of the project

This book is part of Erik Olin Wright's Real Utopias Project.[13] Wright died in January of 2019 after a long battle with acute myeloid leukemia, but he had organized the workshop where these papers were initially presented in July of 2018. Wright began the Real Utopias Project in 1991—the same year that the Soviet Union disappeared from the map. In the context of triumphant global neoliberalism, Wright saw the need for a revival of the utopian imagination as a response to Margaret Thatcher's confident assertion of TINA—There Is No Alternative—to market liberalism.

However, Wright focused on utopias that were real, by which he meant reforms that could actually be implemented within the current political and economic arrangements and that had the potential to weaken the power of existing economic and political elites and increase the capacity and mobilization of oppositional movements. Earlier volumes in this series focus on basic income, gender equality, citizen assemblies, and redistribution of assets.

In two books, *Envisioning Real Utopias* and *How to Be an Anticapitalist in the Twenty-First Century*, Wright elaborates this project's theory of change. He argues that the revolutionary path to socialism is no longer viable or even desirable. However, progress toward socialism is possible through a strategy of eroding capitalism that involves a sustained effort to build counterinstitutions and more effective forms of democratic governance. Wright argues for combining four approaches to accomplish this erosion. There need to be initiatives to tame capitalism through increased regulation, more effective taxation regimes, and more generous transfer payments. There must be efforts to dismantle capitalism by major institutional reforms that socialize resources that were previously under private control. There must be campaigns to resist capitalism through fights for better wages and working conditions and for improving the communities in which poor and working-class people live. Finally, there must be expanded opportunities to escape capitalism by creating worker-owned cooperatives, consumer cooperatives, and other institutions that are not subject to the logic of profitability.

Wright insists that if an oppositional movement or political party were able to coordinate and unify constituent groups pursuing each of these four strategies, significant progress toward socialism could occur. This would take the form of a substantial democratization of society that both increased popular influence over governmental decisions, including particularly those in the economic realm, and expanded significantly the population's capacity to deliberate, to debate, and to hold elected officials accountable at all levels of government.

Introduction

Wright considers the democratization of finance to be a very promising example of a real utopia. On the one side, major financial reforms would represent both the taming and the dismantling of capitalism because they would limit speculative activity and could reduce the role of the profit motive in allocating capital to different purposes. On the other, greater access to finance by the poor and the working class would facilitate efforts to escape and resist capitalist class power.

This project began soon after the global financial crisis. When Wright was elected president of the American Sociological Association in 2011, he announced that the theme of the 2012 meetings would be Real Utopias, and he invited papers on that topic. I wrote a paper for that meeting on "democratizing finance" that was subsequently published in *Politics & Society* in 2014. Wright made many constructive suggestions for that paper, but he was not satisfied that it would serve as an appropriate anchor for a volume in the Real Utopias session.

In 2014, he invited both me and Robert Hockett to write papers for a small workshop in Madison, Wisconsin, held in the spring of 2015. Robert and I wrote early drafts of what have become the anchor papers for this volume, and those papers generated lively response from the assembled group. A decision was made that the two papers together would serve as the foundation for a volume, with ten to twelve other people invited to write commentaries. Revised papers and invitations to that workshop were sent out in the spring of 2017, so the participants would have ample time to write their commentaries.

After the 2018 workshop, there was another round of revisions. Versions of the two anchor papers and some of the commentaries were included in a special issue of *Politics & Society* published in December 2019. In many ways, the long gestation period of this project has been a good thing. When we began, few people were thinking about a radical overhaul of the financial system. Now, however, these issues are clearly on the political agenda.

INTRODUCTION

Democratizing finance

The phrase "democratizing finance" has a number of possible meanings. For some, it means expanding access to formal credit institutions for poor and marginalized segments of the population whose access to credit has been limited to predatory borrowing from loan sharks or pawnshops. For others, it refers to the opening up of savings accounts and investment opportunities for those who have previously been "unbanked" or lacked any savings to invest.

These meanings, however, are politically ambiguous because extending credit or investment opportunities to the poor can be either a project of egalitarian reform, a cover for new forms of exploitation, or a complicated combination that benefits some and hurts others. So, for example, the initial project in microlending carried out by Grameen Bank in Bangladesh appeared to empower women in rural areas of that nation. However, subsequent for-profit versions of microlending have sometimes proved predatory and have entrapped low-income borrowers in endless cycles of borrowing. Similarly, access to bank accounts could facilitate saving for the poor, but it could also be yet another means to extract resources from them and deepen their poverty.

Our use of the term "democratizing finance" focuses instead on reducing inequalities of income, wealth, and power. We start with the recognition that the existing configuration of finance in most developed and developing countries works to reproduce the income and wealth inequality that has become ever more extreme in recent decades. The financial system also enhances the agency of those who are already wealthy and often blocks those in the bottom two-thirds of the income distribution from changing their situation or accomplishing their life goals.

Those who are already wealthy have access to credit on extremely favorable terms, and this empowers them to take actions that deepen inequality. The largest global corporations can easily raise the capital needed to buy up potential competitors, ensuring future profits that are distributed to top managers

Introduction

and investors who are disproportionately wealthy. Private equity firms routinely borrow money at favorable interest rates to buy up existing firms. They then slash costs by eliminating jobs and cutting back on employee benefits before eventually selling the business again at a considerable profit.

In contrast, the poor, working people, and even the middle class, often find themselves constrained by either the high cost of borrowing or the complete unavailability of credit. Farmers or small businesses might want to borrow to invest in their businesses, but they already experience difficulty servicing past debts. Employee cooperatives and nonprofit organizations routinely find it impossible to borrow to finance the start of a business or to build low-income housing. In the US, the cost of borrowing to finance higher education means that some young people give up on college while others face the burden of cumulative borrowing, which now exceeds $1 trillion in loans.

At the same time, the financial system often works to redistribute income upward. Thomas Piketty's research shows that those in the top 1 percent of households have access to investment opportunities that produce substantially higher returns than the investments available to middle-income households.[14] Since they can also borrow at extremely favorable interest rates, they are able to increase their returns further through leverage. Meanwhile, as we saw with subprime mortgage loans to poor and minority households, lending on predatory terms can be extremely profitable for both mortgage brokers and investment bankers. Even the 18 percent interest rate that many working- and middle-class people pay on their credit card debt enhances the profits of banks and their shareholders.

The existing financial system also reinforces the control of elites over the key investment decisions that shape the future trajectory of economic activity. For example, the investment decisions of oil companies and automobile firms dictated continued dependence on the internal combustion engine despite evidence of global climate change. Moreover, even when governments at the local or federal level invest in infrastructure projects, their freedom of action is often constrained by the need to satisfy the financial intermediaries that help them to raise money in the capital markets.

Finally, the financial system works to reinforce the disproportionate political power of the wealthy that can be mobilized to block egalitarian reforms. In the United States, giant Wall Street firms spend hundreds of millions of dollars on campaign contributions and armies of lobbyists on Capitol Hill. So, for example, it is almost universally acknowledged that the "carried interest" provision in the US tax code is deeply unfair because it allows those who run hedge funds and private equity funds to pay only 15 or 20 percent tax on their earnings while their secretaries generally pay at a higher rate. Nevertheless, the political clout of the beneficiaries is so great that efforts to repeal that provision have been easily defeated.

In our approach, the democratization of finance involves several distinct dimensions. One is to narrow the class difference in access to credit at favorable interest rates, so that poor, working-class, and middle-class people have greater opportunities to borrow on a sustainable basis to realize their life plans. This would operate at both the individual and the community level. People would find it easier to finance higher education or to start or expand a small business. But it would also create more opportunities for employee-owned firms, theater companies, or community organizations that were seeking to upgrade the housing and amenities of a previously neglected urban neighborhood.

The second dimension is to weaken the dominance over the financial system of a relatively small number of giant private financial firms. This follows logically since those firms have prioritized lending at favorable terms to those who are already wealthy. Moreover, creating a much more competitive financial system where public and nonprofit institutions would control a significant share of financial flows would also weaken the political clout of those giant firms, and that, in turn, would open up possibilities for more egalitarian legislation.

The third dimension is to increase democratic input into the critical investment decisions that shape the future of the

Introduction

economy. One aspect of this would be to democratize corporations themselves by giving employees greater voice in corporate decision-making. This project, however, while complementary to what is being proposed here, will not be discussed further because of limitations of space.[15] Another aspect is to diminish the share of investment controlled by large corporations, while expanding the share of investment that is organized by small and medium-sized enterprises, employee cooperatives, nonprofits, and public entities. With regard to the public entities, the idea would be to make them more open to democratic input and less influenced by the priorities of privately dominated capital markets. Finally, more of the institutions that provide financing would be subject to democratic input, so that the allocation of credit would increasingly match democratically derived priorities.

This multiplicity of dimensions makes it obvious that the goal of democratizing finance is complex and cannot be accomplished with just one or two key reforms. Moreover, as Michael A. McCarthy makes clear in his contribution, even if the major financial institutions were taken over by the government, there is no guarantee that their financing decisions would match the preferences of a democratic polity, whatever the institutional arrangements for determining those preferences.

Introducing the volume

The volume begins with an anchor essay by Robert Hockett, "Finance without Financiers." His argument is that the provision of credit by banks and by the increasingly important "shadow banking system" is ultimately underwritten and validated by public entities, including the central bank (in the US, the Federal Reserve) and by the Treasury Department of the central government.

Hockett challenges the conventional view that banks are primarily financial intermediaries that connect lenders with borrowers.[16] Instead, he shows that the credit system fits more closely with the model of a franchiser and multiple franchisees.

Government authorities are the franchisers; they are the ones who have the capacity to create legally binding money and credit. Banks and various entities in the shadow banking system can be understood as franchisees that have been granted the authority to expand the supply of credit by the franchiser.

Hockett's argument effectively reverses the usual understanding of the power relations in the credit system. When banks are seen as financial intermediaries, it follows that government regulators must treat them with kid gloves to avoid a potentially disastrous drying up of the credit needed for the economy to function. In the franchise model, however, the government actually has the power, and deference to bankers is unnecessary.

My essay, "Financial Democratization and the Transition to Socialism," builds on the foundation that Hockett establishes. It argues that the government can use its franchising power to underwrite nonprofit financial entities that would be more likely to direct credit flows in directions that serve the needs of the public rather than the profits of financial firms. In fact, as Sarah Quinn has shown, there is a long history in the US of these publicly directed credit flows.[17]

The paper argues that a strategy of expanding existing nonprofit financial firms and creating new ones could eventually diminish the power and resources of the dominant private financial institutions. Moreover, if there were a major shift in public saving from profit to nonprofit financial institutions, this could facilitate a transition to socialism, defined as significantly greater democratic control over the economy.

The next section of the book consists of three chapters that focus on the politics of financial reform. The commentary by William H. Simon focuses on the institutional arrangements for democratizing the economy. Simon identifies four distinct mechanisms for increasing democracy, and he argues that each has specific strengths and weaknesses. Simon ends by arguing that whichever institutional mechanisms are used, standards must be developed for assuring transparency and for assessing the performance of these more democratic financial institutions. He suggests that a process of peer review in which managers

Introduction

evaluate each other's performance and adopt best practices is an essential element in assuring accountability.

David M. Woodruff's commentary argues that a project of democratizing finance must address the independence of central banks. He explains that market liberals have fought aggressively over recent decades to institutionalize the independence of central banks from elected political officials. This independence has had perverse consequences: it created the situation in which elected politicians have been able to pursue fiscal austerity while relying on central bankers to use measures such as quantitative easing to prevent an economic slowdown. His argument is that central bank independence allows elected politicians to evade responsibilities for weak economies with high unemployment. Moreover, persuading the public of the need for major financial reforms requires challenging the false claims that what central bankers do is a technical exercise with no relation to politics.

Michael A. McCarthy evaluates the proposals of Hockett and Block in relation to a number of different strategies for democratizing finance, including the creation of sovereign wealth funds, establishing inclusive ownership funds as suggested by the British Labour Party in 2019, and bank nationalization. He argues that bank nationalization is the strategy most likely to overcome the entrenched power of private financial institutions. But he also argues that for any of these strategies to be effective, new institutions of democratic engagement are required.

The essays in the second section are more centrally focused on the financial dimension of the argument. The commentary by Sarah Quinn and colleagues adds a historical dimension to the analysis by focusing on financial reform proposals made in the late 1930s by Adolf A. Berle, a key figure in Franklin Roosevelt's New Deal. Berle is usually identified by historians as an opponent of the more left-wing New Dealers. This was a stance that prefigured his career after World War II as a fierce anticommunist. But his earlier role as counsel to the Reconstruction Finance Corporation led him to propose a dramatic expansion of the federal government's role in providing finance for a range of different economic activities. Berle's proposals were not acted upon at the time, but they suggest that during the New Deal, just as now, the issue of a significant expansion of the government's role in allocating credit was on the agenda.

Mary Mellor makes the case that democratizing finance requires the democratization of money itself. She challenges the conventional accounts of how money is created in order to imagine an economy in which human and environmental needs come first. She explains how participatory budgeting could be used in a truly democratic society to democratize both the creation and the allocation of financial resources.

Lenore Palladino proposes two additional innovations as part of the project of financial democratization. The first is a public investment portal that would give savers the opportunity to acquire safe financial assets with lower transaction costs than those offered by private banks and brokerage firms. This would open up more financing opportunities for noncorporate businesses. The second is a government-created public investment account that would be a major step in reducing inequalities in the ownership of financial assets. Since wealth inequality is particularly extreme for black, brown, and Native American families, Palladino's proposal is aimed at dismantling systemic racism.

In the concluding observations, I briefly address two important issues raised by the other contributors—questions of the implementation of financial reform and the issue of centralization versus decentralization.

As with earlier volumes in the Real Utopias Project, the papers assembled here are intended as a set of provocations rather than a blueprint. Up until quite recently, discussions of democratizing finance have not been a significant part of left discourse either in the academy or in the political arena. But recent decades have demonstrated that finance can be both an enormously destructive force and a powerful instrument of social reform. Our hope is that these articles help provoke further debate and discussion over the development of a politics of radical financial reform.

I. ANCHOR ESSAYS

1

Finance without Financiers

Robert Hockett

> I see, therefore, the rentier aspect of capitalism as a transitional phase which will disappear when it has done its work ... Thus [we] might aim in practice ... at an increase in the volume of capital until it ceases to be scarce, so that the functionless investor will no longer receive a bonus; and at a scheme of direct taxation which allows the intelligence and determination and executive skill of the financiers ... (who are certainly so fond of their craft that their labour could be obtained much cheaper than at present), to be harnessed to the service of the community on reasonable terms of reward.
>
> John Maynard Keynes[1]

Introduction: Founding myths and funding truths

Many who advocate democratizing finance seem to have either or both of two blemishes in mind when it comes to what democratization would remedy.[2] One such blemish goes by the name of "financial exclusion." The other sounds in "democratic deficit." The grievance, in other words, is that too many have too little access to credit, that the central bank or monetary authority is too insulated from democratic political guidance, or both. Proffered solutions accordingly aim to boost access to retail banking services, to subject central bankers to more exacting legislative control, or, again, both.

Greater financial inclusion and democratic control are, of course, creditable aims where there is insufficient access to credit, or where central banks or monetary authorities are too insulated from democratic decision-making to be expected to do, or to conform to, the will of the polity. But they also are needlessly *modest* aims insofar as those who push them mean by "finance" what contemporary legal, economic, and finance-theoretical orthodoxy means by the term. For orthodoxy hews to a view of finance that, were it correct, would entail that we have much less room for democratization of access and control, not to mention productive investment, than we actually have.

Finance orthodoxy hews to the view that finance capital, as distinguished from the resources that such capital commands, is both privately supplied and inherently scarce. It believes or pretends that such capital is limited to what is antecedently accumulated by rentiers in the form of financial assets held at banks and other financial institutions, which institutions then "intermediate" between virtuous savers and needful end users of capital. This, what I shall call the "intermediated scarce private capital" orthodoxy about finance, is false. It serves rentiers well, privileging their wealth and their "shots-calling" authority as it does, but it is profoundly antagonistic both to democracy and to productive investment and resultant prosperity, not to mention the truth of finance.

I shall accordingly devote myself in this anchor essay to showing how much more room we have for the democratization of both access to and control over finance than orthodoxy supposes, hence how much more "radical" our democratization demands can and ought to be than they typically are. In so doing, I'll demonstrate that a system of forthrightly publicly generated and administered credit for the financing of socially useful and maximally inclusive productive enterprise not only is feasible, but also is effectively what we have now, save for the "usefulness" and "inclusiveness" parts.

This will in turn set the stage for Fred Block's anchor essay. For my analysis shows that our public capital must be both carefully modulated and attentively allocated, and Block's proposed institutions are optimally positioned to guide allocation both equitably and productively, enabling a democratization of finance that facilitates democratization of production itself.

My argument proceeds as follows. Section I sketches the frame of an updated, post-capital-scarcity account of publicly generated finance. Sections II through IV corroborate my revisionist view through careful examination of all corners of the contemporary financial system. Section V sketches three macro-institutional reforms that my revised portrayal of finance shows to be possible and that will afford a congenial financial environment in which Block's more localized development institutions can discharge their appointed tasks. Then I conclude.

I. Financial flows and private roles

I'll begin by indicating in summary form why the dominant intermediated-scarce-private-capital view of finance is incorrect. I'll then briefly sketch an alternative picture that accords with the world we actually inhabit—not to mention the world that Block and I believe we soon *should* inhabit.

Three models of finance

To see where the intermediated-scarce-private-capital view of finance comes a cropper, it is convenient to start with the pre-accumulation-cum-scarcity component of that view—a component readily shown to be untenable. Then we can turn to the role of the public, which is readily shown to be the source of non-scarcity where capital, again as distinguished from that which capital commands, is concerned.

Orthodoxy's scarcity assumption stems from its assumed picture of that which is lent or invested—that is, its view of finance or investment capital—as pre-accumulated. But there are other available pictures, two of which turn out on both theoretical and empirical grounds to be better portrayals of how finance actually "works" in contemporary economies.

The credit intermediation model

Call the first account of finance the "(one-to-one) credit intermediation" model. This is the image assumed by contemporary orthodoxy, and is accordingly the image likely to be familiar to most lay readers, not to mention mainstream economic, financial, political, and legal theorists who ought to know better.

In the intermediation picture, that which is lent or invested is always something previously privately accumulated, hence limited both by the finite stock of the latter and by the willingness of its accumulators to invest it. Private parties primarily borrow from or invest in *one another* on this understanding—the implicit picture is one of "peer-to-peer" (P2P) lending; and one can only invest—hence only borrow—what is "already there," in previously accumulated, privately held form.

Financial institutions accordingly figure into the intermediation picture first as sites of accumulation—venues in which "savers" or "surplus units" hold their accumulated funds. They then figure, as supplemented now by financial marketplaces as well, as sites of intermediation—sites where accumulators and would-be capital users or "deficit units" can inexpensively "find," "transact with," and "monitor" each other.

Things can accordingly be represented as in Figure 1, in which pre-accumulation is depicted when we read from left to right, and in which one-to-one intermediation is represented by the equal sizes of the discs.

Were the intermediation picture an accurate representation of financial systems across the board, all financial institutions would effectively be mutual funds. Financial markets, for their part, would comprise variations on P2P lending platforms—they would be all about brokering, not "dealing" or "underwriting."[3]

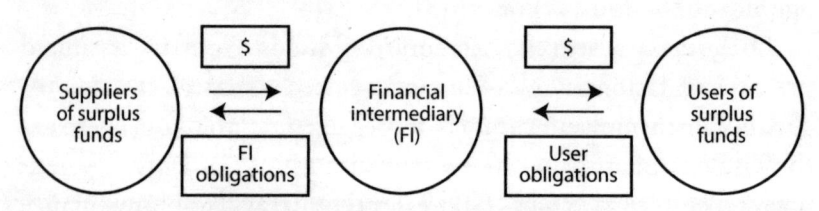

Figure 1. The credit intermediation model

Finance without Financiers

These implications suffice of themselves to suggest that the credit intermediation model might overlook something in modern financial systems. At the very least, it overlooks banking.

The credit multiplication model

A little reflection—or even exposure to a celebrated Frank Capra film—suffices to suggest that the intermediation model cannot be a complete portrayal of the financial landscape.[4] For not all financial institutions are mutual funds.

The most familiar counterexample is the commercial bank, which at least some people know to engage—or in the past to have engaged—in a form of finance known as "fractional-reserve banking." In the fractional-reserve story, banks lend out more than they receive in the form of investor deposits. They hold only enough of the latter, in vaults and reserve accounts, to handle anticipated daily withdrawals, drafts, or similar obligations, and lend out the rest.

"The rest," crucially, serves as the basis of additional lending, such that an originally deposited monetary "base" can be multiplied manyfold. We can accordingly call this picture the "(one-to-many) credit multiplication" model of finance.

The illustration of credit multiplication through fractional-reserve banking typically found in the textbooks begins with a bank that holds 10 percent of its deposit liabilities in reserve. The remaining 90 percent is lent out, with borrowers depositing that lent remainder into their own accounts in the banking system. The banks that receive this 90 percent in the form of deposits then lend out another 90 percent of the 90 percent, then 90 percent of the additional 81 percent, ... and so on, to the point where an initial depository base is multiplied ninefold in aggregate.

Things can accordingly be represented as in Figure 2, in which pre-accumulation is again depicted when we read left to right, and in which multiplication is represented by the larger size of the disc on the right relative to the disc on the left. It should be noted, however, that were Figure 2 to be adapted to represent the financial system as a whole on the credit multiplication model,

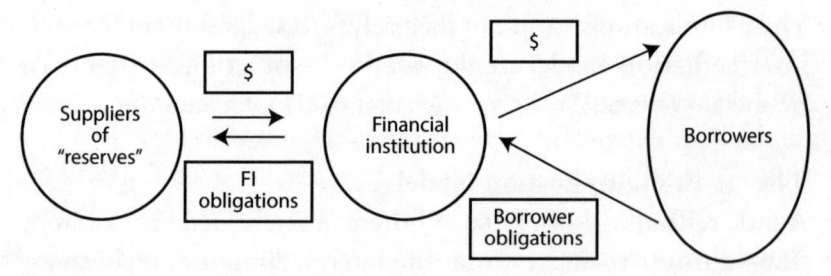

Figure 2. The credit multiplication model

and were credit extensions to take the form of opening or crediting accounts on behalf of the borrowers, as we shall find to be generally the case with banking, then Figure 2 would have to take the form of a two-phase picture.

The first phase, in which pre-accumulated finance capital is required to set the multiplication process in motion, would be represented as in Figure 2. The second phase, in which loans are originated and themselves take the form of deposits, would then be represented by a figure in which the disc at the left grows to be similarly sized to that on the right—as in Figure 3, to which we turn momentarily.

The credit multiplication model, were it accurately to capture much of what occurs in the financial system, would, of course, of itself falsify the credit intermediation model. It assumes with the latter that finance capital must be privately pre-accumulated before credit can be extended, but it does not assume that only that which has been previously accumulated can be lent or invested. The latter figures as a multiple of the former in the credit multiplication picture, with the multiplicative factor inversely proportional to the reserve ratio.

Two entailments of these observations bear noting for present purposes. The first is that, for any x representing the percentage of pre-accumulated funds that financial institutions hold in reserve, $100 - x$ will represent the percentage of credit outstanding that is *not* pre-accumulated finance capital. The multiplicative factor "levers up" that which has been previously accumulated, and diminishes putative capital scarcity proportionally, even if not quite eliminating it.

The second, more far-reaching entailment is that, since the $100 - x$ percentage of credit outstanding is not pre-accumulated and the x can in theory be made arbitrarily small, credit cannot actually be dependent upon privately pre-accumulated "loanable funds" at all. In other words, finance capital need not actually be scarce even in the more limited sense implied by the credit multiplication model. This takes us directly to the third model of finance.

The credit generation model

The fact that x can be made arbitrarily small in the fractional-reserve banking story raises the prospect that credit extension, and hence the supply of finance capital, might not be scarce in any delimitably precise sense at all. Finance capital in the form of credit might instead be more accurately said to be "generated" by lending institutions than "intermediated" or "multiplied" by them. This is the prospect captured by what we can call the "(none-to-many) credit generation model" of finance.

On the credit generation picture, credit outstanding is not really dependent upon—or therefore limited by—pre-accumulated investment capital at all. It is limited only by investment opportunities that certain kinds of institutions—namely those authorized to credit or open borrower accounts whose "contents" are spendable as money—view as potentially profitable or otherwise worth undertaking. Credit is, in other words, endogenously issued rather than exogenously limited, multiplicatively or otherwise, to privately pre-accumulated funds.[5]

Things can accordingly be represented as in Figure 3, in which pre-accumulation now drops out of the picture with what used to be the small disc on the left-hand side in Figures 1 and 2, and in which indefinite extensibility is represented by the growing size of the discs to right and left as loan volume grows on the right, with loan proceeds then deposited in accounts represented by the disc on the left. Note that now, unlike in Figures 1 and 2, causation runs from right to left more than from left to right. As we shall see, "loans make deposits."

The qualifier noted a moment ago—"those authorized to

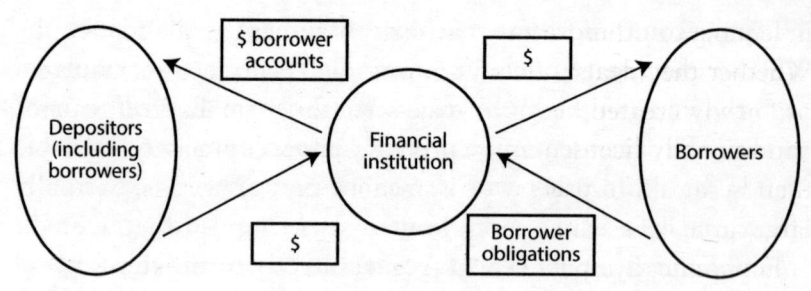

[Figure 3 diagram: Depositors (including borrowers) ↔ Financial institution ↔ Borrowers, with "$ borrower accounts" and "$" flowing to depositors, and "$" and "Borrower obligations" flowing from borrowers]

Figure 3. The credit generation model

credit or open borrower accounts ... spendable as money," whose capacity is represented on the left-hand side of Figure 3 —proves crucial as we turn from the scarcity component to the privateness component of the intermediated scarce private-capital orthodoxy. For the "authorization" and "spendability as money" components of that qualifier signal a central role played by the *public*—that is, *us*, in our collective political capacity—in constituting finance.

Which model? The public core of "private" finance

Where credit flows conform to the credit multiplication or credit generation models, as they do in all contemporary financial systems, the sovereign public inevitably becomes the financial system's prime mover, with privately owned institutions playing at most a publicly delegated, conditionally subsidiary role. I'll first explain why, then explain how—defining and explicating what I call the public "accommodation" and "monetization" of what initially looks like privately originated credit.

Why public underwriting becomes inevitable

I spoke of entities "authorized to credit or open borrower accounts ... spendable as money." "Authorization" and "spendability as money" signal the portals through which the public constitutively operates in the realm even of putatively "private" sector finance.

To begin with "authorization," few institutions are able or permitted, in contemporary jurisdictions, to engage unconditionally in lending or other forms of investing on a large scale for profit. Whether they deal in their own money, "other people's money," or "newly created" money, large-scale financial institutions are conditionally licensed and closely monitored, precisely because their actions affect not only immediate counterparties, but also large numbers of third parties.

Economically speaking, they generate positive externalities upon which vast populations of third parties come to rely, to the point where their failures occasion cataclysmic *negative* externalities. If you doubt this, simply ask yourself what happens if the national payments system—an essential commercial infrastructure—suddenly vanishes with the mass insolvency of the "commercial banks" that supply it through the transaction accounts they maintain on behalf of depositors.

Moving from that unsurprising observation to the perhaps less familiar point about "spendability as money," even fewer institutions than are authorized to invest on a large scale for profit are authorized to open deposits for others that will be publicly recognized as legal tender. If Bentham falsely purports to lend to Anscombe by opening and crediting a transaction account in her name, and then provides her with an impressive-looking passbook or chip card or magnetic stripe card that he says she can use to make payments to others, then Anscombe is in for an unpleasant surprise when she attempts to use either in making a purchase at Melville's across the street. For Bentham must be a publicly authorized banking institution to swap the fiduciary equivalent of spendable public promissory notes (Federal Reserve notes) for Anscombe's unspendable private promissory note.

Only a small number of publicly chartered institutions in any polity have ever been authorized to open transaction accounts for others that will immediately be recognized as legal tender —i.e., as money, good to discharge "all obligations, public and private."[6] If these same institutions are permitted to extend *loans* in the form of such deposits, as has long been the case in all contemporary jurisdictions, then they are authorized to extend what we can call *monetized credit*—something that functions as finance or investment capital in any monetary exchange economy like ours. If in turn these institutions are authorized to extend such credit on their own accounts rather than in the form of one-to-one intermediation as described above, then they are able to issue what is called "credit money," aka Wicksellian "bank money" or "broad money," either in multiplicative or indefinitely generable form as described above.

Finally, if the private liabilities that such institutions take on in issuing credit money are for some reason converted effectively into public liabilities, as again is the case in all contemporary jurisdictions (your bank account, we shall see, is the functional equivalent of a wad of "Federal Reserve notes," better known as "dollar bills"), then that which these institutions are issuing—the form that their finance capital ultimately takes—will in the final analysis be the spendable, hence monetized, full faith and credit of the sovereign that authorizes and backs up their activity. It will be private money made public money.[7]

These publicly authorized institutions will in effect then be franchisees dispensing a resource ultimately provided by a sovereign franchisor—namely that sovereign's own monetized full faith and credit. The sovereign franchisor in such circumstances will have to engage in "quality control" practices of the kind familiar to all franchise arrangements. It will have to take care that its resource not be overdispensed or misallocated, particularly in light of the over- and misallocative incentives that this form of privatized seigniorage, as explained more completely below, always entails when profitability needn't imply productivity. I call these the franchisor's critical money-modulation and money-allocation functions.[8]

"Franchise finance" of this kind becomes all but inevitable when credit flows move from conformity with the credit intermediation picture to conformity with the credit multiplication or credit generation pictures sketched above. One reason is that those public necessities that are an elastic currency and a payments system are fundamentally dependent upon the continued functioning of those institutions that multiply or generate credit money, be they public, as is always possible, or private, as is presently tolerated.[9] It becomes imperative under such circumstances, for an economy that would reap the growth benefits wrought by multipliable or generable yet stable credit money and a payments system, that the sovereign undertake *ex ante* to recognize certain private liabilities associated with credit multiplication or credit generation as liabilities of its own.

For the same reason, it is equally imperative that these accommodated liabilities be spendable as money. This takes us to the twinned public banking functions of "accommodation" and "monetization."

The twin faces of public underwriting: Accommodation and monetization

Accommodation and monetization are the processes through which we the public enable privately issued credit to be indefinitely generated in immediately spendable form, by committing *ex ante* to convert certain private liabilities into public liabilities that function as money. In effect, we in our sovereign capacity commit temporarily to swap public promissory notes (in the US, again, Federal Reserve notes) for private promissory notes (borrowers' contractual promises to repay their loans). Thus, our acting as accommodator, which we must do in order for credit multiplication or credit generation and credit money growth to proceed reliably, is what renders the public a franchisor where even nominally "private" finance is concerned. In effect, it renders all generated, as distinguished from pre-accumulated, finance capital *public* capital.

As Sections II through IV below demonstrate in detail, the principal components of all postmedieval financial systems jointly constitute such franchise arrangements within all jurisdictions that rely upon stable credit multiplication or credit generation to fuel stable economic growth.[10] Under the terms of each such arrangement, we the sovereign public, as franchisor, effectively license private financial institutions, as franchisees, to dispense what we pre-commit to convert into our own monetized full faith and credit. And that means that we charge private-sector institutions with allocating and disseminating public capital.

In the United States, which will serve as my principal exemplar, public full faith and credit—public capital—flow through the financial system in two principal forms. The first comprises directly issued public liabilities: (a) Federal Reserve notes and their bank-depository equivalent, (b) US Treasury securities, and (c) some additional federal agency securities.[11] The second, quantitatively more significant yet less commonly recognized forms of public full faith and credit are publicly "accommodated" and "monetized" *private* liabilities—specifically, spendable deposit liabilities of the kind described just above.

In the US, accommodation occurs when a public authority—typically the Federal Reserve (the "Fed")—takes on a privately issued debt liability—often but not always a bank liability—as a liability of its own. "Monetization," in turn, occurs when the ultimate beneficiary of accommodation—a borrower—is able to spend the proceeds of the accommodated loan as if they were currency, as is the case with bank demand deposits. When a public instrumentality in the US directly or indirectly accommodates and monetizes these private liabilities, it effectively converts them to *our, public* liabilities by extending the full faith and credit of the United States.

Things can accordingly be broadly depicted as in Figure 4, in which a financial institution extends credit money to borrowers in exchange for borrower liabilities, then publicly monetizes those private liabilities through a public institution that "accommodates" the initial credit extensions by crediting lending institution accounts through which drafts drawn on accounts clear.

Note that, in contrast to Figures 1 and 2, where credit flows originate on the left-hand side and work their way to the right, in Figure 4 we have a double movement of sorts. On the one hand, flows originate on the right and proceed simultaneously leftward and upward. On the other hand, the public's precommitting to what occurs at the top enables the great bulk of what occurs below on the right, and hence below on the left, to occur at all.

The Fed and the Department of Treasury ("Treasury"), as Sections II through IV will show, are the two principal federal

Finance without Financiers

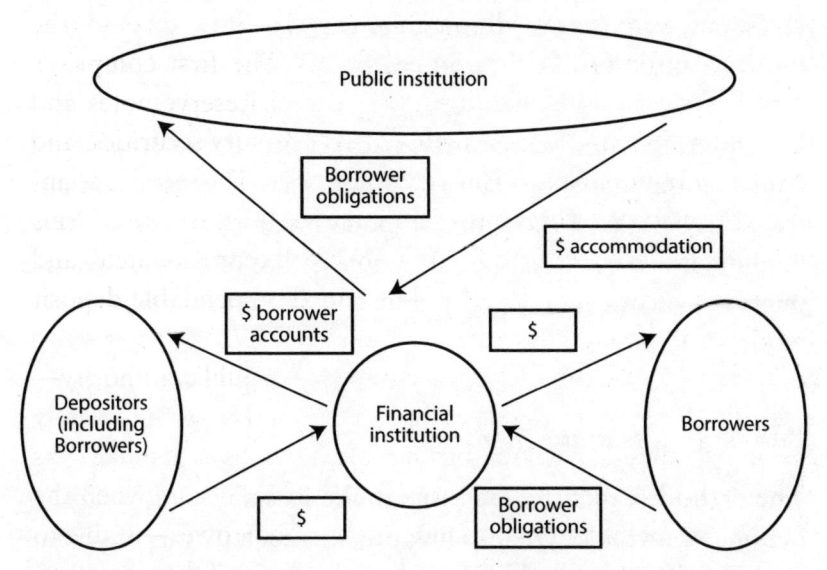

Figure 4. Credit generation and ex ante public underwriting

instrumentalities that act on behalf of the American public as sovereign franchisor in channeling and managing the flow of monetized public full faith and credit throughout our financial system. Their actions are most readily observable in the banking sector, as discussed immediately below in Section II, where the Fed directly and routinely accommodates and monetizes public and private credit alike.

The same dynamics are also at work in the capital and other financial markets mapped in Sections III and IV, however. For US Treasury debt and Fed accommodated bank credit increasingly flow through those markets themselves. And the Fed now directly accommodates the monetized lending activities of much more than traditional banking institutions—so-called shadow banks—in those markets as well. Moreover, directly issued, securitized full faith and credit in the form of US Treasury debt plays a critical role in founding, enabling, and underwriting the non-bank financial markets in the first place. The next several sections trace all these flows in detail, in effect showing that *all* of our financial system is a site of monetized public credit dissemination.

II. Finance at its core: Banks, central banks, public full faith, and credit

The intermediated-scarce-private-capital orthodoxy portrays banks on the model of Figure 1. In this section I show that portrayal to be false. I show that a modern bank's primary—or in banking-law parlance, "special"—role is that of licensed private purveyor of our monetized public full faith and credit on the model of Figure 4.

Banks: Loans make deposits

The orthodox picture: Deposits make loans
In popular mythology, banks link private accumulators of surplus capital with households, firms, and sometimes government instrumentalities that require access to the same. The former is deposited in banks in the form of short-term demand deposits. Banks then lend it out on a one-to-one basis in the form of longer-term loans. Things accordingly flow as in Figure 1.

Interest rates and other financing costs figure as *prices* on this rendering. They amount to money rental rates, determined by the confluence of fund supply and fund demand just as other prices are routinely said to be determined by the confluence of x supply and x demand for any x.[12] This is the vulgar version of the venerable "loanable-funds" model of banking, pursuant to which "deposits make loans," savings determine investment, and funding costs are just rental rates that equilibrate privately provided fund supply with privately and publicly originating fund demand.[13]

The institutional facts of the matter: Loans make deposits
The intermediated-loanable-funds view of banking stands the truth of things on its head, reversing the causal directionality of the great bulk of actual banking relations. The best way to substantiate this claim is by reference to the mechanics of a simple bank-lending transaction.

When a bank receives an application from a creditworthy business or household to borrow, it does not peer into a vault to determine how much in the way of depositors' funds are on hand to lend out to others. Nor does it engage in any contemporary analogue to that act—checking its reserve balance at the regional Federal Reserve Bank, for example, to see "what it can afford." Instead the bank credits a preexisting or newly opened borrower account, then books the transaction as an asset and liability of its own, on the one hand, and an asset and liability of the borrower, on the other.

The transaction books as an asset of the bank because the bank is now owed on the loan—it holds a promissory note issued by the borrower. It books as a liability of the bank because the bank must now honor all drafts drawn on account by the borrower up to the loan amount. The transaction books as an asset of the borrower, meanwhile, because the borrower now owns, and is able to draw upon, a newly credited transaction account. It books as a liability of the borrower because the borrower must repay the bank per the terms of her promissory note.

As a matter of accounting, this transaction does not violate any Newtonian-like law of, say, the "conservation of assets relative to liabilities." There continues to be a one-to-one correspondence between assets and liabilities. Nevertheless, as a result of this simple transaction, there is now more money at work in the economy, as routinely tracked by that measure of money known as "bank money," "broad money," or "credit money." There are, as it were, more promises outstanding—hence, we hope, more productive activities underway, undertaken on the strength of those promises.

The introduction of reserve requirements, capital requirements, or other forms of regulation does not fundamentally alter this picture—or, therefore, the structure of Figures 3 or 4. These forms of regulation are meant to modulate credit aggregates and preserve franchisee "safety and soundness." They do not limit finance capital in any "pre-legal," "pre-political" or "natural" sense.

Central banks: Deposits are money

The central bank accommodates

As if to underscore this last point, the central bank or monetary authority in any contemporary jurisdiction that works to maintain a payments system and manage interest rates will have to accommodate acts of money generation undertaken by privately owned lending banks. This it will do by crediting a "reserve account" in the name of the lending bank, effectively converting the bank's new deposit liability into a reserve liability of its own. Things will accordingly move quickly from the way they are depicted in Figure 3 to the way they are depicted in Figure 4.

That central-bank accommodation of this sort constitutes part of "the business of banking" is an unavoidable result of the fact that, in contemporary economies, the central bank or monetary authority maintains an overnight interbank lending rate target and/or administers a national payments infrastructure on which privately drawn drafts clear at par.[14] Without accommodation, some drafts drawn on lending banks would fail to clear. That would undermine the payments system and, with it, the essential functioning of the real economy in any such economy operating via decentralized exchange among participants. Central banks are accordingly constrained to accommodate to ensure effective clearing, hence to ensure smooth and continuous transacting.

Because this act also enables borrowers to spend out of their new or newly credited demand deposit accounts, the act of *accommodation* here also amounts to an act of *monetization*. The central bank in effect *publicly monetizes* the promissory note privately issued and signed by the individual borrower in favor of the lending bank when completing the loan transaction. In this sense the central bank will be placing the full faith and credit of the nation behind the credit of the individual—publicly monetizing, in the form of Federal Reserve notes, the privately issued financial instrument that is the borrower's promissory note.

Finance without Financiers

In this sense, the private bank is simply assisting the public central bank in deciding which unspendable, privately issued promissory notes to "swap" for spendable, publicly issued promissory notes—ideally for productive purposes.[15] The interest it earns on the loan is its payment—its privatized seigniorage—for assisting the central bank in this way.

The "public" central bank, operating in part through the "private" banks, thus enables us collectively to spot ourselves credit individually, as we jointly and severally work to improve our material lives over time. It is all a matter of *ex ante* gatekeeping by private banking institutions acting pursuant to publicly provided guidelines, followed by *ex post* accommodation and monetization by the public's agent—the central bank or monetary authority.

The central bank monetizes

The discussion thus far highlights something important yet underappreciated about contemporary banking systems. Privately owned banks dispense not privately deposited "scarce capital," but what is effectively an indefinitely extensible, publicly modulated *public resource*—a resource on which they are publicly licensed, moreover, to charge private seigniorage rents. In this sense, the banks are best viewed as privileged outlets for the monetized full faith and credit of the United States—i.e., as dollar franchisees. "Private" banks are effectively purveying public credit.[16]

As privileged purveyors of the monetized full faith and credit of the Unites States, explicitly accommodated and protected by the central bank, privately owned banks constitute the inner core of our financial system. Not surprisingly, other financial institutions and markets tend to grow around, attach themselves to, and even work toward functional *amplification and replication* of the core banking franchise—particularly in boom times, when credit growth tends endogenously and procyclically to self-amplify. How that occurs is the subject to which I turn now.

III. The capital market periphery and the banking core: Public credit underwrites private credit

Those at least passingly familiar with the mechanics of banking and central banking as described above might endorse my account of finance as a public–private franchise thus far and yet now pose some skeptical follow-up questions. Don't the *capital and money* markets constitute a *parallel* financial system that more closely conforms to the traditional picture of finance as one-to-one, intermediated, scarce private capital?[17] Don't they present a case in which unambiguously private "deficit units"— called "issuers" in this new context—really do seek funding from unambiguously private "surplus units" or "investors" who purchase their securities with pre-accumulated funds?

These queries are readily addressed. Note first that there is no need, in light of my purposes here, to deny that financial intermediation occurs in financial markets. Intermediation, like other things mentioned on bumper stickers, happens. My claim is simply that financial intermediation is not the *defining*, or even the *most significant*, form of credit flow underway in our financial system. What flows more importantly through the financial markets is, again, our own monetized public full faith and credit. And this, I'll now show, is as true of the capital and money markets as it is of the banking sector.

The precise channels and mechanisms by which public credit flows and finds use outside the formal banking system are more subtle and convoluted in the tracing than are the mechanics of traditional banking as described in Section II. That might partly account for the persistence of the myth of intermediated scarce private capital among those who study and pronounce on the capital and money markets as distinguished from the banking sector. Nevertheless, these flows are traceable. In this section I accordingly trace them through the capital markets. In the next I will trace them through the "shadow banking sector" and money markets that have developed within and alongside those markets.

The orthodox picture: Capital accumulators finance firms

The received understanding of capital markets takes them for sites at which those who have pre-accumulated scarce private capital "meet" the firms that have need of such capital to finance their operations. Credit thus flows in this picture just as it does in the one-to-one intermediated model of scarce private credit illustrated in Figure 1. All that changes is that (a) the "market" becomes the "financial intermediary" in question, (b) the "surplus units" become "capital investors," and (c) the "deficit units" that seek use of scarce capital come to be called "issuers"—so named because the instruments of their borrowings—their capital market "promissory notes," as it were—are the financial securities that they issue.

But capital markets do *not* conform to the one-to-one credit intermediation model portrayed in Figure 1, even if, as noted a moment ago, "intermediation happens." They conform to the none-to-many credit generation model portrayed in Figure 3, as we'll now see.

The institutional facts of the matter: Public credit finances firms—in part through borrower-investors

There are multiple ways in which the received view of capital markets as sites merely of one-to-one intermediated scarce private capital falsifies the truth. I'll now recite them in sequence.

Begin with the indispensable role played by publicly issued debt in founding and then sustaining all capital markets in the first place. The lion's share of investment securities that trade on the world's exchanges are issued by sovereigns. Securities markets, in other words, are, in principal measure, markets in public liabilities (in the US, Treasury securities) just as are banking markets (in the US, Fed dollars).

The large share of securities markets represented by sovereign debt is no happy accident. Large *sovereign* debt markets are effectively prerequisites to the emergence and sustenance of large *private* debt (and equity) markets. This can be understood and verified both in historical and in functional terms.

Historically, the world's first heavily capitalized securities exchanges—those in Amsterdam, London, Paris, and New York—began their lives either as outright government instrumentalities, or as adjuncts to government instrumentalities, or as sites at which government-issued debt could be purchased and sold. Similar stories are encountered when we turn to smaller but still prominent, or later-founded, securities exchanges with present-day significance. These include Frankfurt, Tokyo, Shanghai, and Seoul.

Turning from historical correlations to functional explanations, it is no mystery why capital markets ride upon Treasury and government-agency liabilities just as bank-lending markets ride upon central-bank liabilities. The reason is found in three related and indispensable roles that sovereign debt always plays in these markets.

The first is the "reserve-asset" role. Securities markets require a liquidity reservoir into which investor funds can be rechanneled during times of turbulence, when privately issued liabilities come to look less reliable than publicly issued liabilities. Sovereign debt obligations, backed by the full faith and credit of their issuers, are the principal form that liquidity takes in these markets, much as publicly accommodated bank-credit money is the form that liquidity takes in other markets.

In this sense, US Treasury debt might be likened to something like our capital markets' reserves held with the Fed—that is, reserves of "base money."[18] This could then account for a striking empirical finding reported in the literature: so-called safe assets—government instruments always chief among them—seem to have represented a constant share of global financial assets over time, even as the latter have grown continuously and enormously over the decades.[19] If the "safe-asset share" is indeed constant, then market capitalization itself would be a constant multiple of treasury liabilities or their perceived equivalents—somewhat in the way credit in the banking system is treated as a constant multiple of central-bank liabilities on the (inaccurate) "multiplier" view of banking.[20]

Finance without Financiers

The second, related role played by public liabilities in the capital markets is that of literally indispensable "benchmarks" in pricing other, more risky privately issued securities. So indispensable is this benchmark role of public debt that the very tools which enabled securities markets to grow as exponentially as they have since the so-called financial revolution of the late 1960s and the 1970s—namely reliable asset-pricing methods from CAPM through arbitrage pricing—require for their operation a postulated "risk-free" asset.

Without the sovereign debt benchmark, pricing even privately issued financial assets reliably is not only impractical—it is impossible.[21] In US as well as global capital markets, this benchmark takes the form of securitized public full faith and credit known as the US Treasury security, universally considered the safest of safe assets in its ready convertibility into cash—that is, into Federal Reserve notes, the other sovereign liability—at par.

The capacity of US Treasury liabilities to play this role requires not only that they be safe, but also that they be bountiful. This is evident in past reactions to cases in which Treasury liabilities have diminished. When the size of the US national debt has shown signs of shrinking in the past, as it did in the late 1990s, for example, the Treasurys' reliability as a benchmark declines. The result is that markets become volatile and market watchers fret at the prospect of there being *too little US federal debt*.[22]

The third role of securitized public full faith and credit in the capital markets stems from the first and second roles, and ultimately carries us into the next section's realm of "shadow banking." This is the role of public debt instruments as what I shall call shadow-bank "base money." As described in more detail below, Treasury securities and other government liabilities serve as collateral in many transactions that constitute money-generating functional equivalents to bank-lending transactions. These instruments are able to play this role only in virtue of their superior reliability, both as claims and as benchmarks in calculating other asset values.

The demand for securitized public full faith and credit—tradable Treasury liabilities—as lending collateral in the securities markets appears to be so insistent that some scholars have attributed the proliferation of securities backed by mortgages and other assets, from the later 1990s onward, to the fact that there was not sufficient Treasury debt outstanding to play the crucial role of lending-transaction technology in the late 1990s or early 2000s, thanks to the vaunted "Clinton surpluses."[23]

The final three reasons to repudiate the intermediated-scarce-private-capital model as a portrayal of the capital markets originate in the private rather than the public sector. First is the fact that firms, through voluminous "stock-buyback" activity, now routinely reveal themselves not to be dependent on investor-supplied capital at all in financing their operations. Second is the fact that the ownership concentration of firms that stock buybacks bring about is taking place among financial institutions —primarily private-equity and hedge funds—that Section IV below shows to have privileged access to publicly accommodated and monetized bank and "shadow bank" credit. They publicly finance their own private buybacks.

Finally, there is the fact that even ordinary individual investors are able to borrow in keeping with the model of banking laid out in Section II *in order to purchase firm-issued securities* in the first place. This means that it is often *"individual investors" themselves* who are the true "intermediaries" in the process of "financial intermediation" between investors and firms, with banks, and hence the sovereign, as the ultimate investors.

In other words, things look as they would were we to combine Figure 3 and Figure 4, as in Figure 5.

It is true that most modern jurisdictions regulate "margin lending" of the kind portrayed in Figure 5—particularly in the wake of financial asset-price bubbles and busts of the kind that procyclical endogenous-money generation facilitated by margin lending brings about. But this is precisely the point. The *reason* why margin lending must be carefully *regulated* is that it is a conduit through which indefinitely extensible public full faith and credit finds its way, via the banking and shadow-banking channels, into the capital markets.

Finance without Financiers

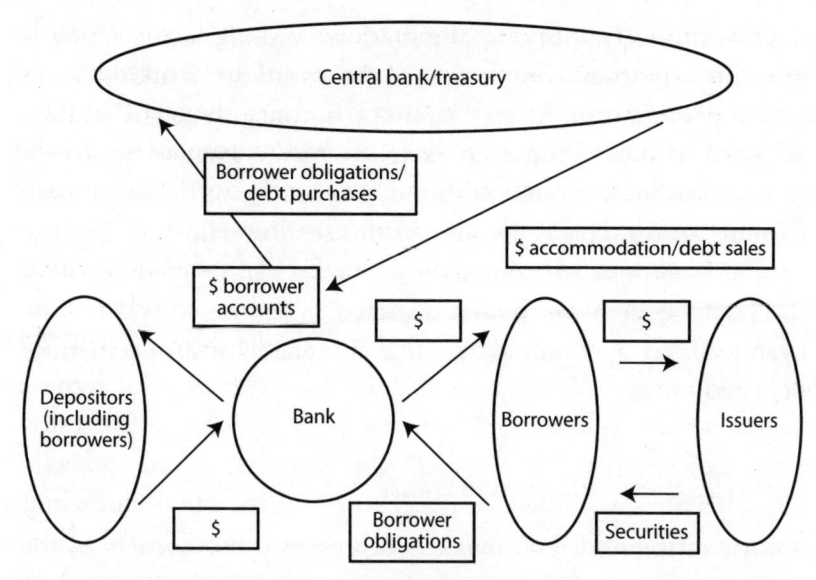

Figure 5. Capital markets with banks and public underwriting

IV. Bank amplification and replication by capital markets: "Shadow banks"

The financial dramas of 2007–2009 drew belated attention to what has since come to be called "shadow banking."[24] The term refers to the amplification and even full replication of traditional bank-lending activity in the nonbanking sectors of the financial system, including the capital markets just considered, without benefit of those forms of regulatory oversight that we the public exercise over the bona fide banking sector.

For my part I will use the term to designate both this phenomenon and one more that accompanies it and is yet more important—namely what I have been calling the public accommodation and monetization of initially private bank-like liabilities, as defined above in Sections I through III. "Shadow banking" will thus designate the specific mechanisms through which capital markets, and now also money markets, amplify and replicate the role of banking and Treasury securities markets as channels for dispensing the full faith and credit of us, the sovereign public.

Quantitatively speaking, the shadow-banking sector is now a critically important complement to the traditional banking sector where proliferation of credit money is concerned. The lending volumes of this sector, even exclusive of the staggering derivative commitments found within it, rival those of the traditional banking sector. This is because, as this section will show, finance capital is supplied through these markets in conformity with the credit generation model depicted in Figure 3, and is now even publicly accommodated and monetized after the manner depicted in Figure 4.

Securitization and repo markets

Securitization and repo markets represent those corners of the capital markets in which bank-reminiscent dynamics are easiest to discern. Securitization is a means by which a bank or other lender removes an asset from its balance sheet, partly in order to enable itself to purchase additional assets and thereby extend further credit, without thereby incurring higher capital-regulatory obligations. In this sense, it can function as what I will call a bank-credit *amplification* mechanism. It enables a bank to issue more credit that ultimately is accommodated and monetized by the Fed in the manner described above in Sections I and II.

Mechanics: Bank-lending amplification and replication

Here is how the process typically works. The bank establishes a "special-purpose vehicle" (SPV) or "special-investment vehicle" (SIV) in the legal form of a trust—essentially a legal entity with no function other than to hold assets, managed by a "trustee" selected by the bank. The bank then "sells" loans to the trust, with the proceeds of the sales thereupon becoming available for further lending activity.

This enables the bank to conduct further lending and, thereby, further credit generation. Hence my term "amplification." The securitization trust purchases the assets that its founding bank sells to it with the proceeds of bond sales to investors—sales facilitated by margin loans taken out by investors as described

Finance without Financiers

and depicted above in Section III and Figure 5. These bonds are commonly known as "asset-backed securities" (ABSs).

In summary, things look as depicted in Figure 6. Use of the SPV as depicted at the bottom of the figure enables the bank to keep lending without falling foul of any capital requirements imposed by regulators to modulate bank-credit generation. In effect, the bank simply transfers some of the loan obligations owed it, not to the central bank, but to the SPV. Note also both that the bank continues to lend to people who invest in issuing firms, as noted earlier in connection with Figure 5, and that the SPV is itself an issuer, some of whose bonds might be purchased by other banks, or by bondholder/investors who borrow from other banks, again as in Figure 5.

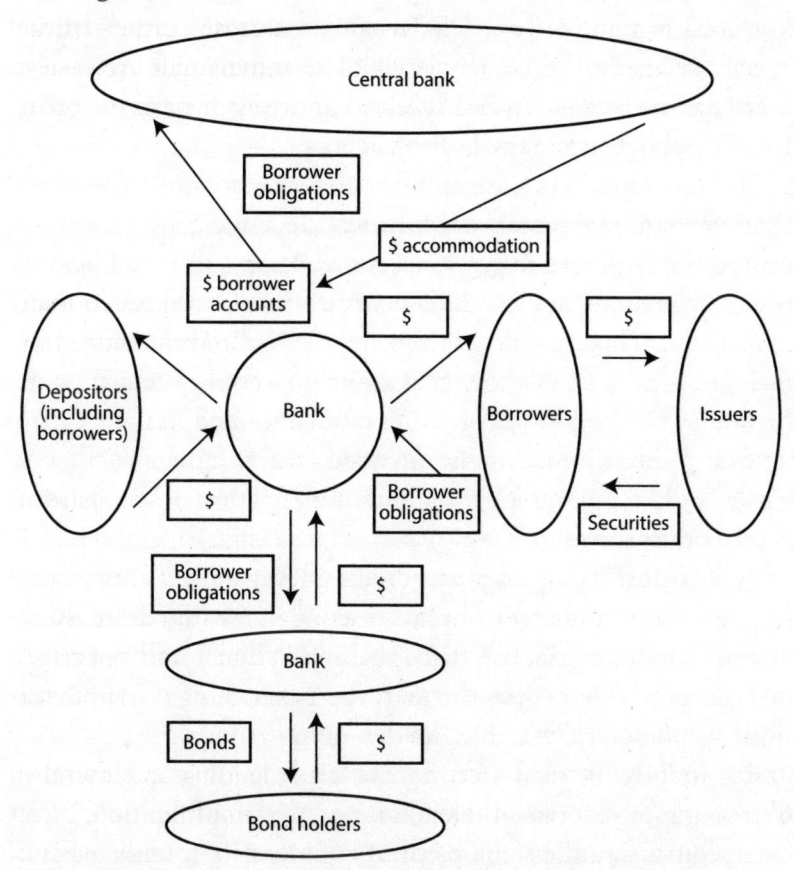

Figure 6. Financial markets with public underwriting and securitization

This takes us to repo transactions, one of the two transaction technologies that are probably the closest substitutes for traditional bank lending and deposit taking in the shadow-banking sector.

Securities sale and repurchase agreements—aka "repos"—are short-term lending transactions pursuant to which a borrower sells certain assets to a lender, while agreeing to repurchase the same assets within a day or two at a slightly higher price. Financially speaking, a repo is a close functional equivalent of a short-term secured loan. The variable "haircut" between selling and purchasing price serves as the (typically very low) borrowing charge. The initial selling price serves as the loan principal. The sold and then repurchased asset serves as collateral. The assets in question typically are US Treasury securities, other federal agency securities, or some species of seemingly safe ABS—e.g., mortgage-backed—that has received an investment grade rating from a publicly accredited rating agency.

The repo markets are probably the largest subsector of the shadow-banking sector, accounting for some $3.7 trillion in transaction volume. Repo transactions do not so much *amplify* ordinary banking activity, like securitizations do, as functionally *replicate* it. This they do both in their so-called maturity transformation properties—low-cost short borrowings accompanied by higher-yielding longer-term investments—and in their capacity first to increase privately extended credit aggregates, then to trigger public accommodation and monetization of the same, as described in Section I.

Repo transactions augment credit aggregates economy-wide in a manner reminiscent of that at work in the "credit multiplication" model of finance discussed in Section I and portrayed in Figure 2. This occurs through the practice of rehypothecation, pursuant to which a lender–cum–temporary purchaser of an underlying repo security can repledge it as collateral in borrowing of its own—thus initiating a chain of multiple credit extensions using the same piece of collateral. The more links in the chain involving this one piece of collateral, the more credit is generated upon its basis.

Finance without Financiers

The concatenation of multiple sequential lending transactions upon the basis of a single piece of collateral, sometimes referred to suggestively as "churning," lends repo transactions a "velocity" akin to the velocity of money circulation first identified as important by Irving Fisher many decades ago. For this very reason, along with the fact that sovereign debt instruments make up the lion's share of repo collateral, some analysts of the global financial system have begun to suggest that rehypothecated collateral chains, on the one hand, and more orthodox monetary aggregates such as the Fed's M2 measure,[25] on the other, are effectively substitutes for one another.

Things accordingly look as depicted in Figure 7. The small size of the disc on the left represents the comparatively small "base" of Treasury and government-sponsored enterprise (GSE) debt—themselves, of course, public liabilities—that can support a much larger volume of repo lending through the practice of rehypothecation. The larger discs to the right correspondingly represent this larger volume of repo borrowing and lending built upon the smaller base of public debt. Note finally that since banks themselves can act as repo lenders and need no pre-accumulated funds to act in this fashion, rehypothecated repo not only *multiplies* pre-accumulated funds but occurs in part with no need of such funds at all. It adheres to the credit generation picture of Section I.

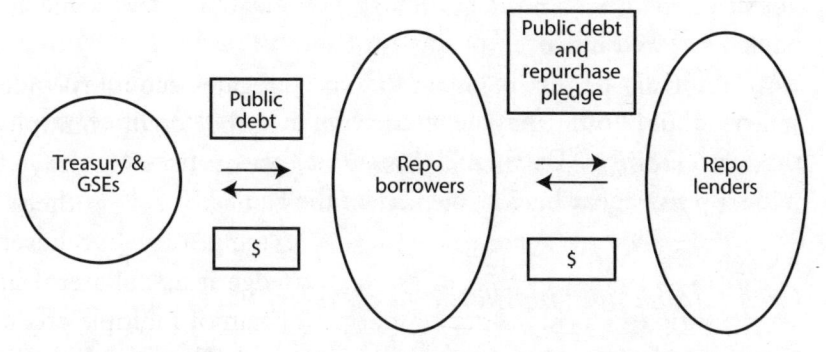

Figure 7. Financial markets with public underwriting and repo

From private to public: Fed accommodation and monetization

Turning from bank replication to public accommodation and monetization, it is first worth noting that the *Fed* actually *invented* repo, as a means of financing World War I expenditures, while the Federal Reserve Bank of New York (FRBNY) now acts as the largest counterparty in repo markets.[26] US Treasury securities, moreover, as supplemented by GSE agency securities, still constitute the principal underlying assets on which repo transactions occur.[27] Hence private repo itself in effect "monetizes" trillions of dollars of *public* full faith and credit that has been previously securitized on the model of sovereign debt as described in Section III.

Where literal *accommodation* in the sense of Sections I and II occurs, however, is, as there, in guaranteed *clearing*.[28] Two publicly guaranteed clearing banks—BNY Mellon and JPMorgan Chase—serve as guarantor/clearing banks for the largest of the repo markets, the so-called triparty market. The significance of this fact is apparent in light of the fact that Fed accommodation of bank lending, as described above, is itself necessitated by the need to ensure clearing of payments. Things look, then, as depicted in Figure 4 above.

An implicit recognition of the fundamental similarity between repo clearing and ordinary bank check clearing, and of the role of public accommodation in repo markets, is found in the Fed's postcrisis efforts to limit *risk taking* by triparty repo clearing banks. The Fed has been pushing for reform in this area with a view explicitly to the linkages between the repo market infrastructure and "other payment, clearing and settlement services that are central to US financial markets" and "operated by the two tri-party agent banks" backed by the Fed.[29]

Credit derivatives markets and clearinghouses

Corresponding in part to the ABS–repo clearance pairing in constituting the shadow banking sector is the credit derivative–clearinghouse pairing. There are more financial derivative types than it would make sense to catalogue here, with a notional value totaling well into the hundreds of trillions of dollars.[30] What is important for present purposes is that many of these complex financial products are used either to construct synthetic lending transactions that replicate bank loans or, by enabling lenders to hedge credit risk, to increase leverage—that is, credit—in already transpiring lending transactions.

In other words, derivative transactions both *amplify* bank lending (as securitization does) and *replicate* bank lending without limit (as rehypothecated repo does). Amplification of bank lending, in turn, necessarily augments public accommodation and monetization, described in Sections I and II.

Mechanics: (More) bank-lending amplification and replication

Again, I'll begin with the amplification dynamic. Where a bank wishes to lend more than risk-based capital requirements currently permit, an alternative to securitization is to reduce asset risk by "insuring" assets on its balance sheet. This a bank can do by purchasing derivative contracts that purport to guarantee payouts in the event of asset defaults or value loss.

In effect, the derivative purchase amounts to a kind of insurance contract. It effects a transfer of risk, for a fee, to a party that is more able or ready to bear it, partly because the party in question is not constrained by regulation to the degree that the bank is. Derivative transactions, then, serve to amplify already publicly accommodated and monetized bank lending just as securitizations do. Things accordingly look as depicted in Figure 6, save with insurance-like derivative purchases from derivative underwriters (typically insurance companies) replacing loan sales to SPVs as the preferred means of off-loading the credit risk that attaches to loan holding.

Use of derivatives to off-load credit risk, as depicted at the bottom of Figure 6, enables the bank to keep lending without falling foul of any risk-weighted capital requirements imposed by regulators to modulate bank credit generation. In effect, the bank simply transfers some of its loan credit risk, not to the central bank but to the insurer. Note also both that the bank continues to margin-lend to people who invest in issuing firms, as noted earlier in connection with Figure 5, and that the derivative underwriter or insurance company is itself an issuer, some of whose financial securities might be purchased by banks or investors who borrow from banks.

But derivative transactions also can *replicate*, rather than merely amplify, bank lending—now in a manner reminiscent of repo rehypothecation. This is readily appreciated by comparing a credit derivative to its insurance-contract counterpart. In essence, the former is a tradable and indefinitely multipliable variation on—that is, a derivative of—the latter.

Consider a fire insurance policy taken out on a house. Such a contract amounts to a bet between the insured and the insurer —a bet that the former "wins" in the event of fire, and that the latter "wins" in the event that no fire occurs during the life of the policy. This transaction is presumably beneficial both to the insured and to the insurer, but is in most cases of negligible significance to the broader public. That is because, under the doctrine of "insurable interest" long operative in the law of insurance, neither party may sell the contract, and no other person may become party to it.

Now imagine a derivative contract whose "underlying" asset is identical to that of the insurance policy—the house that might burn. If we permit as many people as wish to do so to take either side of the fire bet by purchasing or selling tradable contracts that replicate most of the terms of the original insurance contract, things change dramatically. The contracts now become financial securities that are readily monetized, either through sale or through use as collateral in other transactions.

There is no *ex ante* limit to these contracts' issuance. They are subject to no analogue of the doctrine of insurable interest, and there is no reserve or capital requirement or other form of "monetary base" in connection with which they might be quantitatively restricted via some stipulated multiplier of the sort at work in the credit multiplication model of Section I—any more than there is in rehypothecated repo. In this sense, they represent cases of pure credit generation as modeled in Section I and Figure 3.

Like bank loans and repo transactions, moreover, these contracts also tend to proliferate procyclically during boom—i.e., credit expansionary—times, as risk perceptions diminish across the financial system. They are media through which bubble-inflating credit money aggregates can grow "out of control." If such contracts are in any way federally "accommodated" as they steadily boost outstanding credit aggregates, then they too can come to constitute an indefinitely extensible form of securitized, then monetized, full faith and credit of the US.

From private to public: (More) Fed accommodation and monetization

As it happens, credit derivatives *are*, and long have been, publicly "accommodated" much as repo and bank loans are—and again this is through publicly guaranteed clearing. Prior to the passage of the Dodd-Frank Act in 2010, most credit derivative transactions traded "over the counter" (OTC) through large, federally guaranteed dealer banks. These banks often served as counterparties in the derivative transactions themselves.

Since the Dodd-Frank Act, most of these transactions have been required to clear through specifically regulator-approved and federally guaranteed clearinghouses, which effectively assume the risk of failure on the part of the parties to the transactions. The dealer banks that constituted the OTC market prior to 2010, and the clearinghouses that underwrite the lion's share of the market since 2010, accordingly all have been implicitly or explicitly guaranteed institutions considered by all to be "too big to fail."

For the Fed to assure clearing as it does via these guarantees is thus functionally reminiscent of it assuring that checks clear via its accommodation of bank loans, as described in Section II. As if to underscore this point, the major derivatives clearinghouses now have access to Fed emergency liquidity lending in the event of a crisis—a privilege previously restricted to banks.

Once again, then, as with repo, so here we find bank replication and accommodation, which effectively enables private liabilities to proliferate indefinitely even while ultimately coming to constitute public liabilities—i.e., claims on the full faith and credit of the sovereign.

Commercial paper and money markets

A final component of the shadow-banking sector worthy of attention for present purposes comprises the commercial-paper (CP) and money market mutual fund (MMMF) markets. There are nearly $1 trillion in CP instruments and $2.6 trillion in MMMF shares outstanding. For present purposes, MMMFs' and CPs' chief significance is their roles as straightforward bank and bank-loan substitutes that mimic bank activity both in their credit-extending and in their public-accommodation and public-monetization properties.

Commercial-paper mechanics, accommodation, and monetization: (Yet more) bank lending amplification and replication

CP is very short-term debt issued by firms that the US Securities and Exchange Commission (SEC) has effectively deemed high-quality, "investment-grade" borrowers. Both attributes render CP a very low-risk form of lending for purchasers, and thus a low-cost form of borrowing for issuers. For that reason, the CP market is often referred to as a constituent part of the so-called money market for short-term debt instruments—almost as if to verify by popular usage the proposition that those who deal in CP deal in close money substitutes.

CP can be purchased on margin just as other securities can. Hence things can look, as depicted in Figure 5, developed in connection with securities purchases on margin in the capital markets. The public thus indirectly "accommodates" purchases of private CP issuances when it accommodates bank loans that fund such purchases, just as it does purchases of any other financial security on margin as discussed in Section III. In so doing, it monetizes private debt just as it does in accommodating bank loans made in exchange for borrower promissory notes, as discussed in Section II.

The public also "accommodates" CP purchases more directly, however, by providing for direct Fed "discounting" of CP purchased by banks themselves either from issuers or from others who hold it.[31] Figure 8 depicts the mechanics of Fed discounting, whereby our central bank purchases CP from banks that first purchase from issuers. (Depositors have been left out of the picture for the sake of simplicity.)

In effect, the practice of discounting CP amounts to near-direct Fed lending to CP issuers, effected by immediately crediting the accounts of banks that monetize CP and pass it onto the central bank. Public credit money generation could scarcely be more clear or direct.

The public also accommodates CP issuance partly through federally insured banks' guaranteeing the creditworthiness and liquidity of asset-backed CP (ABCP). Finally, the public additionally accommodates CP issuance by guaranteeing certain

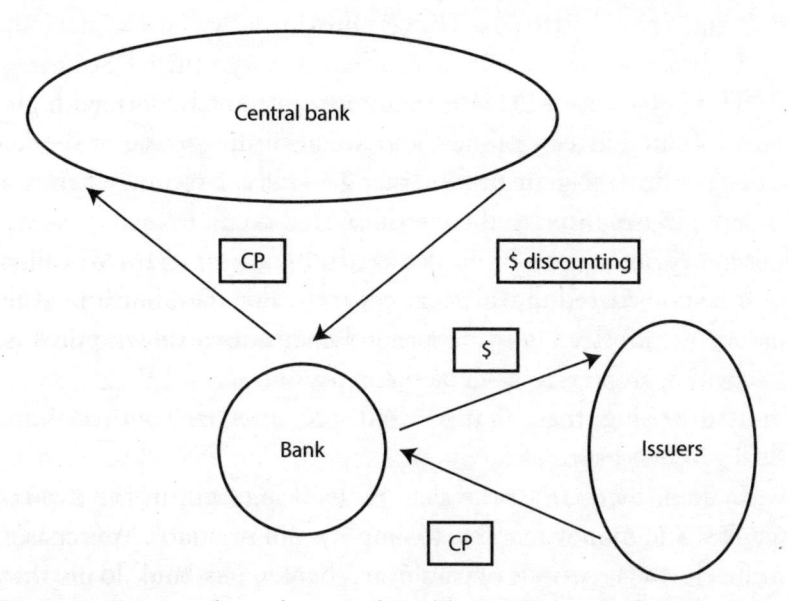

Figure 8. Financial markets with public underwriting and commercial paper

institutions that specialize in investing in this form of debt and monetizing it—money market mutual funds, or MMMFs.

Money market mutual funds: (Yet more) Fed accommodation and monetization

MMMFs are open-ended investment companies that specialize in forming diversified portfolios of CP and other short-term or otherwise "safe" investment securities—in particular, Treasury and agency securities—on behalf of their investors. MMMFs also actively engage in short-term repo lending, as it happens—bringing us full circle inasmuch as we began our treatment of shadow banking with repo.

With some exceptions, special accounting rules continue to permit MMMFs to maintain their value at precisely one dollar per share, while other regulatory provisions permit them to offer check-writing capabilities to account holders.[32] This means that MMMFs effectively *monetize* CP and repo on both sides of the balance sheet, so to speak—on the asset side by doing the purchasing and lending in the first place, and on the liability side by enabling their shareholders to write checks out of shares held in CP and repo portfolios. Things thus initially look as depicted in Figure 1.

This is because MMMFs fund most of their activity with pre-accumulated investor funds, and are accordingly one of the few species of financial institution that generally conform, when considered in isolation, to the intermediated-credit model of finance discussed in Section I and depicted in Figure 1. MMMFs must *not* be considered in isolation, however. For they, like any other issuer, are invested in by people and institutions able to purchase securities on margin as depicted in Section III and Figure 5. It is not surprising, then, that MMMF accounts are counted in the Fed's M2 measure of the money supply.

In sum, then, all of the shadow banking channels enable the capital and money markets to amplify and replicate, in all salient respects, the functions of traditional banks. This they do not only in their maturity transformation properties, as focused on by regulators and academic observers concerned with "panic-proofing," but also in their publicly accommodated and monetized credit generative capacities, as pictured in Figures 3 and 4.

So important has the shadow banking sector become in replicating the traditional banking sector, in fact, that the Fed itself has recently announced an intention to use not only traditional bank channels but also shadow banking channels in conducting its monetary policy through open-market operations in the future.[33] This too brings us full circle in a sense, for, as noted above, the Fed actually invented repo, and of course sits at the center of our banking system and, now, our capital markets and shadow banking system as well.

V. Some programmatic implications: Deliberate public credit modulation and credit allocation

It should by now be quite clear that the intermediated-scarce-private-capital view of finance is erroneous. We the public sit at the center of the financial system, and generate the resource that circulates through that system—our own monetized full faith and credit. This has always been true of our banking system and most of the corners of our capital markets, and is now, via the workings of shadow banks and the public accommodation thereof, true of our system's entirety. This carries with it important theoretical and practical implications. Among these are both newly appreciable opportunities and newly appreciable imperatives.

On the opportunity side of the ledger, we see that there is much more that the public can do where both the modulation and the allocation of credit aggregates are concerned than financial orthodoxy has thus far recognized or admitted. On the constraint side of the ledger, we see that the public not only can but *must* be more active where credit modulation and credit allocation are concerned—such was the principal lesson of 2008 and its aftermath.

Let's start with the latter. As seen in the foregoing sections, the public's critical role in accommodating and monetizing credit extensions in literally all sectors of the financial system now brings with it a significant vulnerability. That is the capacity of franchisee institutions to misallocate and thus overextend credit money during boom times in a procyclical manner—fueling asset price rises that themselves stoke further requests for and extensions of credit money.[34]

This vulnerability can in theory be dealt with through greater franchisor oversight and control over emissions of monetized public full-faith credit by franchisee institutions. Countercyclical capital regulation and other forms of leverage regulation, along with other measures now classified as forms of "macroprudential" financial regulation, are up to the task if employed by determined regulators.[35] That is probably the principal reason why bubbles and busts are not even more frequent and cataclysmic than they have been in recent decades.

The urgency of the modulatory task, however, is rooted partly in inattention over recent decades to what I call the allocative task. A macroeconomic environment that offers few prospects of remunerative investment in the "real" economy is one in which more speculative investments in the secondary markets grow ever more attractive. Yet these are precisely the markets in which endogenously generated credit money can recursively drive prices to dangerous, crash-prone heights.[36] If the lack of remunerative opportunity in primary markets can be attributed to market failure, then there is an obvious sense in which public inattention to its credit-allocative task renders its credit-modulatory task more difficult.

As it happens, there *are* market failures where primary investment is concerned—indeed, very serious ones—meaning that a more active allocative role on the part of the public finance "franchisor" is as necessary as it is possible. Among the failures in question are the inability of private agents to maintain stability with respect to what I have elsewhere called "systemically important prices and indices" (SIPIs)—notably wage rates, energy prices, and certain other commodity prices.[37]

We have as a public long maintained stability with respect to one SIPI—the money rental, or "interest," rate—and could just as easily do so with respect to other SIPIs. We could even use the same modalities—notably open-market operations of the kind that the Fed engages in every weekday morning from the New York Fed trading desk. So long as we don't, however, we leave the returns on long-term investments in primary markets in significant doubt, thereby encouraging shorter-term gambles on price movements both among SIPIs and among other prices in secondary markets.

This suggests two critical allocative measures that the public can and should take, both in the name of more stable and equitable long-term economic development and in the name of a more readily modulated public credit money supply.

First, the public can act directly on SIPIs themselves through open-market operations, as noted just above. And second, the public can reclaim a significant portion of the allocative role for itself by investing directly in, or guaranteeing *privately* made investments in, new firms in vanguard industries currently starved of capital notwithstanding aggregate capital glut. While at it, the public can also afford much greater retail banking inclusiveness, by providing deposit accounts for all citizens on the liability side of the Fed's balance sheet corresponding to the expansion of the asset side of that balance sheet entailed by more public investment.

The following three subsections outline these three mutually complementary proposals in just enough detail to render them intuitively graspable. Other, more technical work that I shall cite provides more detail for those interested.[38]

The summary version is this: with (a) the establishment of one new federal instrumentality of a kind that the US has had before, and (b) two complementary reforms to an institution we already have—the Fed—a much more democratic system of finance, including local institutions of the kind that Block's contribution lays out, can be had with but minimal tweaking of existing institutional arrangements.

A National Reconstruction and Development Council

The new institution I propose is a contemporary rendition of three earlier pairs of productive investment institutions that we once maintained.[39] In view of its additional, now structural similarities to the Financial Stability Oversight Council (FSOC), which aggregates information for and coordinates efforts among the nation's multiple finance regulatory agencies, I'll call this new institution a "National Reconstruction and Development Council" (NRDC, or the Council).[40]

The NRDC will effectively constitute a contemporary analogue to both (a) the War Industries Board (WIB)–War Finance Corporation (WFC) pairing that oversaw and coordinated our national mobilization effort during World War I, and (b) the War Planning Board (WPB)–Reconstruction Finance Corporation (RFC) pairing that oversaw and coordinated first the New Deal and then World War II mobilization efforts. It will also bear similarities to the First Bank of the United States, designed by the nation's first Treasury secretary, Alexander Hamilton, to pair up with Hamilton's Society for Establishing Useful Manufactures (SUM) to coordinate and facilitate our then new nation's financial and productive development.[41]

Indeed, one way to explain our nation's present travails is by reference to our having forgotten that "reconstruction" and "development" are never finished or "done deals." They are never "completed" or "accomplished" tasks, any more than knowledge, science, or history are. Like technology itself, national economies are forever developing, forever self-renewing, forever "upgrading." The NRDC is designed with that truth in view.

Role and functions

The NRDC will bear primary responsibility for coherently projecting and overseeing productive national investment at the federal level. It will develop, and each year will update, a National Development Strategy analogous to the National Defense Posture Statement updated each year by the Department of Defense. In between updates, it will oversee investments nationwide in pursuit of the strategy.

All of this will, of course, involve planning and coordinating in collaboration with other federal agencies, other levels of government, and the private sector—just as was done by Hamilton's

Finance without Financiers

First Bank of the US and SUM, by the WIB and WFC, and by the WPB and RFC during earlier periods of our history. The Council will also coordinate and in many cases secure or provide funding for national development projects, including but not limited to infrastructure projects. This it can do partly with congressionally appropriated funds and partly with bond issuances and purchases, again as was done by its three mentioned predecessors.

Where securing or providing funding is concerned, the Council will have multiple options. It can lend directly to, or purchase equity stakes in or bonds issued by, targeted entities or enterprises. It can also do so for syndicates of financiers, including private ones, which it itself joins. Or it can recommend Fed purchases of such issuances.

As for its own funding, this can come through either congressional appropriations or bond sales of its own, or both. The latter in turn can include general-purpose instruments, sector-specific instruments, and even project-specific instruments. Going the latter route can enable the Council in effect to employ markets' "price discovery" mechanisms to acquire preliminary information as to the likely success or otherwise of particular contemplated projects.

The Council will work closely with the private sector in the grand project of perpetually renewing the national economy. This in turn will involve bringing together the operations of many now diffuse federal instrumentalities. It is easy to imagine the potential for thereby establishing a more seamlessly integrated network of public–private venture capital and small-business financing operations. Various existing federal venture capital funds and other federal agencies and programs targeting innovative start-ups—such as, for example, the Telecommunications Development Fund (TDF)[42] and the Small Business Administration (SBA)[43]—can be organizationally incorporated into the NRDC structure.

As suggested above, the Council will also work in particularly close collaboration with the Fed, the Department of the Treasury, and the specific cabinet-level departments of the federal government whose mandates embrace specific national development projects. The reason for close collaboration with the Fed and the Treasury is that the NRDC's financial and fiscal operations will be adjacent to—indeed, operationally situated between—those of these two entities, respectively, and hence must be conducted in harmony with them. The reason for close collaboration with other cabinet-level units of federal governance, in turn, is that many national development projects will fall within the functional mandates of particular departments.

Renewal efforts in the realm of transport infrastructure, for example, implicate the work of the Department of Transportation (DOT). Efforts in the realm of energy infrastructures similarly implicate the work of the Department of Energy (DOE). Efforts in the realm of pollution abatement and environmental cleanup, in turn, implicate the work of the Environmental Protection Agency (EPA) and the Department of the Interior (DOI). Insofar as the NRDC works to facilitate the establishment of "start-up" companies in the private sector, meanwhile, it will implicate the work of the aforementioned TDF and SBA.

In all of these and other projects, it will be critical that the NRDC on the one hand and other cabinet-level departments on the other not operate at crossed purposes. It will also be important not to waste the considerable expertise and the many collaborative relations with other levels and units of government, as well as with private-sector industries, that these departments have developed over the decades. Much as the FSOC acts as a coordinating body among the Treasury, Fed, Securities and Exchange Commission (SEC), Commodity Futures Trading Commission (CFTC), Federal Deposit Insurance Corporation (FDIC), and other financial regulators, so should the NRDC in collaboration with *its* mandate participants.

Structure and relations with other public and private sector units

There are many ways in which the NRDC might be composed, structured, and both internally and externally governed. One attractive prospect is to think of the NRDC as a "system," by analogy with the Federal Reserve System, and to adopt either a three- or a four-tiered structure along the following lines.

The *first* option for the top tier would be the heads of the various departments and other agencies mentioned above, whose fields of expertise and mandates overlap with or are adjacent to those of the NRDC itself. This can be thought of as a sort of oversight and strategic planning board, roughly comparable to the FSOC, as noted above, and to the Board of Governors of the Federal Reserve System. It can accordingly be called "the Council," as the Fed Board of Governors is called "the Board."

Ideally, the Council will make decisions in a consensual manner, with voting conducted pursuant to the majority-rule principle only when consensus proves impossible to reach. This, too, would largely replicate FSOC and Fed practice. It probably makes sense for the Council to be chaired by a distinct person, appointed by the president for, say, seven-year terms with the advice and consent of the Senate. This would follow Fed practice, though the seven-year terms would, of course, exceed the four-year terms of Fed chairs.

An alternative possibility is to make the Treasury secretary herself the chair, as is done in the case of the FSOC. The advantage offered by this mode of operation is its subjecting the Council to more direct presidential control. But this can also operate as a disadvantage, inasmuch as the investment horizons of the NRDC must be long, and accordingly not overly vulnerable to sudden changes in politically sensitive presidential administrations.

In the final analysis, because the NRDC will be functionally and operationally situated midway between the quite independent Fed and the less independent Treasury, it probably makes sense to confer upon it a degree of independence intermediate between that of the Fed and that of the Treasury. Appointing a separate chair for seven-year terms—longer than those of Treasury secretaries and Fed chairs, while shorter than the fourteen-year terms of other Fed Board governors—seems sensible against that backdrop. Changes can be legislated in the future should seven-year terms come to seem too brief or too lengthy.

Similar considerations to those recommending seven-year

terms might also militate in favor of appointing additional independent members to the Council, as a means of lessening the degree of dependence on the White House that the FSOC model entails. In the alternative, the Council might be made to comprise only independent members appointed by the president for staggered seven- or ten-year terms with the advice and consent of the Senate. Under this scenario, which we can call the *second* option for the top tier, the other agency and department heads mentioned above—those of the DOT, DOE, DOL, and so on—would be impaneled on an advisory or coordination board, with authority only to make recommendations to the Council, not actually to control it.

In the event that this more independent governance model is adopted, it would make sense to choose Council governors on the basis of criteria analogous to those used in choosing Fed Board governors. A seven- or fourteen-member Council might then be assembled, its members possessed both of expertise in particular development fields and of past experience in government, industry, the academy, or some combination of these.

Whichever option for the NRDC's top tier we adopt, it probably makes sense to impanel just below it a more operationally focused tier. It would be at this level that detailed planning and execution of NRDC financing is done. We might call this the NRDC Investment Committee (NRDC-IC), and think of its role in rough analogy to the Open Market Committee of the Fed, the finance committee of any large business concern possessed of a chief financial officer (CFO), and the investment or fund manager of any investment bank or investment fund.

The Investment Committee under this scenario would assess and develop various financing options for various national development projects, running from grants through loans to bond issuances or purchases. It would then present these options to the Council for approval or selection, then execute whatever options the Council ultimately opts for.

The Investment Committee might comprise a simple subcommittee of the Council itself, after the Fed FOMC model, or might comprise mainly or only persons with significant financial management experience, with the chair of the Commission also serving as chair, *ex officio* or otherwise, of the committee. Either way, in view of the mainly technical nature of its functions, the committee members should have, jointly and severally, top-level technical and financial expertise and experience. For the committee will, in effect, be conducting the NRDC's principal funding and investment operations, like any investment or fund manager.

One additional layer of possible nuance is worth noting: it might be well to subdivide the Investment Committee into two subcommittees, one concerned primarily with direct "primary" market investment, the other concerned with indirect secondary and tertiary market operations. In such a case the Primary Market Subcommittee would act much like a contemporary investment bank does in underwriting and capital raising more generally. The Secondary Market Subcommittee, analogously, would function more like a fund manager in purchasing various kinds of securities issued by private and public sector entities.

Needless to say, both subcommittees would coordinate, as the departments of any large broker-dealer firm do, under the auspices of the Investment Committee of which they are part. And the latter committee, as noted above, would operate under the continuous oversight of the Council.

The third tier of the NRDC system would be a cluster of regional offices, housed in the regional Federal Reserve banks as the RFC's regional offices were. The idea behind this arrangement is to afford the system with "eyes," "ears," and operational capacity in regions of the country whose primary industries and economic conditions differ from one another in significant ways, the better to facilitate the operations of the more localized financial institutions that Block envisages in his anchor essay.

The Federal Reserve Bank of New York (FRBNY), for example, has expertise in and jurisdiction over much of the nation's financial services industry, which is, of course, largely headquartered in New York. The Federal Reserve Bank of Dallas, by contrast, has more expertise in energy and agriculture, in keeping with its region's primary industries. It makes sense for the NRDC to have regional locations that are similarly sensitive to regionally varying economies.

The Fed regional structure was developed over a century ago, when the nation's economy and population were distributed rather differently than they are now. This presents something of a dilemma where regionally structuring the NRDC's third tier is concerned. Because the current distribution of regional FRBs is anachronistic in light of regional conditions' many changes since 1913, to house in the FRBs would be to "lock in" the same now anachronistic division of regional labor at the NRDC.

The optimal solution here would be to reapportion the Fed's regional reserve banks in keeping with contemporary regional conditions, and then locate the NRDC regional offices in them. By "reapportion," moreover, I do not mean moving any existing FRBs. I mean instead opening additional ones for territories that simply had not filled in yet by 1913.

However we decide to structure the NRDC's layer of distinct regional offices, it probably makes sense for their roles and internal governance structures to follow a pattern that slightly varies to those of their Fed analogues. The ideal arrangement would probably be that of classified boards with one class of directors chosen by the NRDC, another by affected state or local governments, and a third by regionally important industries and labor organizations—all subject to NRDC veto, as in the case of the Fed.

The function of the regional offices would then be to "interface" with subnational units of government, industry, and labor in their regions for purposes of both communication and finance allocation. In this connection, a particularly important role for the NRDC regional offices will be to work in collaboration with the system of "public banks" elaborated below.

Figure 9 depicts the components, organizational structure, and financial flows associated with the NRDC. Line segments represent administrative linkage, while arrows indicate financial flows. "Appropriations" means congressionally appropriated funds, "remittances" means possible remittances to the Treasury, "Liabs" means financial liabilities (i.e., payment obligations), and "$" means money payment.

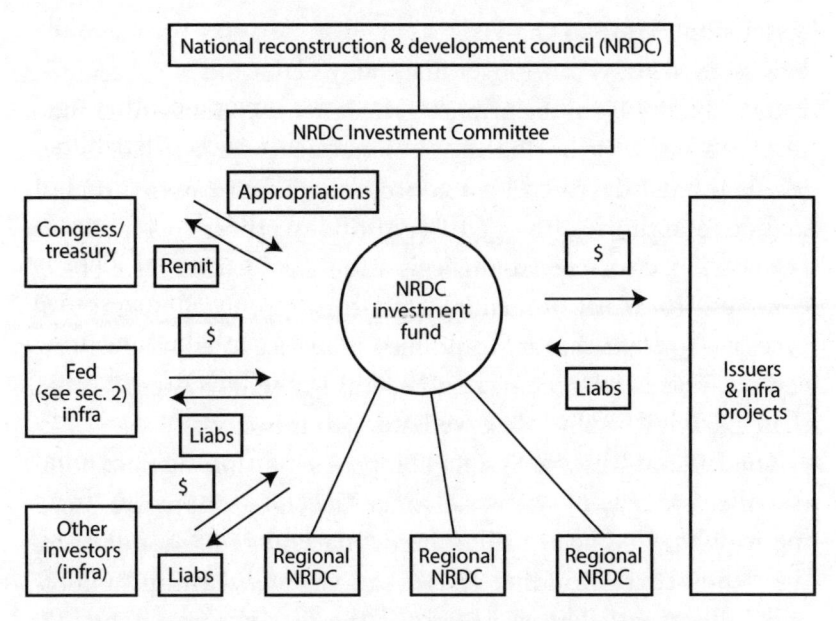

Figure 9. NRDC administrative & financial flow structure

It should be noted that if the division of the Investment Committee into distinct Primary Market and Secondary Market Subcommittees suggested above is adopted, the NRDC Investment Fund depicted in Figure 1 will be correspondingly bifurcated. There might, indeed, be multiple funds, as the committee judges prudent.

Federal Reserve reforms/restorations

As noted earlier, one interpretation of "democratizing" finance is the imperative to foster broader financial, commercial, and economic inclusion on the part of our population. This militates strongly in favor of certain Fed reforms—or perhaps better put, restorations—that will make of the Fed a full complement to the National Reconstruction and Development Council. I call this "Spread[ing] the Fed."[44] The simplest way to organize discussion here will be by sequential reference to the asset and liability sides of the Fed's balance sheet.[45]

Asset side: "Spread the Fed"

Few seem to know any longer that today's DC- and NYC-centered Fed is a far cry from the original. The latter was designed to function as a network of de facto regional development banks (the regional feds) overseen by a coordinating board with Article II executive authority (the Fed Board of Governors).[46] Had it not been designed so, its enabling legislation would never have passed Congress, for many influential legislators opposed a central bank precisely for fear that it would inevitably become DC- or NYC-centric. This is why we have a Federal Reserve "System," rather than a single "Federal Reserve Bank," to this day.[47]

The Federal Reserve System comprises multiple distinct nodes of collective agency at two distinct "levels"—one corresponding to what I've been calling here "macro" and "modulatory," the other corresponding to what I've been calling "micro" and "allocative." The Fed Board is the first of those, while the regional Federal Reserve banks—I'll call them regional Fed banks or regional Feds—constitute the second.

The regional Feds were meant originally to help finance continuous economic development in our nation's multiple economically distinct regions. This they did by monetizing—"discounting"—productive commercial paper.[48] That is a credit-allocative function. It's about productively directing the flow of publicly generated investment capital as defined above—our public's monetized full faith and credit.

The Board was in turn meant to coordinate all of this regional-development financing to ensure that its partial decentralization across separate regions didn't fall prey to recursive collective-action predicaments as defined above, and in consequence generate nationwide modulatory dysfunction—inflation, deflation, hyper-inflation or debt deflation. This is a credit-*modulatory* function—it's about centrally orchestrating, via ultimate control of the national credit pipeline, the coherent functioning of regional public capital disseminators to avoid misallocation and, with it, mismodulation.[49]

This was a brilliant arrangement—maybe more brilliant in potential even than its founders fully realized. In a single organizational stroke, it offered institutional means of solving the age-old allocation/modulation conundrum, while relatedly defusing our age-old national ambivalence about the dangers of capital concentration on the one hand and capital over- or under-generation on the other hand. That conundrum and associated ambivalence had been the twin drivers of a strange national oscillation between central banking and de facto monetary anarchy from the era of Hamilton on down through the Gilded Age, and at last they were institutionally solved—in potential, at least.[50]

The institutional solution, moreover, took a form that bridged not only macro and micro, not only modulation and allocation, but also *public and private.* For productive initiative was left to private sector producers and entrepreneurs, while decisions whether publicly to monetize project-associated private paper were assigned to institutions that were themselves hybrid entities —the regional Fed banks being, as they were, overseen by boards of directors with membership two-thirds determined by private sector entities subject to Fed Board approval.[51]

The story of how we lost this arrangement is a complicated one, but boils down to this. World War I broke out one year after the Fed's founding, with the US entering by 1917. This required establishment of a mobilization board and a specialized financing arm—the WIB and WFC noted above. The latter took on much of the Fed's allocation function in what was meant to be a temporary arrangement, but the need for a smooth demobilization after the war led the WFC to remain in operation until the end of the 1920s.[52]

The Crash of 1929 and ensuing Depression prompted a resurrection of the WFC nearly as soon as it had ended. President Hoover, who had designed the WFC as a cabinet official in the earlier Wilson era, revived it in the guise of the RFC. Roosevelt scaled the institution up upon taking office, making it the central financial planner of first the national recovery effort and then of the World War II effort. This in turn involved housing regional RFC offices in all of the regional Feds, as noted earlier. Hence this was the form taken by resuming the regional Feds' development finance role.[53]

The problem with this was, when Cold War fears led to the winding down of the RFC in the early 1950s, nothing replaced it to handle regional credit allocation, apart from a new Small Business Administration (SBA) without the same fulsome optionality. And so here we linger. But this is as much opportunity as it is loss. For it effectively shows us precisely what to do to direct our monetized full faith and credit (our public capital), whose flows I have mapped in Sections II through IV, toward the local development finance institutions that are the centerpiece of Professor Block's proposals.[54]

All we need do is this: charge the regional Feds with *monetizing local productive paper again*. Do it directly, through purchases of qualified paper issued by local enterprises, or indirectly via private sector banks and public institutions like Block's or the Bank of North Dakota (BND), or all of the above.[55] They know how to do it; their research departments are practically telling them how to do it through the research they generate on local business and credit conditions. All we need to do is instruct them to do it.

The eligibility requirements that the regional Feds impose as conditions for monetizing local paper will no longer sound in mere profitability, which modern capital "markets," as mapped above in Sections II through IV, decouple from production as distinguished from speculation. Instead they will sound in "productive development" as effectively—and democratically—defined by the NRDC's regularly updated National Development Strategy document, described above.[56]

The relevant financial instruments will accordingly become bona fide productive assets in the Fed's portfolio. Add to that portfolio both (a) issuances made by the NRDC Investment Fund as described above, and (b) securities purchased for operations of the price stabilization fund (aka "people's portfolio") described below, and we have a fully augmented and productively deployed new portfolio of Fed assets. These assets will, of course, include the paper issued by Block's institutions. And all other assets will be compatible with and indeed complementary to Block's.

To any augmenting of assets on a balance sheet, of course, corresponds an augmenting of associated liabilities. In the case of the Fed, the most salient liabilities take the form of our nation's money—the Federal Reserve notes that the Fed issues and the bank reserve accounts that it maintains. This means that the liability-side counterparts of the asset-side changes just described will amount to a new system of publicly maintained retail banking, which at this point will be digitized just as private sector banking is now digitizing. To this I now turn.

Liability side: Fed citizen and resident accounts, and a democratic digital dollar

A key role in providing for broad financial and commercial inclusion in the name of both justice and stability will be played by a system of digital Fed citizen and resident wallets that I'll now elaborate.[57] We can think of these reforms as means of converting the Fed from a "bank for the banks," as it is now, to a "bank of the people," which is more consonant both with our nation's founding ideals and with the goals of financial democratization.

Mechanically speaking, the core idea here is very simple. It is to afford every citizen, firm, and unit of government, and any approved noncitizen resident, a digital deposit-cum-transaction "wallet" at the Fed that functions (a) as demand deposit accounts privately held at commercial banks now do, and (b) as Fed "reserve accounts" maintained on behalf of banks and other privileged financial institutions at the Fed now do. Wallet holders will be able to transact both "vertically" with public instrumentalities and horizontally with one another through these wallets. Payee wallets will simply be credited, and payor wallets will correspondingly be credited, as further schematized and depicted diagrammatically below. This will immediately offer a plethora of distinct commercial and financial democratization benefits that are long overdue. I can reprise these briefly, then sketch out a bit more of the operational detail.[58]

The first benefit will be an immediate end to the pervasive degree of financial and commercial exclusion and, with it, economic marginalization that presently characterizes the nation's financial system and broader economy.[59] Gone in one stroke will be the chronic American problem of the "unbanked" and "underbanked," which not only deprives the nation of the creativity and productive talents of a full quarter of our population, but also unjustly subjects the marginalized to the depredations of payday lenders, check cashers, and other species of "loan shark."[60]

The second benefit will be a far more effective channel for the conduct of counterinflationary and counterdeflationary Fed monetary policy—that is to say, credit modulation, as discussed above. The present monetary policy "transmission belt," as it is called, is subject to profoundly wasteful leakages. For it relies indispensably on profit-seeking private sector "middleman" institutions that mediate between the populace on the one hand and its central bank on the other hand.[61]

Expansionary policy during a recession, for example, relies on privately owned banks to lend cheap federal funds to individuals and businesses. Yet these banks frequently use the funds simply to speculate on commodity and other markets, thereby routing funds away from their intended recipients and toward endeavors that actually raise the prices of necessities that ordinary citizens must purchase—foodstuffs and fuel, for example.[62]

"Direct" citizen/central bank banking will sidestep these leakages. Counterdeflationary monetary policy, for example, can be effected through direct crediting of citizen and resident wallets—in effect, a sort of "QE for the people" or "citizen helicopter money" far more effective, and just, than the forms of QE and helicopter drop employed during the Great Recession just over a decade ago. Counterinflationary policy, for its part, can be effected simply by raising interest on citizen and resident wallets—the analogue to interest on required reserve (IOR) currently enjoyed by privileged banking institutions with Fed Reserve Accounts—thereby boosting the attractiveness of saving over spending when this is macro-economically desirable.[63]

Similarly, the system of Fed citizen and resident wallets will allow for far more effective credit modulation and allocation than is presently possible. Modulation will be effected through the newly leakproof monetary policy transmission belt as just described. Allocation, in turn, can be conducted via the same mechanism. A particular firm, industry, state, municipality, or other entity that the Fed or NRDC approves for funding in pursuit of one or another productive enterprise or national development project, for example, can receive those funds directly in its Fed citizen or resident wallet. That can take the form of a transfer from a Treasury account, an NRDC account, or some other account also maintained by the Fed.[64]

A final benefit offered by a new system of Fed citizen and resident wallets will be the opportunity it affords to steer the various new financial technologies now discussed under the heading of "fintech" in salutary, socially beneficial directions. New blockchain and distributed ledger technologies (DLT), along with the digital currencies typically associated with them, are of course undergoing a "revolution" of sorts in their spread and proliferation.[65]

Many of the claims made for these technologies by their enthusiasts are breathless and in some cases even ridiculous. Some of them definitely have the potential to change the financial landscape for good or for ill, however. And many of the world's central banks are now actively experimenting with some of the relevant technologies as they look to upgrade their national payments systems and facilitate digital banking and transacting.[66]

Against this backdrop, a Fed-administered digital dollar—I call it a "democratic digital dollar" (3D)—looks all but inevitable.[67] And this actually can aid in the project of affording greater commercial and financial inclusion. For a system of Fed-administered citizen and resident wallets then can be accessed by their users not only online or at ATMs and teller windows, but also via smartphones and similar devices.

Many underdeveloped countries with past histories of undeveloped banking sectors already are "leapfrogging" into the twenty-first century, skipping over the twentieth, with phone banking technologies. There is no reason the US can't do likewise on behalf of the banked and unbanked. And the Fed's expansion of its system of reserve accounts to embrace citizen and resident wallets will afford an opportune moment to do so.[68]

Operationally speaking, this transition to a full "people's Fed" on the liability side of the Fed balance sheet will occur in two stages. Each stage will visit its own effects upon the Fed balance sheet—that is, again, its book of liabilities and its asset portfolio. The second stage, moreover, will also make of the Fed a seamlessly integrated complement both to Block's institutions and to the NRDC.[69]

During the first stage, current private sector bank deposit liabilities to depositors will simply convert into discount window liabilities owed to the Fed. Banks' asset portfolios will be unchanged. In effect, the Fed will simply be interposed between depositors and commercial banks, with the Fed owing those whom the banks previously owed, and the banks owing the Fed instead of the depositors.[70]

During the second stage, Fed wallets will be the repositories of newly Fed-monetized credit corresponding to productive lending that the regional Feds do both directly and via private sector banks, BND-style public banks, and the institutions that Block designs in his anchor essay. Publicly generated credit growth, as I describe in Sections I through IV above, in other words, will be expressed both in the Fed's asset portfolio and in its corresponding book of liabilities—in this case, Fed citizen and resident wallets.[71]

Several long-term changes that the switch will make both to "the business of *banking*" and to the financial system more broadly, as mapped in Sections II through IV, should be noted.[72] First, neither the capital markets nor the shadow banking sector will be fueled by monetized public full faith and credit as elaborated in Sections III and IV. Instead that credit will flow directly to productive products and enterprises as determined by the NRDC and the regional Feds.[73]

Second, insofar as banks owned by the private sector continue to lend in ways that find expression in the form of newly opened deposits, the latter will be Fed wallet deposits, meaning in turn that the banks will have to borrow through the Fed discount window as effectively administered by the regional Feds.[74] Here again, this means that public full faith and credit will flow only to productive, not merely speculative, projects. For as noted above, discount window eligibility criteria will sound not merely in profit potential, but also in productive potential as defined by the Fed and NRDC.

It bears noting here that the Fed already conditions discount window lending upon bank loans' possessing certain socially desirable attributes. The problem is that these sound primarily in profitability, which Sections II through IV have shown to be decoupled from production by stratified modern capital and shadow-banking markets. All that will change, then, is that discount window conditionality will sound in democratically defined, because Fed- and NRDC-defined, productivity. In effect, then, the discount window will become the "choke point," and thus the "focal point," at which our limiting bank lending solely to productive and inclusive forms of public credit extension takes place.

Note that this does not mean that more speculative bank lending and capital market activity of the kinds mapped in Sections II through IV need be prohibited, or will otherwise come to an end. It means only that this form of activity will not run on monetized public full faith and credit as presently, but instead only on pre-accumulated privately held capital.[75] This is, in effect, to say that private sector finance will be *made* to conform to the intermediated-scarce-private-capital picture to which it now falsely claims to *conform*. We will, in other words, *make* Figure 1 in Section I true of them. Reduced to a slogan: public management of public capital, private management only of bona fide private capital.[76]

Summing up, Figures 10 and 11 depict Fed and private banking operations as, respectively, they now normally operate and will operate under the proposed "Fed-spreading" reforms. Once again, arrows depict flows and "Liabs" means financial liabilities generically considered. "Dep" means deposit liability, and "Debt" means debt liability—two specific species of the genus "liability." Both diagrams ignore for present purposes the flows that run between the Fed and sundry non-bank issuers of liabilities both public and private—e.g., the Treasury and sellers of mortgage-backed securities (MBSs) pursuant to QE3. "DW," added here, refers to the Fed's discount window facility.

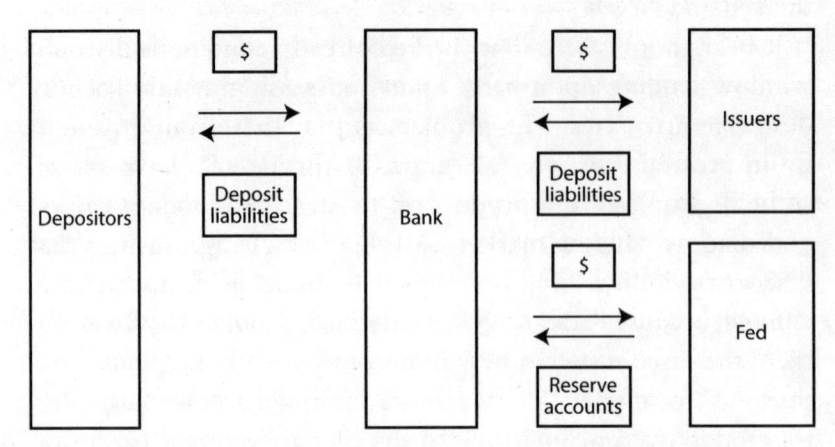

Figure 10. Current Fed/bank arrangements & financial flows

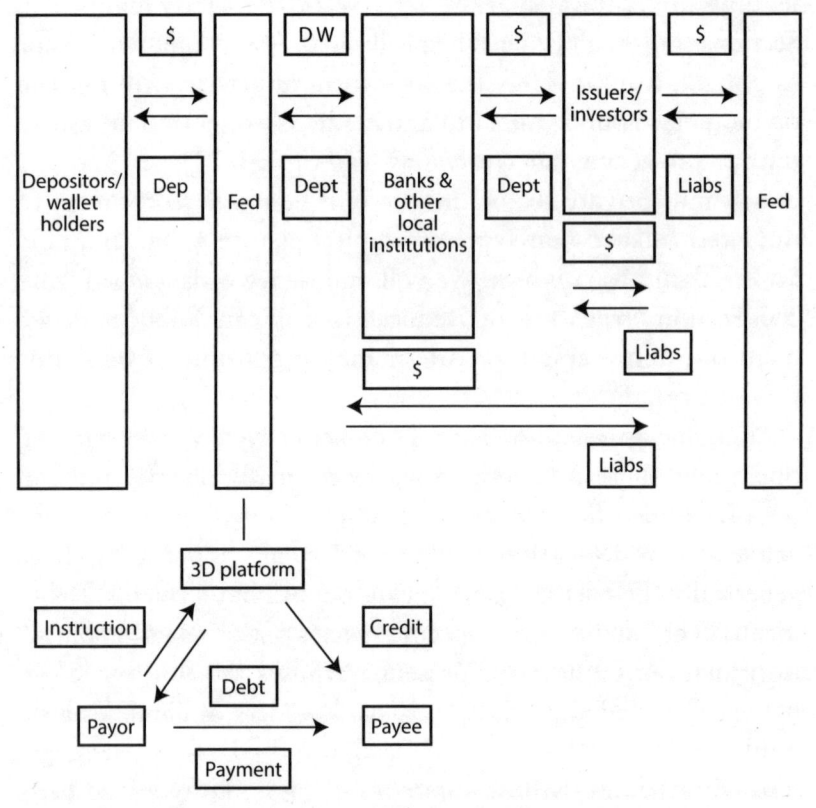

Figure 11. Reformed bank/Fed/NRDC relations & financial flows

A Fed price stabilization fund—aka a "people's portfolio"

Another helpful tool in maintaining optimal credit allocation, and hence price stability too, will be a price stabilization fund (PSF), or "people's portfolio." This fund can readily be made part of the Fed's asset portfolio, thereby further integrating the Fed's mission with the NRDC's mission in a manner that fits squarely within the mandate of each institution.[77]

The idea behind the people's portfolio is for the Fed to generalize its already well-established regime of open market operations with a view to limiting volatility in respect to more systemically significant prices than just interest rates. Labor costs, commodity prices, fuel prices, and others all can be added. Indeed, any sector or subsector in which inflationary or deflationary pressures build can enjoy price modulation through Fed shorting and purchasing activity respectively.[78]

Since the regime of Fed citizen and resident wallets just described will bring additions to the Fed's book of liabilities, moreover, the Fed will be accumulating new assets in any event. Some of these will take the form of new productive paper discounted by the restored regional Feds as elaborated just above. Some will take the form of newly issued NRDC instruments as elaborated further above. The people's portfolio will constitute another such class. Its assets will be those held to enable the Fed to conduct open market operations not only in Treasurys to affect interest rates, but now also in other additional securities to stabilize other SIPIs, as also described above.

What we will have, then, is fully public finance that works on behalf of *all* Americans, on *both* sides—asset and liability—of the public ledger. We will have what I call citizens' finance on what I call a citizens' ledger.

Figure 12 synthesizes Figures 9 and 11 while adding the price stabilization fund. All previously employed terms mean what they've meant in preceding diagrams. Again the diagram ignores for present purposes the flows that run between the Fed and sundry non-bank issuers of liabilities both public and private—primarily the Treasury and sellers of mortgage-backed securities (MBSs) pursuant to QE3.

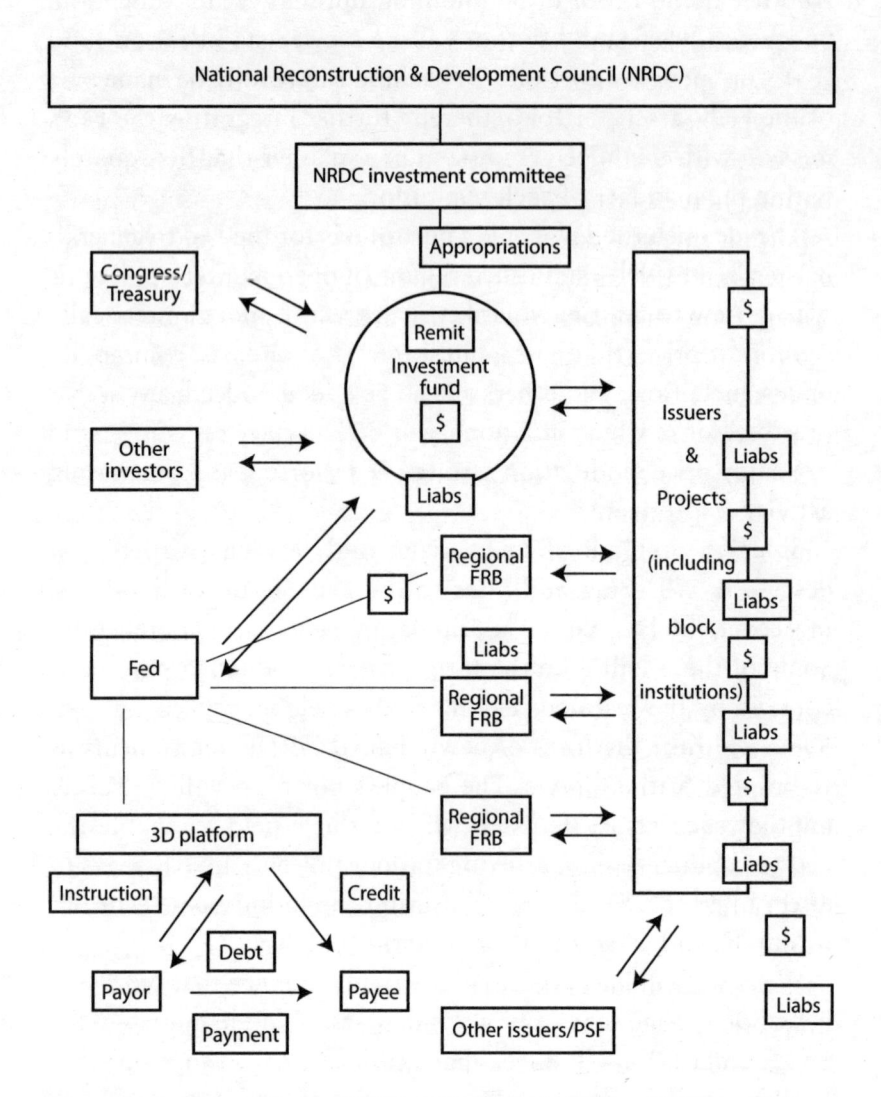

Figure 12. "People's Fed"/NRDC administrative & financial flow structure

Conclusion: Finance without "financiers"

As noted at the outset of this anchor essay, the intermediated-scarce-private-capital view of finance simply mischaracterizes contemporary finance. It stands the truth of things on its head. Much more accurate is a portrayal that captures what intermediation there is, while attending with care to the much more important role played by the public that generates and allocates its own full faith and credit in monetized form throughout the system. From this point of view, the financial system looks much like a franchise arrangement in which the public is franchisor, while the institutions dispensing its full faith and credit are its franchisees.

Reconfiguring our understanding of the financial system in this way is a critical first step toward making that system work in a manner that actually aids, rather than hinders, inclusive, stable, and continuous productive development. It underwrites explicit recognition both of the propriety and of the necessity of the public's taking an active role in allocating and hence modulating its own credit aggregates—its public capital—across the economy that it constitutes. And it opens the door to a bolder, more creative approach to designing—or rediscovering—effective ways of doing so.

The boldest approach not yet taken is the establishment of localized *public* investment institutions of the kind that Block proposes in his contribution below. I hope that the foregoing discussion has made clear just how free we all are to do as he recommends, and how readily we can adapt our existing financial system and the federal instrumentalities that constitute it to that purpose. "A picture," as Wittgenstein once said, "held us captive." That picture is false, and we are now free.

2

Financial Democratization and the Transition to Socialism

Fred Block

This chapter proposes a strategy for radical financial reform that could be implemented in the United States or in other developed market economies.[1] It builds on the argument elaborated by Robert Hockett in "Finance without Financiers" in this volume that credit creation is ultimately dependent on the power and resources of governments. As Hockett shows, that authority has usually been deployed to underwrite the profitability of banks and other for-profit financial institutions. The proposal here is that governmental authority would be used to build up a network of decentralized, nonprofit financial institutions that would significantly improve the allocation of credit with positive results for economic welfare.[2] If these positive economic results were to materialize, radical financial reform might then provide the critical missing element that could facilitate a democratic and gradual transition to socialism.[3]

The radical financial reforms proposed here are intended to extend the influence of democratic decision making into the economy in several distinct ways. First, differential access to credit is now one of the central factors in reproducing social,

Financial Democratization and the Transition to Socialism

economic, and political inequalities.[4] The very rich can borrow tens of millions of dollars at extremely favorable interest rates, whereas low-income households might be able to borrow a few hundred dollars from payday lenders or loan sharks at confiscatory interest rates. By improving credit access for poor and working-class people and for their organizations, these reforms could narrow that gap. This, in turn, could increase the ability of people to pursue both individual and collective plans, such as starting a new business that might be for profit or collectively owned, pursuing more education, or working to upgrade a neighborhood.

Second, as private financial institutions are incrementally displaced by public and nonprofit ones, there would be an increase in democratic input into decisions about what activities are financed at the most favorable interest rates. At present, flows of finance at low interest rates favor hedge funds, private equity funds, and speculative investments in financial instruments. These flows have created "a winner-takes-all economy" that has significantly increased employment insecurity and income and wealth inequality and created the concentration of wealth and income documented by Thomas Piketty and his colleagues.[5]

The alternative envisioned here involves two significant changes. First, there would be a dramatic increase in the financial resources held by locally based and nonprofit financial institutions that would prioritize the borrowing needs of those communities, resulting in more financing of affordable housing, small businesses, nonprofits, and employee cooperatives. Second, large-scale investments in research and development, infrastructure, clean energy, and energy conservation would be financed by a network of nonprofit financial entities structured to be responsive to public input.

Through these two channels, an ever-greater share of the investment flows in the economy would be responsive to the preferences of the public.[6] To be sure, this shift would require an ongoing process of social learning—a different kind of financial literacy. People would need to understand the different consequences for society of subsidizing investments in speculative financial instruments versus subsidizing investments in affordable housing.[7] Nor is the goal that *all* investment decisions would be determined by public deliberation; there would still be significant room for private investment. Rather the idea is a gradual democratization of decisions about critical investments that shape society's future. Over time, the public would have a greater voice in decisions governing investments in infrastructure, energy use, land use, transportation, education, health care, and new technologies.

This radical reform agenda has become politically relevant now because the process of financialization over the last four decades has channeled credit creation into several narrow tracks, so that a number of increasingly vital economic activities have been left without sufficient access to credit at reasonable interest rates. If these reforms were implemented, the federal government would provide enhanced subsidies, making it possible for both existing and newly created nonprofit financial institutions to develop the expertise required to finance these critical economic activities sustainably.

The debate in the United States over the Green New Deal that began after the 2018 midterm elections suggests that there is now a political constituency that favors major structural reforms to the US economy to address the global climate crisis and the ever-intensifying inequality of wealth and income. If that constituency were to achieve greater levels of political support, the financial reforms proposed here would dovetail with the Green New Deal agenda.

In fact, the US federal government has a long history of creating new credit channels to finance previously neglected types of economic activity. It happened in 1916 with the Farm Loan Act and in 1932 with the passage of the Federal Home Loan Bank Act, which became the basis for the New Deal's dramatic expansion of financing for home mortgages.[8] More recent federal initiatives expanded the availability of credit for small businesses, student loans, community development, and alternative energy initiatives. In short, what is proposed here represents a deepening of earlier efforts rather than a completely new direction. Moreover, as a legacy of earlier reform projects, the United States has

Financial Democratization and the Transition to Socialism

a remarkably strong infrastructure already in place to provide support to nonprofit financial institutions.

The full version of this financial reform agenda includes reforms to the global financial system that would work in synergy with the domestic reforms.[9] I will not address those global reforms at any length for reasons of space, but they embrace three key elements. First, there is a need to reduce the dollar's global role and to create a global credit institution along the lines of Keynes's proposal in the 1940s for an international clearing union.[10] Second, the amount of lending organized through nonprofit global development banks would be greatly increased. Finally, a global transaction tax and other measures would lower the flows of private global capital. Suffice it to say that those global reforms are plausible because the current international monetary and financial system is plagued with very serious problems. The system almost collapsed in the 2008–9 global financial crisis, and the subsequent decade has seen a slow and precarious economic recovery.[11] The stance of the US government has been the major obstacle to global reform, since there is broad interest around the world in revising what has become a dysfunctional global set of rules and institutions.

The argument of this chapter will be developed in five parts. The first section places the proposals in the context of historic debates over financial reform. The next section lays out two critical factors that have opened up the possibilities of a new financial reform politics. The third section describes the reforms and explains why it might be possible to mobilize majority support for them. The next sections lay out the standard dilemmas of socialist transition and show how radical financial reform could make it possible for a socialist government to manage that transition successfully. The last section is a brief conclusion.

Financial reform in historical context

Recent events in Greece suggest the possibility of a surprising convergence between radical financial reform and socialist politics. Starting in 2010, austerity policies imposed by the European Union produced high unemployment and economic misery. On

January 25, 2015, Syriza—a left-wing party opposed to austerity—won the Greek parliamentary election and was able to form a government. What followed were months of painful negotiations with the Troika—the European Commission, the European Central Bank, and the International Monetary Fund—over the terms of a new loan that Greece needed if it was to stay in the eurozone. The Syriza finance minister, Yanis Varoufakis, a leftist economist, became extremely unpopular with the Troika negotiators because of his unrelenting insistence that Greece be released from the prison of austerity. Ultimately, Varoufakis was replaced as finance minister, and the Syriza government conceded to a continuation of austerity.[12]

After leaving the government, Varoufakis revealed that his department had been working on a contingency plan if Greece could not come to terms with the Troika. The plan responded to the threat that the European Central Bank would stop providing lines of credit to Greece's banking system, which would force Greek banks to close their doors. The resulting absence of credit would bring the entire Greek economy to a standstill.

Varoufakis and his team planned to use the nation's tax identification system to construct a parallel credit system that could function while the Greek banking system was out of commission. In the absence of the clearing of checks by banks, individuals and businesses would be able to pay their bills by having this newly created parallel banking system debit or credit their tax account by the amount required. Those with continuing debt positions would have to pay some interest, but many of those who were economically active would see their debits offset by inflows of payments from others. Once this system was in place, ordinary economic activity could continue even without a banking system, and it might even be possible to reverse years of austerity in Greece if those running the parallel system made access to credit available at favorable interest rates. Some businesses that had been previously starved for credit could conceivably expand their operations. The idea was to use the government's authority to create a public system of credit creation.

To be sure, this plan was never implemented, and its mere

existence was seized on by other political parties in Greece to tell voters that the Syriza government was reckless and dangerous. Nevertheless, the incident is important because it represents a rare moment of convergence between two political and intellectual currents that have been deeply at odds for many decades. The first is the tradition of Marxian socialism that has historically adopted quite orthodox positions on questions of finance. Polanyi, for example, argues that after World War I, socialist intellectuals were virtually unanimous in advocating a return to the gold standard; even when socialist parties won national elections, they were usually quite reluctant to engage in deficit financing or other unorthodox policies.[13]

The second tradition is more heterogeneous; it includes thinkers of both the right and the left who imagined that redesigning the mechanisms through which credit is allocated in the economy could be a path to significant economic and political improvements.[14] We can call this group radical financial reformers; representative figures include C. H. Douglas, who inspired "social credit" parties in a number of English-speaking countries and various left-wing proponents of local money systems based on labor time.[15] In *The General Theory*, John Maynard Keynes pays tribute to Silvio Gesell, a German-born thinker who lived for a time in Argentina and proposed the concept of stamped money.[16] According to Gesell, currency would lose its value unless it was stamped each month, and the cost of the stamps would provide a powerful incentive against hoarding.[17]

With a few notable exceptions, there has been little love lost between these two traditions.[18] For one thing, fascists in the 1920s and 1930s often made use of these alternative credit ideas as part of their effort to blame whatever economic hardships people were suffering on the machinations of Jewish bankers.

Moreover, Marxists historically argued that reforms of the financial system were unlikely to make a significant difference as long as the existing system of private property remained unchanged. Even in critiques of finance capitalism, the argument was that financial firms were exerting greater ownership and control over the production process.

However, the Syriza incident suggests that there is now a possibility of a creative synthesis between these two traditions. This possibility is facilitated by the centrality of financialization in the current world economy and a willingness of socialist intellectuals to recognize that the power of private property can be diminished through regulatory initiatives and the creation of alternative institutions.[19] I will suggest here that radical financial reform could actually provide the means to overcome the formidable barriers to a democratic transition to socialism. Elected left governments from the 1930s onward that promised radical change have had to contend with capital flight and capital strikes when they try to implement measures that threaten the interests of property holders. This kind of disruptive resistance generally results in a downturn in economic output that undermines political support for the leftist government. Wright uses the concept of "transition trough" to describe these periods of diminished output that have repeatedly frustrated democratic socialist advances.[20]

But what if an elected left government were able to take advantage of an incremental program of financial reforms that had created a parallel financial system alongside the existing financial structures? It might be possible that after a ten-year interval, when these parallel financial institutions became rooted in the economy, the left government would be able to survive a direct conflict with propertied interests because the historical weapons of capital strikes and capital flight would no longer be sufficient to cause a sharp economic downturn. In short, radical financial reform could weaken the structural power of capital to resist a broader program of socialist transition. In this sense, the democratization of finance would be the paradigmatic real utopia because, over a decade or two, it might transform the balance of power in the struggle to shape the social order.

What has changed?

There are two reasons why a synthesis between socialist theory and radical financial reform might now be feasible. The first is that changes in the economy have created a serious mismatch between the existing financial system and actual investment needs. One key change has been a shift in the role of large corporations in the economy. To be sure, the United States and other developed market economies continue to be dominated by giant corporate entities; several of these firms now boast market capitalization exceeding $1 trillion dollars. However, this continuity obscures some important changes.

Today's dominant firms, such as Facebook and Apple, employ far fewer people and account for a much smaller share of aggregate investment than did such firms as General Motors and General Electric a generation ago. Facebook employs fewer than 40,000 people, and Apple has only about 90,000 employees in the United States.[21] To be sure, they accomplish this leanness in different ways. Facebook relies on hundreds of millions of users to produce content, while Apple depends both on subcontractors in Asia who produce its products and on networks of independent developers to produce new apps for its mobile devices.

The tendency to off-load risky and expensive investments to others has become a standard corporate strategy in this period. Uber, Lyft, and Airbnb expect drivers or homeowners to purchase new automobiles or upgrade their rental units. Many of the biggest firms have embraced "open innovation," meaning that they depend on small and medium-sized enterprises to do the difficult and risky work of innovation.[22] When a big firm sees a new product or process that has potential, they either license it or simply purchase the firm that did the development work.

Another element of the relative decline in corporate investment is the growing importance to developed economies of infrastructure investment. Infrastructure is, almost by definition, a public good; private firms are usually unable to make these investments on their own. The public sector must either pay most of the cost itself or make deals with private firms that assure them a future flow of profits. Either way, financing infrastructure involves a fiscal burden on the public sector.

The urgent reality is that the cost of needed infrastructure has been rising relentlessly. Populations are increasingly concentrated in urban areas that require much more infrastructure per capita in order to manage flows of goods, people, energy, water, and sewage. Moreover, new transportation and communication technologies usually do not displace earlier ones, so simultaneous investments in multiple systems are needed. Transportation now requires infrastructure spending for waterborne transport, roads, railroads, air travel, and space travel. In communications, we have landlines, broadcasting, cable systems, mobile phones, the existing internet, and plans for a much more advanced system for transmitting vast amounts of digital data. Furthermore, most infrastructure projects—both maintenance and new construction—are labor intensive compared to manufacturing, which drives up their relative cost. Finally, climate change is necessitating major new investments to make communities more resilient and protect populations from deadly storms and rising sea levels.

These trends that diminish the corporate role in investment create a mismatch because the existing financial system is structured to direct the flow of capital toward large firms. Much of society's savings, such as pension funds, are invested in the stock market. However, big corporations in the aggregate no longer raise money by issuing new stocks; they have been returning money to investors through dividends and share buybacks.[23]

Government entities at all levels continue to have access to capital at very favorable interest rates, but the public sector's ability to fund critical infrastructure spending has been constrained by fiscal crisis and conservative anti-spending ideology. Republicans have repeatedly created huge federal budget deficits by passing massive tax cuts that benefit big firms and the very rich. However, when the Democrats control the presidency, the Republicans have fought ferociously against public spending programs that would increase the federal deficit.

For nongovernmental entities such as households, nonprofits, and small and medium-sized firms, credit might be available, but it is usually at very high interest rates. This is critical because an investment financed at a 4 percent interest rate might have a very high probability of success, but the same project financed at 14 percent is likely to be far riskier. Think, for example, of

Financial Democratization and the Transition to Socialism

a nonprofit agency wanting to build affordable multifamily housing. The higher interest rate translates directly into higher rent charges that could easily undermine the original intention of making the units affordable. In short, the consequence of the mismatch is that many potentially productive investments do not occur, resulting in less aggregate investment and slower growth in economic output.

We can identify four distinct categories of economic activity in the United States that are chronically constrained by the absence of credit at reasonable rates.

Infrastructure spending including green investments

Estimates from the American Society of Civil Engineers (ASCE) are that the United States will have an infrastructure deficit of something in the order of $4.6 trillion over the next decade.[24] Governments at the federal, state, and local level have been experiencing fiscal stress for a generation and are reluctant to take on the increased debt burden required to finance vitally needed infrastructure maintenance and improvement. There have been limited experiments with public–private partnerships to address infrastructure needs, such as privately financed toll roads, but the results have not been particularly promising.

Moreover, the ASCE estimates do not include the huge costs of the clean-energy infrastructure required to address climate change. There is now ample evidence that a variety of outlays by households and firms to reduce energy consumption or to install solar panels or wind turbines will produce a high return on investment.[25] For example, replacing incandescent bulbs with LED bulbs can pay for itself in a year, and insulating walls and attics in single-family homes can often recoup the expenditures in two to four years. In some states with prices at current levels, solar panels will pay for themselves in four or five years. Making these types of investments could have a huge effect in reducing greenhouse gases, but many are not being made because households and firms lack sufficient cash reserves and most existing financial intermediaries have shown little interest in these forms of lending.

Lending for small and medium-sized businesses and nonprofit groups

Repeated surveys show that many small and medium-sized businesses feel credit constraints that limit the opportunities to expand their activities.[26] Again, the major barrier is the rate of interest that they have to pay for credit. If one has to borrow on a credit card at an annual interest rate of 18 percent, very few opportunities for expansion exist that are likely to produce returns that would cover that debt burden. However, if the rate of interest were closer to 4 percent, for example, there would be a far greater menu of opportunities.

One of the key issues in this kind of lending is the question of collateral. Financial intermediaries are generally far more interested in lending when the loan is backed by assets that can be forfeited in the event of a default. The consequence is that lending in this sector tends to be tilted in favor of those engaged in real estate development. Firms in other sectors of the economy face much higher hurdles in gaining access to credit.

The problem of credit is particularly vexing for high-tech start-ups seeking to produce new products or new processes. Firms that have grown from start-ups to major corporations are widely celebrated as central to the vitality of the United States economy. But the reality is that many start-ups fail to cross what is called "the valley of death"—the interval between proving the concept for a new product and having a commercial prototype.[27] For many high-tech firms, this period can be five to ten years. Although a variety of federal programs, such as the Small Business Innovation Research Program, help firms through the early years of the process, survival becomes more difficult with every passing year.

Non-predatory lending to households

The deepening economic inequality in the United States has meant that many households in the bottom half of the income distribution are effectively excluded from any kind of nonpredatory

Financial Democratization and the Transition to Socialism

access to credit. As Jacob Hacker has shown, household income for many is highly unstable. Dramatic ups and downs are common as a result of health crises, spells of unemployment, encounters with the legal system, or marital instability, and such shocks are usually not offset by government transfer payments.[28] This instability of household income leads to extremely low scores on measures of creditworthiness.[29]

Beyond the sheer misery of being denied credit on reasonable terms, the consequence is that it is far harder for millions of households to engage in "bootstrap" operations that have historically been routes to upward mobility.[30] For example, small-scale entrepreneurial efforts such as running a food truck or fixing up decaying housing are impossible without some source of cheap credit. Similarly, it is difficult for adults to finance the acquisition of new skills without borrowing.

Nonprofit development of affordable housing

The United States faces an acute crisis of affordable housing.[31] The focus of developers has been on building high-end apartment towers that produce high economic returns. Those who are not rich have to compete for older housing, much of which is located in less desirable neighborhoods. And population pressure on this existing housing stock has driven rents to unprecedentedly high levels. Many households are forced to pay more than half of their income in rent for apartments that are small or poorly maintained; younger people have returned to the parental home in increasing numbers. If capital at reasonable rates were available, many more nonprofits could enter this field and either build new units or upgrade existing structures.

This mismatch has become so acute in the United States, in part, because of a series of mergers and takeovers that have given a relatively small number of very large banks a dominant role in both consumer deposits and outstanding loans. As of 2018, the top ten banks were responsible for 53.7 percent of outstanding loans.[32] Moreover, there is evidence that the very largest of these banks have significantly reduced their small business lending since the 2008 crisis, with the consequence that such borrowers face even higher interest rates.[33]

Financial mismatch

In summary, the financial mismatch is blocking huge amounts of productive investment that would improve the lives of millions of people. At the same time, the mismatch encourages destabilizing speculative activity and destructive financial practices. Since the corporate sector is no longer in need of outside capital, the financial sector directs ever-growing quantities of cheap credit to speculation in financial assets. The consequence has been the spectacular growth of hedge funds, private equity funds, and trading in complex derivative instruments. As was clearly demonstrated in the global financial crisis in 2008–9, this increased speculative activity can be deeply destabilizing.

This financing mismatch creates a political opportunity for radical financial reform, since the growth of speculation is dangerous and accelerates the growth of income inequality. At the same time, the lack of finance for needed productive activity makes millions of people worse off than they would be otherwise and slows the response to the crisis of climate change.

The second factor that facilitates a new synthesis between socialism and radical financial reform is that we now have a better perspective on the workings of the credit system than did earlier generations of left theorists. This new understanding, outlined by Hockett in his contribution to this volume, is basically the franchise theory of credit creation. In the modern era of central banks as lenders of last resort, the state basically grants a franchise to private actors to engage in the process of credit creation. Without the state's ultimate agreement to protect these franchise holders from failure, they would not be able to engage in the process of creating credit out of thin air. But this process of credit creation is essential; without it, economic activity would quickly decelerate in the absence of access to credit at reasonable rates.

The critical feature of the franchise model is that it makes clear where power actually lies. As franchisees, the private financial

Financial Democratization and the Transition to Socialism

intermediaries that create credit are obviously dependent on the government. Without the franchise arrangement, the risky activity of credit creation would sooner or later lead them to fail. However, these institutions also have a very strong interest in hiding the reality of this dependence because government authorities must also regulate the financial sector and place limits on the riskiness of their portfolios. Since the banks and other financial institutions make greater profits by taking on higher levels of risk, they are constantly facing conflicts with regulators about the appropriate level of risk.[34]

Their main strategy for gaining leverage on the regulators is to insist that the dependence runs in the opposite direction. They do this by arguing that banks and other financial institutions engage in the critical task of intermediation—connecting lenders and borrowers. They further claim that if they are unable to engage in the vital task of intermediation, economic activity would slow to a crawl and government revenues would fall precipitously. It follows that financial intermediaries must be granted maximal freedom to direct credit where it is needed. Excessive regulation of finance will "kill the goose that lays the golden eggs." Of course, the argument gains force because of the widely held belief that the fastest route to prosperity is to depend on the self-regulating dynamic of markets.[35]

Because the franchise model cuts through this ideological haze, it opens up a whole set of alternative policy options. One is to replace the current framework of financial regulation with the public utility model. That model is based on the idea that when a private firm is granted monopoly rights to provide electricity or natural gas to homes and businesses in a certain geographical area, it is appropriate for regulators to control the amount of profit that the firm can earn from that business. In exchange for giving a particular financial institution the franchise to create credit, the government should set a maximum amount of profit that the firm can earn. Such an approach would have the great advantage of discouraging financial institutions from taking on higher levels of risk, since they would not be able to retain profits in excess of the government-set ceiling.

The more radical option is for the government to expand the category of franchisees that are authorized to create credit to entities that are not organized to pursue profitability. This expansion can happen in two ways. One is for the government to create in-house franchisees that would be public sector agencies with the ability to create credit. The other is to encourage the creation of nonprofit institutions or entities organized by local or state governments that would be credit-creating franchisees. In both these scenarios, granting the franchise would have to be accompanied by regulatory measures, since public or nonprofit entities would still have incentives to engage in irresponsible or unsustainable credit creation.[36] But as we have argued, the United States has implemented parts of this scenario in the past. Hence the reforms that are proposed do not create something fundamentally new but simply expand the scale of what already exists.

Another advantage of the franchise framework is that it highlights how much agency governments already exercise in shaping their nation's financial system. In the United States, for example, there was a very long history of a highly diversified banking sector with thousands of small and medium-sized banks. That changed in the 1980s when the Reagan administration decided that insufficient industry concentration was hurting the competitiveness of US banks in the global economy.[37] Government policies drove a huge wave of mergers and takeovers over a quarter century that ended with a handful of giant banks controlling more than 50 percent of all consumer deposits. In Germany, in contrast, a very different set of government policies worked to preserve a tripartite structure in which the terrain was divided among private banks, *Landesbanken* (state banks), and cooperative banks.[38]

The point is that even theorists who draw on a Marxian framework for understanding the dynamics of capitalism have to acknowledge what we can call the relative autonomy of the financial superstructure.[39] The logic of extracting surplus value at the point of production does not dictate a particular form or structure for a society's financial system. There is great diversity in the structure of financial institutions in differently developed market societies, with some relying heavily on public sector financial entities and others demonstrating considerable regulatory effectiveness in keeping destabilizing speculative finance in check. In short, state policies have been and continue to be critical in determining what a nation's financial industry looks like. All of this suggests that reform initiatives in this sphere could be successful.[40]

The reform proposal

The franchise framework alerts us to the reality that the federal government has repeatedly mobilized to finance activities that were otherwise facing prohibitively high interest rates. Financing for the first intercontinental railroad in the US was organized through federal land grants to the railroad companies. The firms then used the land as collateral to float bonds in the United Kingdom that financed the actual construction. In 1916, after decades of agrarian protest over the lack of cheap credit for farmers, Congress passed the Federal Farm Loan Act, which funded cooperative lending institutions for agricultural credit. In 1932, the Federal Home Loan Bank Act created the infrastructure for the development of savings and loans to provide mortgage credits to homeowners.[41] In 1958, federal legislation created small-business investment companies that had access to guaranteed financing through the Small Business Administration. This was the mechanism that created the modern venture capital industry.

In 1994, the Clinton administration pushed through legislation that created the Community Development Investment Fund, which makes equity investments in institutions that have been qualified as community development financial institutions (CDFIs). Many of these began as grassroots initiatives to revitalize impoverished communities. As of 2018, there were 1,000 CDFIs with total assets of $130 billion. In 2010, additional legislation made it possible for these CDFIs to float bonds that were guaranteed by the federal government.[42]

Also in 2010, the US Congress approved a $30 billion Small Business Lending Fund that provided low-interest loans to community banks that were willing to increase their small-business lending. Ultimately, only about $4 billion of government lending was approved, but it is estimated that the program boosted small-business lending by $19 billion.[43]

The reforms proposed here are intended to operate on a much larger scale than those previous initiatives. But the point is that Congress, usually as a result of grassroots pressure, has repeatedly shown a willingness to use federal franchising power to create credit to finance activities that were neglected by established financial institutions. This could happen on a much larger scale with sufficient pressure by an organized movement.

The specifics

The reform project involves creating a complete set of new or revitalized nonprofit financial institutions with the ability to provide the credit required to fund the four systematically underfunded activities described earlier. The government would extend its financial franchise to permit the scaling up over a ten-year period of these alternative financial institutions. Moreover, as these institutions matured, they would provide attractive savings and investment instruments for people who wanted an alternative to giant banks and mutual funds. As this parallel system expanded, it would finance high levels of productive activity, and it would change capital flows to reduce the size and power of entrenched financial institutions.

Before we get to the details, an important issue needs to be addressed. At the core of conservative rhetoric is the notion that governments should live within their means and authorize only expenditures that are equal to revenues in any given year. But this notion, of course, is contrary to how both businesses and households operate. Private economic actors distinguish between current expenditures and capital expenditures, and they routinely borrow to finance home purchases or the building of new productive capacity on the theory that such outlays produce a flow of services over a long life span that will exceed the annual payments required to pay off the debt. Governments, of course, also make capital expenditures such as building new airports or roads or sewage treatment plants. It follows logically that governments should also maintain separate accounts for current and capital expenditures and that it is appropriate for them to borrow to finance some share of these capital outlays.

Over the last thirty years of fiscal crisis and heightened anxieties about government borrowing, there has been a strong tendency to rely on gimmicks to finance urgently needed capital outlays. In some states, for example, governments have made deals with private firms to build new highways with the promise that the firm will be able to collect all of the tolls for fifty or hundred years. In Chicago, for reasons that are unclear, the city turned over the collection of revenue from parking meters to a private firm. Such measures have been justified with the rhetoric of privatization, but they make neither economic nor political sense.

In short, there are certain vital government outlays that should be financed entirely out of current revenues or through direct government borrowing. Off-budget mechanisms, such as financing through a public infrastructure bank or loan guarantee arrangements or credit creation by nonprofit entities, are appropriate for other categories of outlays where risks are greater, returns are uncertain, or the mix between public and private benefits is more complicated. But, of course, establishing decision rules concerning which expenditures should be financed through which type of mechanism ought to be the result of a process of democratic deliberation.

Finally, it is important to emphasize that both government deficits and reform of the financial system are not substitutes for an effective regime of taxation. Forty odd years of market fundamentalism have both created an ongoing fiscal crisis and allowed an enormous concentration of wealth in the hands of the top 1 percent of households. As Thomas Piketty has repeatedly emphasized, a return to truly progressive taxation is the best means to overcome the fiscal crisis while also significantly reversing the maldistribution of wealth and income. The historical data he and his team assembled show clearly that taxation played a key role in reducing wealth and income inequalities in the period from 1914 to 1970.[44]

With these important qualifications, we can establish three design principles for the process of radical financial reform. The first is that the newly created institutions should be structured as not-for-profit. This is critical for two reasons. First, profit maximizing is the fundamental source of financial instability identified by Hyman Minsky.[45] Financial institutions that seek to maximize profits face the constant temptation to increase the riskiness of their loan portfolios because higher risk equals higher returns. For Minsky, the only way to hold this temptation in check is through regulation, but both the power and zeal of regulatory institutions tend to fluctuate with changes in the political balance of power and fading memories of the last financial disaster. Nonprofit institutions are not immune to this temptation; there are examples of nonprofits that have been overly aggressive and bid up the salaries of their executives. But the combination of a nonprofit orientation, some mechanisms of democratic accountability for these entities, and strong regulatory institutions will reduce significantly the danger of Minskyan instability.

The second reason these institutions should be nonprofits is that lending is basically a labor-intensive activity. Face-to-face work is usually needed to extract from borrowers the disclosures that are necessary to evaluate their creditworthiness. And it is here that profit-making financial intermediaries run into problems. Hiring loan officers is expensive, and the number of transactions that each loan officer can handle in a given day or week is limited. When banks compare the profits to be generated by loan officers with the profits generated by portfolio managers who buy and sell various securities, the portfolio managers invariably win.

For-profit banks have addressed this problem through automation. They have eliminated the high staffing costs of various forms of lending by using computer programs to score and evaluate loan applications. But such techniques tend to redefine creditworthiness as resemblance to a statistical norm. If the applicant looks similar to people who have paid off loans in the past, then he or she will receive credit on reasonable terms. If not, he or she will be denied credit or, as with subprime mortgage lending, be required to pay a substantially higher interest rate than other borrowers. Since failure rates of small-business loans are high, the computerized algorithms tend to limit credit to firms that have already proved themselves or to firms that have collateral in the form of real property. This practice tends to bias credit availability toward real estate development and away from other endeavors.

But nonprofit institutions with a mission defined as facilitating economic development in a particular geographical area will be motivated to employ loan officers who develop the skills necessary to provide credit to individuals and firms who fall outside the parameters of the standard lending algorithms. Such institutions are far more likely to employ criteria of creditworthiness that emphasize the particular history of an individual or firm. With appropriate government support, they would also be in a position to engage in synergistic lending by extending credit to multiple firms in the same area.

The second design principle is decentralization, which will vary from extensive to moderate depending on which niche these institutions are seeking to fill. In the case of lending to households and small businesses and funding clean energy, for example, the idea would be similar to the 1916 and 1932 legislative initiatives—to encourage the creation of many new financial institutions at the local level that would rely on local knowledge to distinguish between promising and risky loans. In the case of infrastructure spending or support for high-technology start-ups, the idea would be to divide the work across five or ten institutions with some degree of regional specialization. The goal is to avoid re-creating the centralization and giant size of the dominant Wall Street institutions. Maintaining decentralization is also a way to assure that none of these institutions grow too large and that there continues to be some element of competition, so that those seeking funding have multiple options.

The final design principle is specialization: each of these financial institutions should focus on one or two niches in the market. They would not attempt to become financial generalists.

Financial intermediaries require specialized knowledge to become proficient in distinguishing between prospective borrowers with a reasonable chance of success and those likely to fail. Moreover, the criteria for distinguishing between meritorious and deficient proposals are quite different for energy retrofits, small-business loans, or infrastructure projects.

One can see this logic at work in the field of venture capital, where a handful of relatively small firms have been extraordinarily successful in providing critical financing to firms that ended by being spectacularly successful. The venture capital partners have been deeply rooted in Silicon Valley for decades, so they have developed a strong intuitive sense of what is likely to work and what is not. Moreover, the transaction is not an arm's-length one: the venture capital partners play an ongoing role in giving the firms they support advice, network connections, and other types of help. Nevertheless, success is probabilistic. Venture capitalists make their money from the 5 or 10 percent of supported firms that end up experiencing rapid growth and successful stock market offerings.

In short, venture capital is a knowledge industry that works because partners accumulate a deep understanding of the challenges that firms in their market sector will face.[46] In the same way, loan officers or cooperating entities in this network of nonprofit financial intermediaries will develop parallel forms of expertise that allow them to become more effective over time in deciding which loans to approve and which to deny. Moreover, as their knowledge develops, they will also be able to give loan applicants useful advice that can help improve their success in using the funds productively. But such expertise is far more likely to develop in the context of specialization, where loan officers are dealing repeatedly with, for example, infrastructure projects or the retail sector, so that they are able to learn from past experiences.

Alternative financial institutions

The proposal here involves four distinct elements that are designed to work together to produce a highly effective parallel credit system. In each case, legislation will be needed to create or expand existing institutions. In addition, ongoing government efforts, including new regulatory measures, will make sure these efforts are successful and do not produce perverse consequences.

An expanded sector of nonprofit retail financial institutions
There are numerous models for nonprofit financial institutions that collect deposits from a geographical area and then relend the funds for mortgages and to finance local business activity. Schneiberg describes how mutual banks were created in the pre–New Deal period as part of an infrastructure of local bottom-up institutions that played an important economic role, particularly in the upper Midwest.[47] Deeg describes the important role that public and cooperative banks have played in financing economic activity in Germany, especially investments by small and medium-sized enterprises, over recent decades. Mendell and her coauthors describe the complex web of locally based financial institutions that have supported the development of the social economy in Quebec starting around 1996.[48]

The main emphasis here is on credit unions because they already have a significant presence within the US financial marketplace. Credit unions are nonprofit financial institutions organized as cooperatives, in which each member has one vote and the opportunity to elect the organization's leadership. As a consequence of the historical popular distrust of Wall Street in the United States, much of the regulatory and support structure for credit unions to play an expanded role already exists. The US government has a dedicated system of deposit insurance and regulation for credit unions, and credit unions are eligible to be part of the Federal Home Loan Bank system that provides small banks with credit lines to help them through temporary liquidity crises. Furthermore, credit unions have accumulated a strong track record of functioning well even in economic downturns.

However, it also must be recognized that, on the whole, credit unions in the United States have not been particularly dynamic or innovative in recent decades. Part of the issue is that existing legislation tightly restricts small-business lending by credit unions. But even credit unions originally created by the energies of social movements tend to become routinized and limited in focus as they age. Finally, until the process of computerization had progressed quite far, credit unions simply could not compete with commercial banks in the range of services they provided.

Now, however, even very small institutions of this type—organized in networks—are able to provide clients with a broad range of financial services. Credit unions can, for example, provide access to a network of automatic teller machines and the ability to wire funds to other destinations. And these small institutions need not hire all of the staff required to do the appropriate due diligence for small-business lending; they could contract with small nonprofit consultancies that develop expertise in particular business domains and work with a range of different financial intermediaries.

Another possible and complementary strategy would be to rely on networks of public banks, building on the example of the Bank of North Dakota. Activists across the country are trying to persuade city governments to establish local public banks that could both hold the many accounts of municipal agencies and significantly expand the availability of credit for small businesses, nonprofits, and affordable housing. Although organized to be independent of city hall, these public banks would have diverse boards that represented different local constituencies. As with credit unions, networks of these local public banks could provide customers with the full range of financial services.[49]

Whatever the combination of credit unions, public banks, and community banks, the idea would be that the federal government could set off a wave of entrepreneurial effort by pursuing two steps.

Step 1 would be a federal matching-funds program set up to capitalize or recapitalize new or existing nonprofit financial intermediaries. Given the enormous costs that society has paid for its dysfunctional financial system, an outlay of $50 billion over five years would be a small price to pay to create a vigorous, locally oriented financial system. The idea is that local investors would raise $10 million to capitalize a new credit union or nonprofit

Financial Democratization and the Transition to Socialism

bank or public bank and the government would provide an additional $10 million—in the form of a low-interest thirty-year loan. Or similarly, a sleepy bank or credit union would be recapitalized with an additional $20 million that would be matched by $20 million from the federal government. The matching funds would simultaneously signal the government's strong support for these institutions and create strong incentives for grassroots efforts to build this new sector.

Step 2 would be a new system of loan guarantees to support lending by these institutions. Along with the capital infusion, the federal government could also immediately provide loan guarantees for these institutions to lend to households, businesses, nonprofits, and government agencies for conservation or clean-energy projects. The value of these investments has been well documented. Again, the urgency of a green transition would justify the relatively small budgetary commitment that would be involved since these loans for energy saving should have a very small failure rate. But this would be an efficient means to underwrite a dramatic initial expansion in the loan portfolios of these institutions.

On a less rapid timetable, a system of loan guarantees must be built to support long-term lending to small and medium-sized businesses. The design requires care because these loans are riskier and the dangers of abuse and fraud are substantially greater. The goal would be to create something similar to a guarantee program that exists in Germany where the risks are distributed across different institutions. One might imagine, for example, 25 percent of the risk being covered by the Federal Home Loan Bank Board, 25 percent by the Federal Reserve System, 25 percent by the Treasury, and the final part carried by the originating institutions. Because these guarantees are designed to support somewhat risky loans at the local level, it is assumed that there will be periodic losses from businesses that fail, but those losses would be spread across strong institutions whose revenues would be increased by the stronger growth resulting from more vigorous lending to small and medium-sized firms.

One complexity here is that many small local credit unions or community banks are unlikely to be able to develop the expertise in-house to engage in this kind of business lending. However, nonprofit consultancies that develop this kind of expertise can and should emerge and work with a network of credit unions to identify worthy projects eligible for the government loan guarantees. To protect against fraud, it would also make sense to license the nonprofit consultancies and subject them to some ongoing regulatory scrutiny.

The success of this strategy ultimately requires that millions of citizens be willing to change the way they invest their savings. At present, roughly 92 million people belong to credit unions in the United States, and these institutions control about 10 percent of consumer deposits—about $600 billion. With such a strong starting base, it is plausible that people would be willing to move much more of their savings from big commercial banks to credit unions once they saw a broad effort to revitalize the sector. The goal at the end of a twenty-year transition period would be to reverse the current ratio: 90 percent of deposits in the credit unions and only 10 percent left for commercial banks.

Nonprofit investment banks

These new institutions could be created as nonprofit entities jointly owned by large public pensions funds or by other nonprofit financial intermediaries. They would compete directly with existing investment banks that underwrite bonds. This would give local governments and public agencies an alternative to dealing with existing Wall Street firms when they decide to issue new municipal bonds. This alternative is important because the relationship between municipalities and Wall Street has been marked by both predation and corruption.[50] These institutions would also be able to finance large-scale infrastructure projects. But in evaluating these infrastructure projects, these nonprofit investment bankers could add an additional creditworthiness criterion. They would also consider whether the planning of the project involved sufficient democratic input and engagement from citizens in poorer and more marginal communities.

Financial Democratization and the Transition to Socialism

Finally, these new institutions would also be able to securitize loans written by nonprofit financial intermediaries. For example, loans to individuals and businesses to finance solar power or to build multifamily housing could be consolidated into bonds that would be sold to investors. Through this instrument, the credit unions would have an infusion of new capital to expand their lending activity further. To be sure, this securitization process would have to be carefully regulated to prevent any participants from playing the "pass-the-trash" game that was so central to the subprime mortgage disaster. But with all of the key participants operating on a nonprofit basis, the incentives for large-scale fraud would be diminished.

The issuance of these bonds would provide individual investors, pension funds, and other institutions a safe and socially productive outlet for their savings. The intuition here is that most people are not looking for outsized returns on their personal saving; they want primarily security and predictability. Bonds that reliably paid 3 or 4 percent per year would be attractive, especially when people understood that these investments were contributing to sustainable economic growth that was improving their own communities.

The consequence over time would be a dramatic transformation in the structure of most people's retirement portfolios. Instead of the current mix, which is heavily weighted toward equities, the bulk of retirement savings would be made up of various types of publicly issued and safe bonds. As the public gradually retreated from corporate stocks, there would be a decline in share values, and proponents of significant reforms in corporate governance would gain significant leverage. In order to make their shares more attractive, big firms would now be forced to compete in a process of "definancialization." This would include bans on share repurchases, significant reductions in executive compensation, improvements in corporate governance that included recognizing other stakeholders, and an abandonment of the short-term time horizons associated with maximizing shareholder value.

A public investment bank

Given the centrality of infrastructure spending, there is also the need for a national investment bank that would be able to create credit to fund needed infrastructure projects. On the principle of decentralization, this should be organized through five or six regional units that operated with a high degree of autonomy while also being able to share knowledge about the complexity of particular types of infrastructure projects. This bank would be able to raise capital by selling bonds to the public through one or another of the public investment banks.

But the principle of competition would also operate in that a city, a state, or some kind of regional entity would have several different options for funding a particular infrastructure project. It might go to one of the public investment banks to sell bonds or it might arrange to finance the project through the closest office of the public investment bank. The competition would reinforce the need for all of these entities to develop staff expertise, and it would maintain pressure on them to make the loans available at the lowest possible interest rates.

However, the public infrastructure bank also requires arrangements to assure democratic accountability. Both the headquarters and the regional offices would have management boards that included representatives of various constituencies such as business, labor, community groups, and elected officials. Congressional oversight would also be required to assure that the institutions were consistently serving the public and that large-scale infrastructure projects were carried out in ways consistent with both social and environmental impact studies. Since some large-scale infrastructure projects can reshape entire geographic regions, procedures must be developed to assure broad public involvement in these decisions.

A nonprofit innovation stock market

A final measure is needed to assure a higher level of investment in innovative small firms working at the technological frontier. Such firms have been chronically starved of capital, and they have been heavily dependent upon various government programs for their survival. Moreover, since the path to long-term survival is so difficult, many of these entrepreneurs see little choice but to sell their firms to large corporate buyers, with the consequence of less diversity and competition in the economy.

Since the chances that any one of these firms will survive and be profitable are relatively low, a strategy is needed that allows investors to hold stakes in several of these firms with the idea that success by a small minority of firms would compensate for losses by all of the others. This is the principle on which venture capital firms operate, but venture capital is extremely labor intensive and thus very difficult to scale up to provide resources for a much larger number of firms.

The solution would be for the government to work with the nonprofit investment banks to create a new stock exchange where high-technology start-up firms would be rigorously screened and have the opportunity to sell shares up to some limit, such as $10 million. The shares would not compromise the existing ownership structure of the firm, but they would entitle shareholders to a portion of the profits that the firm might eventually earn. Specialized mutual funds would then put together diversified portfolios that would take positions in hundreds or possibly thousands of these firms. Individual and institutional investors would then be able to have a stake in future innovation by purchasing shares in these mutual funds.

Some successful firms might decide to graduate from this stock market to the major stock markets, assuring a large return to those holding their shares. But other firms, including those organized as cooperatives or B corporations, might opt to remain listed and continue using the market periodically as a way to raise capital for expansion.[51] Here again, the idea is that a relatively small institutional change could have broad consequences in significantly expanding the diversity within the business environment. Most importantly, high-tech start-up firms, regardless of their form of business organization, would face improved prospects for long-term survival.

Economic synergy

This set of financial reforms is designed to accomplish several distinct goals. They would contribute significantly to a more dynamic and more environmentally sustainable economy by generating a higher rate of productive investment in infrastructure, multifamily housing, clean energy, conservation, and small businesses. This would result in new job creation and expand the flow of services that people really need. This set of reforms is also intended to weaken the dominant position of existing financial institutions, including both giant banks and huge investment management companies such as BlackRock and Vanguard. This weakening would happen through an incremental shift of consumer savings from for-profit to nonprofit entities. Currently, something close to 90 percent of consumer bank deposits are with large commercial banks, but with the reinvigoration of credit unions and nonprofit banks, we could expect a large-scale shift of these deposits toward more locally based institutions as consumers recognize the benefits of reinvesting in their communities. At the same time, savers would have attractive alternatives to putting their retirement funds in mutual funds and common stocks. They would be able to shift to a variety of bonds issued by nonprofit investment banks or the public investment bank, and they could acquire mutual funds invested in the innovation stock market.

The combination of the new institutions and changed consumer behavior would help move the United States away from the stock market–centered model of business development. Small and medium-sized firms would have a much richer set of financing options than aspiring to become publicly traded firms. By relying on finance from nonprofit institutions or the innovation stock market, such firms would be able to raise significant amounts of capital without the risk of takeovers that occur with stock market funding. This would make it far easier for new firms to compete directly against incumbent firms. Such a diversified funding environment is far more appropriate in the era of the vanishing corporation than continuing a system of financing that was linked to an earlier historical period in which large firms accounted for a very high percentage of economic activity.

Finally, this process of reorganization would weaken the political clout of large financial institutions. With less control over consumer deposits and retirement savings, giant institutions would have to shrink and make do with reduced flows of profits. This, in turn, would reduce the resources they had to invest in campaign contributions and right-wing think tanks. It would become harder for them to push back against regulators and harder for them to stop the advance of their nonprofit competitors.

The problem of socialist transition

The recent experience of Greece's Syriza government exemplifies the problem faced by leftist parties that have promised their supporters a definitive break with "capitalism," defined as the rationality of a market economy based on the pursuit of profit. Such governments generally face a combination of domestic and foreign opposition that fundamentally weakens the domestic economy, with the usual result that the leftist government retreats from its transformational agenda. In Chile in 1973, the elected government persisted in its project despite economic troubles, but mounting domestic turmoil provided the excuse for a US-backed military faction to seize power. One way or another, every time an electoral path to socialism has been attempted, it has ended in defeat.

Wright has theorized this problem in terms of the "transition trough" that an elected socialist government is likely to face.[52] The new administration is elected with a promise to raise living standards for a majority of the population, but domestic and foreign resistance generally leads to an economic downturn that inevitably erodes the government's support because the promised increases in output and more equitable distribution fail to occur. So the critical issue is whether there are means by which both the depth and the duration of the transition trough can be minimized. If the trough is shallower and briefer, the chances are greater that the government can consolidate its domestic support and move forward with its transitional program.

The trough is generally created through the confluence of domestic and global pressures. At home, resistance to the government's proposals means that businesses and wealthy individuals are likely to forgo new investments and large firms might begin layoffs in anticipation of weakening demand. At the same time, both foreign and domestic groups are likely to start shifting liquid capital out of the country in anticipation of a fall in the value of the national currency. The government's ability to offset this capital flight with increased foreign borrowing is likely to be limited because of the hostility of international banks and global organizations. The result is invariably a currency crisis where the government has to take action to prevent a dramatic fall in the value of the nation's currency.[53] The government might impose controls to slow the flight of capital, but it usually has to raise domestic interest rates in an effort to slow the outflows. Then the tighter monetary policy generally has the effect of further slowing domestic economic activity so that the transition trough becomes even deeper.

This combination is powerful because the domestic and foreign opponents are able to continue the pressure month after month. It makes sense for firms to withhold investment and make do with lower profits for a year or longer in order to defeat the leftist threat and guarantee larger profits in the future. At the same time, the outflows of capital are likely to continue, so the government has little respite from the ongoing currency crisis. The possibility of a reform-driven domestic economic expansion gets pushed off into the future as the transition trough becomes longer and deeper.

However, the kinds of financial reforms proposed here have the capacity to reduce the severity and duration of the transition trough. The central mechanism is the expansion of the nonprofit portion of the financial system and the shrinking of the for-profit segment. The nonprofit financial institutions could be expected to maintain and expand their lending in order to blunt any kind of investment slowdown by large firms and for-profit financial institutions. Given the growing importance of infrastructure spending and the fact that employment by large corporations has already dropped, there is a distinct possibility that expanded lending by the more democratic financial institutions would maintain employment at pre-transition levels.

Even if there were little or no domestic investment slowdown, however, the pressures of capital flight would continue. But it is here that the growing size of the nonprofit financial institutions would become relevant. Not only would they be reluctant to participate in the capital flight, they would also have the ability to increase their borrowing abroad to offset the pressures on the national currency. So, for example, a public infrastructure bank and large nonprofit investment banks, with established track records of operating effectively, would retain their capacity to borrow on global capital markets. They might in this transition period have to pay a somewhat higher rate of interest, but their increased borrowing could give the government some respite from pressures on the currency.

Moreover, if the level of domestic economic activity did not fall substantially during the transition, the government would have more legitimacy in denouncing the flight of capital as a deliberate effort at economic sabotage. As long as the economy was doing reasonably well, the claim that investors were shifting capital abroad to protect themselves from economic disaster would be less credible. This would create a political context in which the government could legitimately impose more effective capital controls to slow the outflows. The combination of those controls and increased international borrowing by large nonprofit banks might be sufficient to avoid a currency crisis.

With this additional breathing room, the left government might be able to sustain its reform agenda long enough that the electorate would begin to experience real gains. If a reform-driven economic expansion were to begin, then some of the domestic and foreign opponents might decide that a boycott strategy no longer made sense. As some private firms and international lenders began to relent, the government would have growing room to maneuver, and its economic successes would grant it greater political legitimacy. Once past the transition trough, there would still be the possibility of reversals, but some of the critical reforms could become firmly institutionalized.

This narrative is the core claim for why radical financial reform represents a real utopia. It shows that it might be possible for an elected leftist government to make the transition trough shallow and short enough that the government could survive and win the next election. But it leaves open the question how the left government would organize the stages of its reform projects and shape the rhetoric it uses for both its base and its opponents.

The strategy proposed here operates in two stages. In the first stage, the left would push through a program of radical financial reform designed to expand significantly the scope and reach of the nonprofit financial sector. The movement's energy would focus on nurturing these new institutions since it will take time and considerable effort to grow the network of nonprofit institutions to enable dramatic increases in its lending capacity. The second stage, in which the movement broadened its reform agenda and risked a direct confrontation with big business, would then come some ten or fifteen years later. How could this scenario play out strategically and rhetorically?

At the rhetorical level, the movement would define socialism as simply the extension of democracy to include the economy.[54] In this formulation, there is no single moment of transition from a profit-oriented economy to a socialist economy; it is, rather, an evolutionary process through which there is an ever-greater and ever-deeper extension of democracy into economic decision-making.

The movement would also affirm its commitment to democratic institutions and democratic norms, including competitive elections fought against parties with very different political commitments. Within this framework, the movement can be quite open with its opponents and its supporters about its commitment to a gradual and deep socialist transition that will preserve democratic institutions and practices.

The movement would also explain that one of the most

Financial Democratization and the Transition to Socialism

important planks in its socialist agenda is the democratization of the financial system. It would insist that the existing financial system, despite being underwritten and guaranteed by the government, serves oligarchic interests and fails to work for the vast majority of the population. The reforms would mean that large private financial firms would face increased competition from a network of nonprofit financial institutions. However, the theorists of the market always stress the value of competition, so what could be wrong with subjecting entrenched financial firms to some healthy disruption by new market entrants?

In raising the banner of radical financial reform, the movement would work to build a broad coalition, including small and medium-sized businesses that could be persuaded of the advantages of a more democratic financial system. With sufficient electoral support, the movement could then implement the first-stage reforms. Intense opposition to those reforms by the existing financial institutions is to be expected, but the strategy to dampen such resistance would be to threaten private sector banks with the public utility model. Their choice would be either to let the financial-reform legislation go through or to face much tighter regulation that would immediately threaten their profits. Since the threat posed by the reform legislation lies well in the future and is even then only a theoretical possibility, it seems unlikely that the financial interests would mount a full-scale campaign of resistance that included capital strikes and capital flight.[55]

The victorious movement would also pursue other reforms that are familiar parts of the repertoire of left governments, which would include enhanced programs to transfer resources to people in the bottom half of the income distribution through progressive taxation, strengthened labor rights, measures to combat racial and gender inequality, improved environmental regulations, a push to increase democratic participation in governance, and modest increases in taxation on corporations and the rich. The movement would, however, avoid pursuing reforms that challenged the power of big business directly, such as very large tax increases or requirements that corporate boards be restructured to include stakeholders such as employees and customers. The movement would stress its commitment to incremental improvements that made the economy work for all citizens.

If the scenario of capital flight and capital strikes began to unfold even with relatively modest reforms, the movement could retreat while working to hold on to the financial reforms it had implemented. It would mobilize energy at the grass roots to make sure that the network of nonprofit financial institutions was developing according to plan. In the event that the movement was voted out of office during this period, the new decentralized system of financial institutions would continue to grow if they were meeting the real needs of a variety of constituencies.

When the movement felt that the time was right, it would campaign for office with a promise to make deeper reforms that would challenge the power of the rich and large corporate entities. This is when issues of restructuring corporate governance or a major escalation of redistribution through the tax system would be on the agenda. In short, the movement would provoke a confrontation in the hope that the transition trough would be short and shallow. Having weathered this storm, the movement would then be able to create an economy that truly worked for all citizens.

Conclusion

For most of the last century, political movements committed to radical financial reform and those favoring a socialist transformation have been at odds and have often worked at cross-purposes. Today, however, it is possible to see a creative synthesis of these two traditions in which radical financial reform becomes the critical measure that makes it possible for a government committed to a democratization of the economy to survive. The argument is that both the duration and the depth of the transition trough could be minimized if a successful process of radical financial reform had previously been implemented and given the time to mature.

This article has focused almost entirely on a reform process within a particular nation. However, the vision elaborated here also has an important global dimension. At the same time as leftist political parties within nations were fighting to implement radical financial reform domestically, they would also exert pressure for reforms of the global financial and economic order. In that arena as well there is a significant opening for reform; those arrangements have become increasingly dysfunctional. The point is that winning even partial reforms at the global level, such as a global financial transaction tax, would work in synergy with domestic efforts. Such a tax, for example, would mean that those shifting capital abroad to destabilize a leftist government would have to pay a substantial up-front fee for the transaction. Moreover, as the global reform process advanced, those further steps would create a more favorable environment for these domestic transitions.

But the critical step in this real utopia is the rejection of the conventional account of the role of financial institutions in market economies. As long as people believe that such institutions are intermediaries who play the critical role of connecting savers with investors, it is very difficult to challenge their institutionalized power. But when it is understood that they are franchisees that have been granted a privilege by the government to create credit, it becomes possible to challenge that privilege and demand that it be extended to other institutions that are not preoccupied with the maximization of profits. Such a reform is essential to democratize finance and ultimately to democratize the entire economy.

II. THE POLITICS OF FINANCIAL REFORM

3

Economic Democracy and Enterprise Form in Finance

William H. Simon

The institutional design of "democratizing finance" could play out in either or both of two trajectories. First, there is what Fred Block in his chapter in this book, titled "Financial Democratization and the Transition to Socialism," calls the "public utility model." This approach would tighten the regulation of enterprises that would continue to be organized as for-profit or investor-owned corporations. The second would transfer responsibility and resources to organizations constructed to internalize public goals and values. Robert Hockett's updated Reconstruction Finance Corporation, Block's local nonprofit banks, Michael A. McCarthy's sovereign wealth fund, and Lenore Palladino's "public investment platform" are examples.[1]

The first course is less radical. The public utility model is basically the one that is now in place. Block would tighten regulation, but only one of his proposals seems a major departure from current practice—limitations on profits. The alternative institutions emphasized in the second approach currently exist in various manifestations, but moving them to the center of the financial system would involve an epochal change.

To the extent that reform is guided by democratic ideals, the two approaches involve different instantiations of democracy.

In the regulatory approach, actors accountable to general electoral processes impose external constraints on organizations that retain discretion to pursue private goals within the constraints. In the second approach, political responsibility is imputed to actors within the organization, and they are expected to use their discretion to further public values as well as the private interests of the organization's constituents.

I propose to consider the rationales for the second approach and the forms that democratized, ground-level financial institutions might take. There are two relevant types of democracy—general electoral democracy and stakeholder democracy. And with each of these types, it is worth distinguishing between relatively direct and relatively indirect forms of democratic control. I suggest reasons for thinking that the most directly democratic forms are not necessarily the most promising.

The key rationale for the move to more democratic forms is to encourage the better alignment of managerial incentives with public interests. Such alignment requires not only redirection but also a broadening of incentives. Thus, effective enterprise reform requires the creation of techniques of monitoring and performance assessment that accommodate multiple, complex, and competing goals. Such techniques do not exist in any fully developed form; they are in the process of creation. These techniques have further implications for institutional configuration. They suggest that informal lateral connections among peer institutions may be as important as the internal structure of the institutions.

The problem with the business corporation

The call for democratization at the enterprise level arises from dissatisfaction with the business corporation, the critical defining features of which are (a) the attachment of control rights to capital rights and (b) free transferability and accumulability of ownership interests. In the 1980s, these features produced two critical phenomena: (a) the market for corporate control and (b) legal recognition of maximizing shareholder value as the meaning of managerial fiduciary duty.

The for-profit corporate firm lodges control in the firm's investors, that is, those who have the residual claims on its income and assets. This fact creates uniquely powerful incentives for maximizing profits. It gives strategic discussion within the organization what Claus Offe and Helmut Wiesenthal call a "monological" character.[2] From the investor's perspective, this characteristic is advantageous; it reduces "decision costs."[3] Offe and Wiesenthal, writing from the left, and Henry Hansmann, writing from the center, attributed the dominance of the business corporation over competing forms to its superior ability to devise and commit to a coherent strategy. It is easier to agree on a strategy to maximize profits than on one to optimize multiple conflicting goals of various constituencies.

However, from a social perspective, there is a disadvantage. To the extent that the corporation's activities generate negative externalities, powerful internal incentives push against taking account of them. Public concerns can be addressed through regulation to the extent that officials can formulate and enforce regulations effectively. But the powerful incentives of the for-profit form can induce activity designed to defeat effective formulation and enforcement.

The conception of the corporation as single-mindedly devoted to profit maximization has been around for a century and a half, but it has only recently been embraced by the law, and business elites were quite divided about it for much of the twentieth century. In the mid-twentieth century, most lawyers and many economists advanced a different view, according to which the "separation of ownership and control" arising from the dispersion of shares meant that shareholders had limited practical opportunities to discipline management. (The main practical opportunities were the proxy contest and the derivative suit, both of which were expensive and rare.) Managers thus had a good deal of discretion. They could use this discretion to benefit themselves, but they could also use it to benefit non-shareholder constituencies, such as organized labor, local communities, and customers. Some interpretations of the large mid-century corporation portrayed the manager's role as mediating among shareholders and those other constituencies to hold the enterprise together in some productive collaboration. That portrayal was, to varying degrees, both normative and descriptive.[4] The courts generally upheld management discretion to act in the interest of non-shareholder constituencies.

Since the 1980s, however, the courts and the corporate elite have embraced the monological conception. On the legal scene, the key development has been the hostile takeover. Before its advent, the monological conception would have been difficult to enforce. Managers could assert that benefits to non-shareholder constituencies served long-run shareholder interests in reputation and collaborative relations. Courts did not feel able to second-guess such rationales. But the takeover allows enforcement of shareholder primacy by the market for corporate control. Entrepreneurs who believe management is failing to maximize profits can earn their own profits by acquiring control and replacing the incumbents. The courts, as they cleared the way for the takeover, began to speak about "shareholder value" as the governing norm with unprecedented clarity.[5]

The social disadvantage of the organization's single-minded focus on profit is especially acute to the extent that there is asymmetry of information between public regulators and the organizations. If the risks that regulation addresses are caused by technology that is exceptionally complex, evolves rapidly, or varies locally, then regulated actors are likely to have better understanding than officials. Their incentives are to use their superior understanding to further profits for the enterprise at the expense of exacerbating risks that are substantially borne by others.

In banking, the most pertinent challenges arise from government subsidization of risky activities through such mechanisms as deposit insurance, last-resort lending, and implicit "too-big-to-fail" bailout insurance. The banks push against regulatory constraints to take on more risk because the government subsidizes it. They finance speculative investment at the expense of investment in the real economy despite the fact that social returns to the latter are higher. And they are indifferent to positive externalities that come from investment in underdeveloped regions or disadvantaged people or the environment.

A further concern is the potential arising from the relative complexity of even routine financial transactions for the exploitation of unsophisticated customers. The increased exposure of banks to competition since the 1980s has improved customer service in some ways, but customers are egregiously exploited in others. The recent Wells Fargo scandal that led to the firing of 5,000 employees is one of the most extensive consumer frauds in history.

Banking is not the only area where the social desirability of the for-profit form is being questioned. In the late twentieth century, in several areas where public or charitable provision was customary, experiments were undertaken with for-profit enterprise. Efforts were most notable in health care and education. More radical initiatives founded on the same logic occurred with prisons and military services. In all these areas, aggregate performance of for-profit enterprise has disappointed proponents, and there have been many scandals.

Varieties of enterprise democracy

In the enterprise context, democracy can be understood as greater accountability to the general electorate on the one hand or to stakeholders on the other. And within the general and stakeholder fields, we can distinguish relatively direct and relatively indirect forms of accountability. These two parameters yield four types of enterprises: state corporations, state agencies, charitable nonprofits, and cooperatives (Table 1).

In the next two sections, I assess the relative advantages of the different types, considering first the relatively directly democratic forms and then the relatively indirectly democratic ones. In general, I suggest that the indirect approach is more promising in most relevant contexts.

Table 1. Democracy and form of enterprise

	Type of democracy	
	General	Stakeholder
Intensity of public control		
Indirect	State corporation or authority	Charitable nonprofit
Direct	State agency	Cooperative

Source: Author's elaboration

Relatively directly democratic enterprise forms

Legally, the incidents of relatively directly democratic enterprise control are, first, the power of elected officials or stakeholders to remove enterprise directors at will, and second, strong control by elected officials or stakeholders over the organization's resources. In other words, the enterprise is dependent on elected officials or stakeholders for frequent budget appropriation or expenditure approvals. The key relatively directly democratic forms are the state agency and the cooperative.

The state agency

The state agency is an organization governed by directors appointed by elected officials. If we take the form in which democracy—here, electoral control—is strongest, the directors would serve at the pleasure of elected officials, and the entity would rely entirely on annual appropriations from a general government. Its resources would be redeployable at the will of the general government. It would have neither taxing nor borrowing authority of its own. Its contracts would be subject to approval by the general government.

This description fits many public entities exercising regulatory authority, such as the Environmental Protection Agency or local zoning boards, and entities providing services, such as Veterans Affairs or most public schools or police departments. However, whether such entities are well suited to play major roles in financial or economic development has often been doubted. The reasons relate to problems with this kind of democratic control. First, it is difficult under strong electoral control to execute long-term plans or projects that extend over many election cycles. Voters can be shortsighted, and their attention can wander. Only a few issues can be salient in a general election, so electoral decisions may be inconsistent over time, as attention flits. And, of course, politicians may use their control opportunistically to get short-term electoral benefits. Think of Richard Nixon pumping up the money supply in 1972 or Governor Chris Christie of New Jersey canceling the Hudson River tunnel to protect tax cuts in 2012.

An individual or a private organization can undertake long-term projects by making long-term contractual commitments. But government long-term commitments compromise strong electoral democracy. Or at least that is one influential view. It explains the current constitutional rules in most states that require balanced budgets or the common nineteenth-century rule that precluded many municipalities from committing to contracts that extended beyond the terms of the officials approving them. On a larger scale, it explains the resistance to independence of the central bank. Independent monetary authorities compromise democratic control. And they are accused of favoring dogmatic or class-biased tight-money policies. But popular pressures for alternative policies can cause harmful inflation or interest rate rises.[6]

The general effects of direct popular control seem unclear, but there are ample grounds for caution. Nathan Jensen and Edmund Malesky, for example, recently reported a study of local government incentives for business investment. They echo the view widely held among economists that such subsidies tend to be ineffective or unnecessarily generous and to have regressive fiscal impacts.[7] They looked at the relative effects of direct and indirect electoral control on the propensity to offer such subsidies, comparing cities managed directly by elected officials—mayors and city councils—with cities in which elected officials manage indirectly through an appointed city manager. City manager regimes were inaugurated in the Progressive Era out of concern that direct management by elected officials was susceptible to voter short-sightedness and official corruption. The study vindicates at least the shortsightedness part of the hypothesis. Mayoral regimes are substantially more disposed to offer pointlessly generous subsidies to attract businesses than city manager ones. The authors suggest that voters penalize officials when enterprises leave or fail to come in, but not when subsidies conferred on them turn out to be ineffective or unnecessary.

The cooperative

The second version of direct democratic enterprise is the stakeholder-controlled corporation. The paradigm here is the cooperative, a private entity controlled by its "patrons," who have some active connection to the enterprise in addition to investment, typically as customers, workers, or suppliers. The patrons are the residual claimants on the firm's income and (although there is some ambiguity here) assets. In uniting control and residual economic claims, the cooperative resembles the business corporation. But there are key differences. The patron's economic claims cannot be transferred independently of their control claims, and, since their control claims are premised on some active participatory role, new owners must be approved by the remaining owners. So shares are not freely transferable. There is thus no possibility of a hostile takeover.

In addition, control rights in the cooperative are generally distributed equally without regard to investment. Each member gets one vote. Financial reward is distributed on the basis of a combination of investment and economic participation ("patronage").

The cooperative is the enterprise form that most embodies democratic ideals. But it has disadvantages, and experience with it has been mixed. Two problems arise from the incompleteness of representation. Typically, only one set of stakeholders is represented, although others are affected. For example, agricultural marketing cooperatives, which are controlled by suppliers (farmers), have engaged in anticompetitive practices that harm consumers. And the democratic promise is fulfilled only when stakeholders who are represented devote effort to governance. Passive or indifferent patrons are vulnerable to exploitation, as illustrated by some cooperative (mutual) insurance companies that have been reorganized to allow management to appropriate patron capital.

Moreover, cooperatives have difficulty expanding because they cannot provide controlling interests (equity) to outsiders.[8] They can expand only through debt or capital contributions and the retained earnings of patrons. In many organizations, patrons will have limited ability to finance themselves.

Still another problem arises from the distributive disjunction between control and reward. Control is distributed equally, but there can be wide variation among economic shares. So the problem arises that members with poor economic endowments may use their control in ways that redistribute away from those with relatively rich claims. If there is inequality, the poor may have different preferences about retaining and distributing earnings and about consumption within the enterprise. These differences can produce the kind of internal conflict that threatens the enterprise.[9] A relevant phenomenon recently seen in law firm general partnerships—which used to and still can resemble cooperatives—is disagreement over retirement programs. High-billing partners may object to firm-wide pension programs, which tend to be relatively egalitarian. If they are outvoted, they may leave, sometimes causing the partnership to collapse. Alternatively, if the members with relatively large accounts have voting control, they may use it to alter the enterprise form to enable them to cash out the full value of their equity. The prohibition on outside equity narrows the class of buyers for the shares of retiring members to newcomers willing to be and acceptable as patrons. This fact lowers their value. Older members of successful cooperatives may have strong incentives to push to convert the enterprise out of the cooperative form so that it can be sold to outside investors. The remaining owners then become employees.[10]

Perhaps the most distinctive disadvantage of the cooperative form from a democratic perspective is a bias toward exclusion.

The bias has two sources. First, because the cooperative relationship is a relatively thick one involving multiple dimensions, cooperators may be choosy about new entrants in a way that corporate shareholders (assuming we mean public corporations) would not be. Second, cooperators may worry about internal redistribution. If new entrants generate less income, they will still have equal control rights. So new entrants who seem likely to perform below the average of incumbents will be disfavored.

An extreme example of the bias is the New York City housing market, where for a long time building-wide resident cooperatives were favored over individual condominium ownership. The cooperative form meant that residents were mutually responsible for the building mortgage, which made them reluctant to admit newcomers with less than average financial resources. That problem, however, could have been mitigated by adopting the condominium form, where collective responsibility applies only to the common areas. Nevertheless, the cooperative form was favored because it not only encourages but also legitimizes certain forms of discrimination that might otherwise be difficult to achieve. Condominium owners have no standard mechanism to veto people to whom their neighbors wish to sell. And the law makes it difficult to achieve such vetoes contractually by severely limiting enforcement of "restraints on alienation." The cooperative form, on the other hand, requires a collective judgment before a sale can occur.[11] Residents can use their veto to exclude people they dislike for virtually any reason. In theory, they are still bound by antidiscrimination law with respect to race and other protected characteristics, but it is very difficult to prove that a decision was based on such considerations.

In the financial sector, cooperative banks, or "credit unions," as many are called, typically limit lending to depositors and often require, in addition, that depositors and borrowers have some further relation, such as employment by a common employer. This arrangement makes for trust and information sharing and is associated with lower borrower default rates. But it limits the range of potential participants.

Relatively indirectly democratic enterprise forms

The drafters of the US Constitution rejected "democracy," their term for relatively direct forms of popular rule, for "republicanism," their term for relatively indirect forms.[12] The president is not elected directly; voters choose electors who in turn choose the president. And until the Seventeenth Amendment, senators were chosen by state legislators.

The drafters' suspicion of popular control arose in large part from the fear that voters would be shortsighted or reckless in financial matters. Their solution—indirect control—was designed to "refine and enlarge" the views of public officials by attenuating their accountability to the electorate.

The specific processes of indirect control in the Constitution are not highly regarded today. The indirect election of senators has been eliminated, and hardly anyone defends the Electoral College. But if we look at the institutions that have developed to combine public accountability with financial or economic development, something like the idea of indirect control is prominent. The key examples are the government corporation and the charitable nonprofit corporation.

The government corporation

I use the term "government corporation" to describe a range of entities that are sometimes called corporations—for example, the Reconstruction Finance Corporation—but also go by other names, especially "authority," as in the Tennessee Valley Authority or state and local redevelopment and transportation authorities.

The government corporation is an entity treated as a separate accounting unit with authority to take various actions (e.g., contracting, holding property, borrowing) in its own name and on its own initiative. However, ultimate control and financial rights are retained wholly or mostly by the general government. The governing board of the corporation is mostly appointed by elected officials. They may include stakeholder representatives, but they have fiduciary duties to the entity as a whole, not to the narrow interests of a specific constituency.

Typically, electoral control is attenuated by two sorts of mechanisms. The first are governance procedures. The tenures of board members may be staggered across electoral cycles, and removal may be precluded except for demonstrable cause. Thus, elected officials can change control of the corporation only gradually and sometimes only over more than a single electoral cycle. At the subnational level, insulation can be achieved by sharing control of a corporation across separate municipalities, counties, or states. If control is divided among members chosen by different jurisdictions, no single electorate can induce a change of control unilaterally.

The second kind of insulating mechanism concerns finance. The corporation can be given borrowing authority and control over income or assets. Using the assets or income as collateral for borrowing removes them from control of elected officials. And if the corporation controls income flows that exceed its operating and debt service costs, it may have substantial discretion to undertake projects free of electoral oversight.

Transportation and development authorities at the subnational level illustrate the advantages and disadvantages of such arrangements. The authorities are able to execute long-range plans that require commitments across many electoral cycles and coordination across multiple jurisdictions. Without their relative autonomy from the electoral process, shortsightedness or inconsistency and parochialism might preclude valuable initiatives. On the other hand, political insulation is also associated with arrogance and contempt for nonelite interests.

The advantages of the state corporation are displayed in the story of the massive cleanup of Boston Harbor in the 1980s and 1990s. For decades the harbor was scandalously polluted. Efforts to remedy the situation failed, despite the illegality of much of the contributing conduct and broad political support for remediation. A major obstacle appears to have been the extreme fragmentation of authority. Effective intervention occurred only after an ambitious lawsuit, and its centerpiece was the creation of the Massachusetts Water Resources Authority—"a new independently financed state authority to take over the roles of planning, constructing, and administering" the cleanup.[13] Having proved intractable to electoral institutions for decades, the problem was solved with the interventions of two nonelectoral ones—the court and the independent authority.

Of course, the dark side of the independent authority is even better known, especially through Robert Caro's account of how Robert Moses turned the Triborough Bridge and Tunnel Authority into an empire more powerful than the elected government of New York. Moses created a modern, automobile-based transportation infrastructure at a cost that included neglect of public transportation, the destruction of many vital neighborhoods, and the herding of poor people into dysfunctional and undermaintained high-rises.[14]

The charitable nonprofit

The other relatively indirectly democratic enterprise form is the charitable nonprofit corporation.[15] The charitable nonprofit is an extremely flexible instrument. Anyone can form one, and the law permits many control arrangements. Members of the governing board can be appointed by public officials or private individuals, elected by members (if there are members, but there need not be), or filled by remaining incumbents as others depart. Officers and board members must act disinterestedly. They may not use control to benefit themselves at the expense of other stakeholders.

The government subsidizes the organization through tax exemptions for the organization and tax benefits for donors. It polices the organization to make sure that (a) its activities are confined to areas that could broadly be characterized as charitable (i.e., perform some social good not adequately served by for-profit enterprise), (b) it is not being used for private inurement, and (c) it is devoting donated resources consistently with its undertaking to donors. But within these broad constraints, directors and officers have discretion to pursue the organization's public-regarding goals comparable to the discretion of for-profit managers to pursue profit maximizing.

Viewed individually, charitable nonprofits are not necessarily democratic, although they can be. Nonprofits need not have members at all, and their boards can be self-perpetuating oligarchies. However, excessively narrow control groups may raise doubts about whether activities are truly charitable or involve private inurement and are thus discouraged by the prospect of regulatory scrutiny. Moreover, nonprofits can be strongly democratic, and both private and public contributions to them can be conditioned on democratic governance. For example, nonprofits wishing to be characterized as "community development corporations," in order to qualify for certain grants, must admit all interested members of their catchment areas to membership and allow them to elect a portion of the board.

Viewed collectively, the nonprofit sphere has democratically attractive features. Since it accommodates initiative so easily, it makes diversity and experimentation possible.

Governance aside, accountability can arise to the extent that the enterprise depends on public financial support. The law is ambivalent about the degree of economic autonomy nonprofits should have. An enterprise that starts out with or accumulates a large endowment can operate on its passive income without any need to raise more. Many view this situation as problematic. Just as control over public resources can insulate the state corporation from political accountability, so control over their own capital can insulate nonprofits from the accountability that arises from the need to convince current donors, contractors, or patrons of the value of their services. Thus there are doctrines designed to limit this kind of insulation, although they tend to be halfhearted. One rule measures how much of a nonprofit's income comes from "public support" (current donations, fees for charitable services, government contracts), as opposed to passive income, and imposes some disadvantages on those who fail to meet a minimum. Another requires "private foundations" (enterprises that make grants from endowment income) to spend at least 5 percent of their endowment each year.

The influence of dialogic assessment on enterprise form

The four alternative forms either demand or permit control structures more conducive to democratic accountability than those of the business corporation. They also prescribe or encourage enterprise norms that are diverse and public-regarding. They require "dialogic" assessment that considers and reconciles multiple values. (The cooperative is a partial exception to the need for public-regarding ends. In principle, cooperatives maximize the welfare of their members, but as their members have multi-stranded relations with one another—as both capital suppliers and patrons/participants—their interests are diverse and may diverge less from public ones.)

In addition, all four alternative forms depart from the incentive structure of the business corporation. They eliminate or, in the case of cooperatives, limit the opportunities of managers to profit from capital gains and their ability to benefit from increases in the enterprise's income. Thus, high-powered incentives to evade regulatory restrictions or create negative public externalities are blunted. There are, of course, disadvantages. There are no material incentives for innovation or cost minimization comparable to those in private enterprise. And "decision costs" may be higher because conversations about goals or performance are longer and more complex.

The main material incentive for such enterprises is the continuing need to attract new resources without the ability to offer capital shares. The enterprises must convince people to pay for their services (on either a first-party or a third-party basis) or to make donations, which will usually mean convincing them of the value of their efforts. As a purely economic matter, these incentives are not high-powered. Donors have limited ability to monitor performance, and large endowments or underserved reputations sometimes allow organizations to escape pressures for accountability.

Granting that the alternative forms avoid the limitations of monological assessment, the question remains how the more complex assessment that they make possible is to be organized.

To begin with, how do we limit the assessment criteria so that they provide some discipline? If the criteria are too vague and too numerous, it will be hard to generate meaningful conclusions about performance. If the criteria are limited and specified, they will have to be revised to take account of unforeseen consequences—counterproductive adaptation (e.g., "teaching to the test"), collateral consequences, or technological innovations. Once we allow for the need for continuing reconsideration of the criteria, every unflattering measurement can be interpreted as either an indication of poor performance or a symptom that the metric needs revision.

Another problem has to do with learning. The for-profit form creates strong individual incentives for firms to learn, but it also encourages them to hide much of the knowledge they acquire from their competitors and to distort the information they provide shareholders and regulators. The market deals with slow learners by eliminating them, not by helping them learn. The alternative enterprise forms are more conducive to information sharing. The problem is that there is some trade-off in the design of an assessment regime between facilitation of learning and motivation of effective effort. The criteria that have the most diagnostic value, and hence point the way to improvements, may not be those that most readily facilitate rankings or threshold determinations that can justify sanctions, such as withdrawal of resources.

There is no definitive solution to these problems, but responses to them have tended to converge in a distinctive architecture.[16] Assessment takes the form of a kind of deliberative engagement across firms or organizations. The organizational structure is neither a market nor a bureaucracy but a set of shifting and informal networks.

The most distinctive mechanism is peer review. Organizations are assessed by teams of outsiders from organizations performing tasks similar to theirs. The practice is pervasive, but it is most fully developed in medicine, especially with respect to hospitals.[17] Peer review strives to combine learning with comparative assessment. Metrics tend to emphasize diagnosis and are explicitly provisional. A central focus of inquiry is the organization's capacity to adapt to new circumstances, learn from its mistakes, and integrate new knowledge generated elsewhere. Such reviews can also generate rankings and comparisons. Rankings and comparisons have diagnostic value because they indicate where the best practices are to be discovered. But they also can serve accountability purposes.

The term "peer review" connotes a horizontal dimension, but the process has hierarchical elements: it must be organized across firms by a coordinating organization. That organization can be controlled collectively by the firms under review themselves. More commonly it is a nonprofit corporation with the substantial representation of those under review but with the significant, often controlling, representation of other stakeholders.[18]

A further hierarchical dimension arises from the use of the peer-review process as an indicator or requirement by regulators, funders, and customers. In medicine, for example, participation in the Joint Commission on the Accreditation of Hospitals (JCAH) process and minimally satisfactory ratings are conditions of various professional licenses and reimbursement by Medicare and private insurers.

The peer-review process presupposes a willingness to share knowledge across firms and thus is limited in the for-profit sector. True, there is quite a bit of knowledge sharing in the for-profit sector, as many of the hospitals in the JCAH network are for-profit. Nevertheless, for-profit firms will not freely share information on matters on which they are competing intensely. Conversely, it is an advantage for a nonprofit organization that its form lessens this inhibition.

The most developed performance metrics in the financial sector are the traditional accounting norms of profitability and "safety and soundness." Efforts have begun only relatively recently to develop metrics that take account of other social goals. There is, for example, the Global Impact Investing Rating System overseen by the Global Impact Investment System. Such approaches, however, have a long way to go to achieve the sophistication of the hospital regime or to provide the requisites of accountability for a broadened nonprofit financial sector.

Peer-review regimes generate accountability in two distinctive ways. First, such regimes implement accountability directly at the firm level. Practitioners account to peers. This is a somewhat different accountability from that overseen by either public officials or stakeholders. Peer reviewers typically do not hold public office and are not electorally accountable. Although they may have stakes in the industry, they do not have stakes in the firm under review, and they are supposed to be disinterested, not representative in the political sense. Part of the rationale for these regimes is that the duty to explain one's practices and submit to the judgment of peers contributes to responsibility both by forcing articulation and reflection and through mechanisms of pride and shame.

At a second level, the regimes induce accountability by making the organization's operations more transparent to outsiders, including both stakeholders and electorally accountable officials. The review generates reports that can be made available publicly or distributed to stakeholders, and it can generate conclusions in forms that permit comparisons across firms. The outsiders can use this information to make much more plausible judgments than they otherwise could about what support to give the organizations.

Of course, there are many ways in which such regimes can go wrong. One pathology is a tendency for peers to cover for each other through reciprocally lenient evaluation and grade inflation. With luck, the tendency will be limited by counterpressures. Outside funders and regulators may be able to identify the problem and refuse to accept the inflated ratings. Poor performance by the regime may induce entry of new ones that compete on promise of providing more effective signals. Alternatively, the better performers among the firms being evaluated may resent the efforts of the laggards to blur signals and rankings and insist on more rigor, or they may break away and affiliate with a more effective regime.[19]

The key point, for immediate purposes, is that attempts to democratize the financial sector depend at least as much on the development of mechanisms of transparency and responsibility as on a choice among alternative enterprise forms.

Conclusion

The business corporation became more narrowly profit-focused at just the moment when changes in the financial sector generated opportunities to earn large returns by shifting risks to the public sector. Tightened regulation is one response to this situation. But especially in a technologically dynamic industry, regulators have trouble adapting to new contingencies and detecting innovative forms of evasion. So an alternative approach to aligning private and social incentives—a change in enterprise structure—has some appeal. This move is sometimes characterized in terms of economic democracy and could involve democracy in two ways: by enhancing electoral control over the enterprise or by providing more control to people with interests other than profit. All the relevant enterprise forms have disadvantages, however, and it can be argued that the ones affording the most direct democratic control tend to be the least effective. In any event, no matter which nonprofit form is chosen, accountability will depend on effective modes of assessment and information sharing across enterprises.

4

To Democratize Finance, Democratize Central Banking

David M. Woodruff

More than one hundred years ago, Georg Simmel wrote,

> One might say that money becomes increasingly a public institution in an increasingly strict sense of the word: money consists more and more of what public authorities, public institutions and the various forms of intercourse and guarantees of the general public make of it, and the extent to which they legitimize it.[1]

And he was right![2] In developed countries, states enjoy a thoroughgoing monopoly on what counts as a legal means of payment. Bank deposits, transferred to settle legal obligations at parity with cash, are issued by legally constituted entities in legally delimited ways. Bank deposits' parity with cash and their reliable flow through the financial system depend on state institutions. In effect, as Robert Hockett's contribution to this volume demonstrates, commercial banks exercise public power by operating a state-sanctioned and state-sustained "franchise" to issue money effectively interchangeable with that directly issued by the central bank. Even when its issue and circulation are managed by private organizations, money is indeed a public institution, our most pervasive and all-embracing one.

To Democratize Finance, Democratize Central Banking

If a public institution facilitates what both Fred Block and Hockett term a "financial dictatorship," then democratic legitimacy would seem to demand its reform. This chain of reasoning is logically unexceptionable, but its political impact is open to question. Developed and convincing analyses of the intertwining of public power with the institutions of capitalist exchange have been available at least since the 1920s, but they have proved no barrier to the rise of neoliberalism since the late 1970s. One reason for this, I suggest below, is the way that persistent, prevalent, and emotionally resonant convictions about the role of individual desert in driving market earnings deny or obscure the state's formative role for market institutions. The tenets of such "everyday libertarianism," which implicitly assume a stateless market, are unlikely to be dispelled by a proposal to broaden the monetary franchise to nonprofit banks, even if it is popularly accepted.[3]

Efforts to reform finance must consider not only the ideological context but also the broader economic and political context. Here it proves essential to understand the role of independent central banks. Promoting the independence of the central bank was a core aspect of the broader neoliberal push to insulate markets from democratic control. Eliminating the direct influence of elected officials over monetary policy and tasking central bankers with the pursuit of price stability, neoliberals insisted, would inhibit the profligacy of politicians and permit the unpopular monetary restriction necessary to bring an end to inflation.

In the aftermath of the financial crisis of 2007–8, central bank independence had unanticipated but highly significant effects. Throughout the developed world, fiscal policies to stimulate demand in response to the crisis were manifestly inadequate in scale and pursued only briefly before giving way to a contractionary austerity.[4] But central bankers' mandate for price stability, designed with inflation in mind, also required them to fight deflation. Central banks were left with little alternative but to seek to mitigate the effects of fiscal austerity through creative efforts to prompt new lending.[5] This pattern had the perverse political consequence that the architects of austerity were at least somewhat insulated from a potential electoral backlash, bailed out by a second-best replacement policy of which there was little public awareness.

I argue below that public purpose lending, if established, could easily contribute to this damaging political configuration as another makeshift substitute for appropriate fiscal policy. More generally, given these ideological and political circumstances, a reform aimed at deploying the money franchise in service of public policy goals must be joined to a second reform: the reversal of central bank independence. For reasons explored below, by making monetary policy and its effects an object of regular debate, democratization of central banking would make everyday libertarianism much harder to sustain. And a transparent connection between monetary and fiscal policy would also improve democracy's capacity to make coherent policy choices, including those about the appropriate contours of the money franchise. In sum, democratization of central banking would help create a permissive environment for a socialism understood in Polanyi's sense as "subordination of the market to democratic politics."[6]

Ignoring the state in the market: Everyday libertarianism

Hockett's institutionally precise exposition of the public character of private banking recalls a critical American perspective on the place of the state in a market economy that is too often forgotten. Highlighting the pervasive, intrinsic role of legal institutions in capitalism was a key part of the program of what Barbara Fried has termed "the progressive assault on laissez-faire," spearheaded by legal realists and the so-called old institutional economists (OIE) from the late nineteenth century, which flourished especially in the interwar years.[7] Their analysis charted the myriad ways in which legal institutions shape exchange through authorizing some acts and forbidding others, with contract, property, and tax law putting the state in the backdrop of every transaction (even the illegal ones) in modern capitalist economies. As the brilliant (but profoundly morally tainted) economist John R. Commons put it, "Each individual is a 'public utility' to the extent that the public powers are employed in his behalf against others."[8] From an OIE perspective, the activity of fractional reserve banks in creating "new credit," which is equivalent to creating "new money," was just another example of how a capitalist legal system grants "a certain share of collective power" to those engaged in legally authorized transactions.[9] A bank, Commons stated, deals

> in promises to pay lawful money. And the volume of its promises to pay on demand may be as great as the risks it is willing to take on the chance of having enough lawful money on hand to meet a run of outgoing checks presented by customers and other banks in excess of the run of incoming checks deposited by customers and drawn on other banks.[10]

Commons thus recognized that banks were not usefully understood as intermediaries between savers and borrowers and that their creation of money—like any other capitalist transaction—involved the delegation of public power.[11]

Such arguments are at least as compelling now as they were when Commons wrote in 1924. Indeed, in the specific case of finance, given intervening developments that strengthen central bank support for private credit, they are more compelling. Nonetheless, despite a dominant position in the US academy before World War II, the OIE's influence in the years after the war saw a rapid, near total decline. Legal realism likewise rapidly waned within the law academy, and the renaissance of its key ideas with the critical legal studies movement proved, unfortunately, relatively circumscribed.[12] The effort to use recognition of the public character of private capitalist transacting as a springboard for a political strategy should reckon with this history. Within the academy, sociology-of-knowledge factors certainly played a role in marginalizing the two schools of thought, but that does not explain why their key insights failed to embed themselves in broader political practice and discourse despite a period of near hegemony in the academy.

Innumerable causes could be cited, but I would like to focus on what I believe is a significant ideational one: the power of what Liam Murphy and Thomas Nagel have termed "everyday libertarianism." Everyday libertarianism refers to the sense that our net market income "belongs to us without qualification, in the strong sense that what happens to that money is morally speaking entirely a matter of our say-so"; this moral confidence derives from an intuition that market rewards are deserved. Given that incomes depend crucially on the morally contingent contours of state-provided market-shaping institutions, even "cursory critical reflection" should dispel the claims of everyday libertarianism. Yet "the instinctive sense of unqualified ownership has remarkable tenacity."[13] Everyday libertarianism exercises a corrosive effect on the capacity of political discourse to absorb an analysis of how private economic institutions embody authorizations to invoke public power, for any such analysis foregrounds the market-shaping processes that everyday libertarianism must ignore if its moral position is to have any coherence. Its strength is thus a significant barrier to socialism understood as democratic control over the contours of markets, as it makes a reasoned public discussion of the core issues all but impossible.

Can the franchise model disrupt everyday libertarianism?

From an intellectual standpoint, money, the public institution that constitutes the object of private acquisitiveness, is a particularly telling illustration of the incoherence of everyday libertarianism. But how to make use of this insight politically is another question. Murphy and Nagel do not really expand on why everyday libertarianism is so pervasive despite its intellectual vacuity. (We will leave to one side efforts by the rich and powerful to promote more explicit versions of the same ideas.) They imply that it is reinforced by the quotidian experience of getting and spending, and the practical experience of exclusive control over net income, to which a mandate, say, to pay additional taxes appears an unwelcome exception. However, this is only part of the issue. It would not in itself explain why everyday

To Democratize Finance, Democratize Central Banking

libertarianism should also embody ideas of market income as *deserved*. For Murphy and Nagel, the answer seems to be one of logical implication. If incomes are not deserved, then there can be no justification for the sense of absolute ownership over net income. However, insofar as we are dealing with intuitions rather than reflective thought, ascribing causal power to logical implication seems dubious.

The "market-incomes-are-deserved" aspect of everyday libertarianism does, however, resonate with a widely distributed psychological tendency to seek a meaningful moral order in the world. As Max Weber put it,

> The fortunate is seldom satisfied with the fact of being fortunate. Beyond this, he needs to know that he has a right to his good fortune. He wants to be convinced that he "deserves" it, and above all, that he deserves it in comparison with others. He wishes to be allowed the belief that the less fortunate also merely experience[s] his due. Good fortune thus wants to be "legitimate" fortune.[14]

In the context of market outcomes, one can suggest, this desire for a sense of moral worthiness pushes for an indication that income is deserved, what I have called elsewhere a "theodicy of markets."[15]

In the closing chapter of *The Great Transformation*, Polanyi provides a penetrating analysis of how the entwining of market outcomes with moral self-satisfaction interferes with the perception of the ways in which incomes reflect the application of public power. His argument, albeit laconic and at times obscurely phrased, reveals clear appreciation of OIE arguments. Legally constituted markets inevitably involve compulsion (e.g., to collect debts or enforce property rights), a compulsion obscured by the formal freedoms of choosing consumers. To choose one product rather than another, for instance, inevitably exposes unchosen producers to financial consequences ultimately backed by the power of the state. Yet, in a market economy, any decent individual could imagine himself free from all responsibility for acts of compulsion on the part of a state which he, personally, rejected, or for economic suffering in society from which he, personally, had not benefited. He was "paying his way," was "in nobody's debt," and was unentangled in the evil of power and economic value. His lack of responsibility for them seemed so evident that he denied their reality in the name of his freedom.[16] In other words, the market supplies a seductive language of moral adequacy —paying one's way, in nobody's debt—that draws a veil over the organization of public authority that constitutes the market in the first place.

In the light of this diagnosis of the roots of everyday libertarianism's tenacity, we can inquire into both the prospects for promoting the franchise model and its capacity to transform discourse around constructing markets even if successful. On both counts, there are grounds for skepticism. Certainly, it is easy to present the ability of banks to create money as inconsistent with the idea that incomes must be earned. However, a criticism in this vein does not naturally lead to ideas about profit regulation of banks or broadening the money franchise, since either of these would challenge the theodicy of markets just as radically. In other words, promoters of a modified franchise model would have to direct the stream of political indignation stemming from the realization that banks create money away from the channels most deeply worn in popular economic discourse. Limited experience indicates that efforts to promote broad public knowledge of the fact that banks create money can easily go in the direction of full-reserve banking, as in the recent failed Swiss *Vollgeld* (full-money) referendum, closely linked to the international movement for sovereign money. The key idea of the sovereign money school is to deny banks the ability to create deposits that would trade at par with central bank money on the basis of fractional reserves. One result, as advocates stress, is that banks would earn money only through actual intermediation. Advocates of sovereign money regularly invoke the idea of undeserved incomes to win support for their proposals, reinforcing the tropes of everyday libertarianism.[17]

Suppose, however, that communication to a broad public of the franchise model built support not for its abolition but for its reconstruction, as Block proposes, to limit bank profitability and facilitate creation of nonprofit banks subordinated to public purposes. Although that would certainly be very welcome, whether it would become an effective beachhead for a further pushback against everyday libertarianism is open to doubt. A discussion of how to employ the full faith and credit of the public does not logically entail an analysis of the construction of the markets within which it is employed. Borrowers from a nonprofit bank would still have to repay their loans, based on the ability to make effective commercial use of them against the backdrop of a price system shaped by large and pervasive inequities in bargaining power. Even loan officers well placed to observe the extortionate effects of those inequities would be unable to disregard them in making lending decisions. The difficulties that have plagued microfinance in maintaining developmental purpose and avoiding a slide into predatory lending, absent a broader structural transformation of the circumstances in which small borrowers are located, can serve as a metaphor for the challenges involved.[18] To single out the excessive profitability of a single sector—banking—on the basis of the implicit public subsidy involved in fostering the exchange of bank deposits at par might even have the effect of inadvertently legitimating the profitability of other sectors, although, as the OIE reveals, this profitability is similarly inseparable from the exercise of public power. In short, promoting the franchise model runs a substantial risk of falling into a portrayal of banking as an exceptional violation of the moral strictures of everyday libertarianism, thereby implicitly endorsing their validity and coherence.

Another reason for skepticism about the transformative potential of the franchise model can be drawn from Block's observation that a system of nonprofit banks serving a public purpose does not represent a radical break with US traditions. As he notes, "The U.S. has a long history of democratizing financial reforms. In this sense, it is the last thirty year period that has been exceptional."[19] Block makes a strong case that changing circumstances mean there is an economic base for a more democratized credit system, but the fact that this tradition failed to embed itself on an ideological level, even when institutions persisted, suggests that the scope of the challenge involved in reversing the sway of everyday libertarianism is very large.

Disrupting everyday libertarianism through democratizing central banking

The more general lesson of the considerations above is that assessing the political potential of promoting the franchise model requires understanding how this effort would intersect with the broader context of economic policy. As noted, in the decade since the economic crisis of 2008, the predominant policy stance in the developed world has combined inadequate fiscal stimulus, or outright fiscal austerity, with extraordinary expansionary efforts by central banks. Although indispensable during a financial implosion, and much better than nothing in a profound slump, monetary activism proved inadequate compensation for fiscal passivity or perversity. Even in the most fortunate countries the result was a slow and arduous recovery from crisis, weighing heavily on lower-income groups; in the less fortunate countries, such as Greece, the outcome was simply catastrophic.

The most prominent and significant example of these dynamics took place in the United States. Barack Obama's administration, enjoying unified control of Congress on his accession to power, launched a program of fiscal stimulus in early 2009. Although it was underpowered, the stimulus certainly reduced the depth and longevity of the recession. However, it did very little to help consumers laboring to repay debts, especially housing mortgages, built up in the years before the crisis. Modifications of bankruptcy rules to aid borrowers hit by the massive fall in home prices were blocked by the influence of financial interests in the Senate.[20] Other programs aimed at aiding mortgagees barely got off the ground.[21] There were manifest political and practical difficulties in promoting such policies, but it is also clear that the Obama administration did not make their pursuit a priority.

Nonetheless, even these limited efforts caused a backlash. A symbol of and to some extent a catalyst for this backlash was

To Democratize Finance, Democratize Central Banking

Rick Santelli, a CNBC commentator who made an impassioned call for a "Tea Party" to resist the administration's efforts at mortgage relief. Speaking from the floor of the Chicago Board of Trade, Santelli said,

> The government is promoting bad behavior. Why don't you put up a website to have people vote on the Internet as a referendum to see if we really want to subsidize the losers' mortgages; or would we like to at least buy cars and buy houses in foreclosure and give them to people that might have a chance to actually prosper down the road, and reward people that could carry the water instead of drink the water?[22]

The implicit moral standpoint here was that individuals deserved to live with the consequences of their choices. It was a classic example of the theodicy of markets and the seductive self-righteousness of "paying one's own way." The mix of material and ideal interests animating the Tea Party movement that subsequently emerged was complex, but a self-image as "productive members of society" in contrast to "moochers" provided an important part of its emotional energy.[23] The power of the rhetoric of deservedness was particularly apparent when, on the eve of the 2010 midterm elections, Obama gave a retort to Santelli limited to the defensive assertion that some owners losing homes when unable to pay mortgages were "real people who worked really hard for that house."[24]

The Tea Party's energy, alongside the disappointing results of the Obama administration's insufficiently bold economic policies, certainly contributed to the Democrats' loss of control over the House of Representatives in autumn 2010. Once in power, House Republicans waged a campaign of fiscal obstructionism, culminating in cliff-edge negotiations over increases in the Treasury's authorized borrowing limit. Those showdowns brought an end to the systematic use of fiscal stimulus to cushion the crisis's impact. However, and very importantly, the Federal Reserve retained its independence. And, in line with its mandate to avoid deflation and promote employment, it compensated for fiscal restriction (and market uneasiness over the debt-limit brinkmanship) with innovative expansive monetary policies in the form of quantitative easing (QE), which involved the copious provision of money issued directly by the central bank to offset weak private sector money creation. It was all but impossible to find an argument for QE that did not imply that a fiscal expansion would be more effective, but politics foreclosed such an approach. Republicans sympathetic to the Tea Party held little love for the Fed's activism, which nevertheless continued, obscuring the costs of fiscal austerity. Although many uniquely American institutions and attitudes figured in this outcome, the eurozone and the United Kingdom found their way to a similarly incoherent combination of fiscal restriction and monetary stimulus.[25] And although the specific pathways of political causality were different, arguments based on deservedness played an important role in these cases as well.

We are now in a position to consider how the presence of public purpose banking, legitimated by the franchise approach, might have affected these political dynamics. The most plausible answer is very little. In fact, accounts of money broadly consistent with the franchise view gained ground during this period, but they facilitated rather than challenged the tight-budget–loose-money outcome. Benjamin Braun has argued that before the crisis, central bankers had long found it convenient to endorse what he terms the "folk theory" of money—a theory that fails to recognize the "public–private partnership" governing its issue, regarding banks as intermediaries and ascribing full, exogenous control over the money supply to the central bank.[26] The folk theory of money made monetarism seem a feasible policy and kept the actual practical struggles of adjusting stimuli to achieve expansionary or contractionary bank lending well out of the public view. From the perspective of the folk theory of money, or crude amateur versions of monetarism, central banks' increase of their money issue to many multiples of its precrisis level was alarming. Braun argues that the rise of QE pushed central banks to give a more realistic account of the money-creation process to dispel inflationary fears, noting a 2014 paper issued by the Bank of England (invoked also by Hockett as supporting the franchise model).[27] In 2018, Claudio Borio, a leading analyst at

To Democratize Finance, Democratize Central Banking

the Bank of International Settlements, an influential citadel of central banking orthodoxy, adopted a similar point of view.[28] Although as of early 2019 it would have been an overstatement to say that central banks generally had become protagonists of an effort to convey a more realistic view of the money supply process to the broad public, they certainly were not resisting it.

On a practical level, central banks struggled mightily during the postcrisis period to get commercial banks to lend more freely. In Europe, those efforts progressed to the point where the European Central Bank (ECB) in effect paid banks that would lend to small business, with careful efforts to avoid spillover of those funds into real estate speculation or subsidies for lending that would have taken place anyway.[29] In effect, then, the ECB was seeking to channel banks' money creation to public purposes, if narrowly defined. Nonprofit banks with an explicit public purpose might have been more responsive to such encouragement, but to the extent that they were constrained to avoid losses, they would have experienced similar reasons to hesitate in their lending.

In short, ideas close to the franchise view, and policies with at least a family resemblance to the proposal for public purpose banking, did emerge in the aftermath of the financial crisis. But in the presence of independent central banks with a mandate to avoid deflation, those ideas and policies facilitated, however indirectly, the perpetuation of a political formula that used hypertrophied monetary activism to permit atrophied fiscal policy. The experiment is far from perfect, but the record suggests that, on its own, an effort to promote the democratization of finance via a reconfigured franchise model will at best leave untouched—and at worst actively perpetuate—a political context for economic policy that has proved hostile to socialism—even, remarkably, after capitalism's biggest catastrophe in eight decades.

The broader political situation thus requires that promotion of public purpose banking should be paired with a push for direct subordination of the central bank, and therefore organization of the money supply process, to democratic authorities. This would have at least two positive effects. First, it would remove the incentives for political arbitrage between fiscal and monetary policy. The absurdity of cutting spending "to reduce debt" while the central bank, far from the public eye, is issuing money to purchase government debt at a breakneck rate would become manifest. Rather than focusing on commercial banks as centers of money issue, and asking whether their activities are aligned with the public purpose, democratic discussion could encompass all forms of money issue—including that involved whenever a government makes payments out of a bank account. Instead of promoting an implicit program of loose money and fiscal austerity, parties comfortable with that policy stance would have to embrace it explicitly. As currently organized, a program of monetary stimulus says, in effect, that we in the central bank want to improve the economy by encouraging those enjoying the money franchise to lend more actively and profit by doing so. Defending *that* program in an explicit public forum in which votes must be won could plausibly do a great deal to educate public opinion on banking and open political space for public purpose banks.

A second potential benefit of eliminating central bank independence is that the publicly deliberated making of monetary policy could spill over into broader reforms involving a thoroughgoing challenge to everyday libertarianism. This might happen as follows. A common dynamic in monetary policy practice is that central bankers find the effectiveness of their policies limited or undermined by the organization of the financial markets through which they operate. In reaction, central banks seek to restructure financial markets to facilitate their monetary policy role.[30] But it is not only *financial* markets that condition the effectiveness of monetary policy. As central bankers struggled to raise inflation rates to target levels in the postcrisis decade, the failure of declining levels of unemployment to pass through to substantial wage gains proved an important barrier. However, independent central banks had no levers by which to reverse deunionization and other structural and policy changes that had weakened labor's bargaining power (even if the relevant officials had been inclined to do so). By contrast, elected institutions grappling with the ineffectiveness of monetary policy would have available to them a much broader range of possible reactions and be stimulated to rebalance bargaining strength across a range of economic sectors.

Those to whom this seems a far-fetched prospect might consider some precedents. FDR's effort to shape a monetary policy that could reverse price declines, which had limited direct success, prepared the way for a reversal of his advocacy of budget balance and was part and parcel of the broader effort to restructure markets that constituted the New Deal.[31] In the 1970s, before the primacy of central banks in fighting inflation was firmly established, efforts to tackle the issue frequently involved changes in the authorizations of transactional autonomy granted to private parties. In the United States, for example, the Nixon administration imposed direct controls on wages and prices. UK governments spent years in futile efforts to coordinate incomes policy. These policies were not successful, nor always progressive, but they do illustrate how elected authorities grappling with issues of monetary policy found themselves drawn into a much broader engagement with market structures. This dynamic shone a political spotlight on the functioning of capitalism's legal institutions and underscored the incoherence of everyday libertarianism. The drive to depoliticize such issues was, of course, an important part of the broader neoliberal push that also enshrined central bank independence (CBI).

Naturally, a reversal of CBI would guarantee neither more rational coordination of fiscal and monetary policy nor a progressive market restructuring. But eliminating CBI would have at least one other powerful political benefit. Drawing on the lessons of the Syriza experience in Greece, Block highlights the importance of avoiding a punishing capital strike during the transition to socialism and suggests that a network of nonprofit banks could be a buffer against such a strike. However, as Block recognizes, Greece's participation in the eurozone, and thus the lack of a central bank over which its government had even arm's-length control, was absolutely central to the Greek story.[32] The prospect of financial panic on Greek bond markets, and runs on Greek banks, depended critically on the ECB's expressed willingness to permit such a catastrophe. This situation reprised a broader pattern from the acute phase of the eurozone crisis, when the ECB successfully used the threat of allowing market panics to rage unchecked as a means of promoting austerity.[33] Although the absence of a corresponding fiscal or governmental authority for the eurozone as a whole makes the ECB's degree of independence unique, the pattern in which an independent central bank channels the prospect of market panic to curtail radical political aims can hold in the more common nation-state configuration as well.[34]

All of this suggests that the capacity to resist a transitional capital strike will depend crucially on government control over the central bank. Without lender-of-last-resort support, and without the central bank's continued underpinning of the franchise model, a network of nonprofit banks will be vulnerable to unmediated shifts in market sentiment and a drying up of reserves. Direct subordination of the central bank to elected authorities is thus a crucial institutional precondition for the sort of transition to socialism that Block envisages. Efforts to make establishing control over the central bank part of such a transition, because of the public signal they would send to financial markets, would only strengthen the prospect for a capital strike. Reversing CBI thus plausibly needs to come before an effort to transition to socialism.

Prospects for democratizing central banking

Democratizing central banking is, obviously, not a trivial political challenge. The mainstream consensus on CBI has become deeply rooted over the last several decades. Even some critics of austerity and advocates of "helicopter money" have proposed building the possibility of this policy into the design of independent central banks.[35] However, shifts in economic and political context suggest that the crumbling of this consensus is a realistic prospect.

Codification of an explicit case for CBI dates from the high-inflation period of the 1970s. Whatever the relevance of the key

To Democratize Finance, Democratize Central Banking

arguments in those circumstances, their contemporary pertinence is very difficult to defend.[36] Consider, first, the "time inconsistency" argument, deriving from the claim that economic agents who *expect* inflation will rapidly raise prices in response to any expansion of nominal demand through monetary policy, negating its effect. However, if inflation is *unexpected*, a period of "money illusion" will allow an increase in nominal demand to be interpreted as an increase in real demand, prompting an expansion in production and hiring. Thus a promise to maintain low inflation, once believed, creates space for effective monetary stimulus—and with it, a politically irresistible temptation to violate that promise.[37]

However, the causal mechanism is impossible to credit after years (or, in the case of Japan, decades) of unsuccessful efforts to stimulate in the face of expected low inflation. The same empirical record undermines a second prominent rationale for CBI. Kenneth Rogoff argued for the benefits of appointing central bankers whose distaste for inflation exceeds that of the public, as the prospect of ferocious monetary restriction in the face of price rises would dampen inflationary expectations. Yet if central bankers may be called on to accelerate inflation as well as to reduce it, picking a hyper-conservative central banker could easily prove counterproductive.[38]

The last of the three major justifications for CBI derives its arguments from the supposed monetary dangers of fiscal profligacy. Thomas Sargent and Neil Wallace suggested that the volume of government debt would at some point exceed the willingness of investors to hold it, especially if growth in the stock of debt is accelerated by high interest rates. At this point, they argued, the central bank would face irresistible pressure to use money issue to cover government expenditure—unless the central bank is able independently to determine its policy in a way that "effectively disciplines the fiscal authority."[39] The argument hinges, then, on the proposal that unconstrained fiscal authority will eventually issue debt on a scale that overwhelms the public's appetite to hold its bonds. Yet as long as economic growth outstrips the interest rate on government bonds, as is predominantly the case, there is no reason to assume a looming cliff edge in the capacity of fiscal authorities to place their bonds.[40]

Whether governments do shrug off the shackles of defunct economists and take back control over monetary policy will depend, ultimately, on politics. The prospects and relevant processes will depend on the specific features of different polities as well as capacities to withstand potential negative reactions from financial markets. In the United Kingdom, the unconstrained power of the executive—the lack of "checks and balances"—made CBI relatively easy to introduce and would make it relatively easy to reverse. CBI's prospects thus depend on the costs and benefits for the governing party. For Labour politicians Gordon Brown and Ed Balls, who orchestrated the sudden switch to CBI after Labour's 1997 electoral victory, the arrangement had a dual purpose. To "the markets," CBI underscored New Labour's rejection of radical policies, but the specter of bank rate rises was also meant to ensure that fiscal conservatives would have the whip hand in internal party disagreements.[41] Later, when the Conservative-led coalition government took over in 2010, pre-deflationary economic conditions meant that the Bank of England's inflation target required expansionary policy; this allowed the Tories to implement their preference for austerity, secure in the knowledge that the central bank would mitigate some of the economic impact.[42] Given low world interest rates that reduce the prospective borrowing-cost consequences of a reversal of CBI, and Labour's ambition to reverse austerity, resubordination of the Bank of England to the Treasury is a real prospect should the party return to power. In the UK general election of 2015, Labour Party leader Jeremy Corbyn proposed "QE for the People," which would have involved using central bank monetary issue to fund an investment bank.[43]

Reversal of CBI faces a much more challenging path in the eurozone, and not just because of individual member states' ample capacities to obstruct any revision of the treaty provisions establishing the European Central Bank. The attenuated link to electorates of relevant executive authorities, including the European Commission and the influential but secretive

To Democratize Finance, Democratize Central Banking

"Eurogroup" of finance ministers, as well as the circumscribed powers of the European Parliament and the macroeconomically trivial fiscal role of EU-wide spending, all underscore the absence of democratically responsive agents to which the ECB could be subordinated. Without a strengthening and democratization of Europe-wide institutions, restoration of democratic sovereignty over money will have to take place at the level of individual countries. However, the prospect of bank runs and the significance of euro-denominated obligations make exit from the euro unattractive. There is, though, an alternative route involving the use of fiscal powers—taxation and spending—to facilitate monetary issue. Fiscal authorities can spend in an alternative or surrogate currency, which they agree to accept in taxes. Historically, this is a well-trodden path.[44] In 2011–12, Spain came very close to implementing a version of this approach via netting government debts to suppliers against their tax obligations, although eventually it found a way to accomplish a similar end via channeling a commercial bank's franchise to issue official money.[45] Yanis Varoufakis, Greece's former finance minister, promoted the issue of fiscal surrogate currency during the country's standoff with other eurozone countries.[46] More recently, in the context of sustained stagnant growth, Italy's Lega Nord proposed issuing a parallel currency that could retire budget debts and would be accepted in the payment of taxes, and the coalition government of Lega and the Five Star Movement floated the idea of requesting that Italian debt purchased by the ECB be retired.[47] (It is pertinent that there are reasonable suspicions that shifts in ECB policy and rhetoric helped touch off sharp rises in interest rates on Italian bonds and thus contributed to a substantially less provocative formulation of financial policy by the coalition government.)[48] In sum, the potential conversion of fiscal into monetary powers is a specter that will continue to haunt the euro, although implementation requires more radical politics than have so far emerged.

Finally, in the United States, Hockett's primary focus, the entrenchment of CBI, is somewhat less than is often imagined. Sarah Binder and Mark Spindel note that Congress has repeatedly shown a willingness to change the laws governing the Fed and demonstrate that Fed officials are cognizant of the potential consequences of provoking legislators' discontent. "At best," they argue, "the Federal Reserve earns partial and contingent independence from Congress, and thus, we conclude, barely any independence at all."[49] This is a vast exaggeration; given the multiple counter-majoritarian veto points of the US legislative process, the barriers to curtailing independence are high. Indeed, Binder and Spindel must concede that on many occasions, including during the post-2007 financial crisis, the Fed undertook actions that would never have won congressional approval.[50] Nonetheless, they are correct to emphasize that what Congress has enacted, Congress can, and sometimes does, change. Postcrisis legislative changes focused on narrowing the Fed's discretion in emergency circumstances, including requiring approval from the Treasury for certain policies. This does not undermine, indeed it probably strengthens, the Fed's main potential source of power in crisis circumstances, namely the threat not to act and to permit catastrophe to unfold. But it does slightly extend democratic control over what action is taken, without significant change to the overall model of Fed independence constrained by pursuit of a mandate. A more significant challenge to the model was a 2015 episode in which Congress in effect required the Fed to create new money to fund spending, albeit on a one-off basis.[51] Against that backdrop, political circumstances in which elimination of CBI becomes possible can certainly be imagined. Such circumstances would very likely overlap with those necessary to enable a radical expansion of public purpose banking, so that the two reforms might be passed at the same time.

How to design a democratically appropriate central bank for the United States is a complicated issue, given the country's broader democratic defects. Polanyi's penetrating quip that the US Constitution deployed Montesquieu's "separation of powers ... to separate the people from power over their own economic life" retains its relevance.[52] However, even without a constitutional revolution, democracy would still be strengthened by bringing monetary policy under direct control of the executive branch. The ways in which congressional fiscal policy connected to monetary policy—for instance, excessive spending restrictions prompting a presidential decision to fund deficits via seigniorage rather than debt—would become much more politically transparent. When congressional Republicans were threatening a catastrophic refusal to raise the government's debt ceiling in order to force spending restrictions, some progressives urged the Obama administration to use an obscure legal provision authorizing the executive to mint platinum coins as a means of expanding money issue to meet government obligations.[53] In direct macroeconomic effect, this would have been little different from borrowing via Treasury bonds subsequently purchased by Fed money issues. But it would have been vastly more politically salient and contributed to an honest processing of the fiscal-monetary policy mix within elected institutions.

Conclusion

Block proposes that because "the franchise model cuts through [the] ideological haze [portraying banks as part of the self-regulating market of intermediaries connecting savers to borrowers], it opens up a whole set of alternative policy options."[54] Yet this ideological haze is not so easily dispelled. The brief intellectual history of the OIE given at the beginning of this article suggests that clear-sighted perception of the delegation of public power to private business by legal institutions does not by itself create political opportunities. Furthermore, confusion about the nature of banking is built on a broader base of everyday libertarianism—an intuitive grouping of views that is resilient to exceptions. Certainly, the franchise model shows present-day banking to be an excellent example of the fallacies of everyday libertarianism. But for those able to perceive them, such examples abound. Effectively confronting everyday libertarianism—which creates innumerable points of resistance to promoting socialism understood as the subordination of markets to democratically determined public purposes—plausibly requires continuous discussion that brings its implicit claims into the open. Discussion of the institutions bearing on the effectiveness of monetary policy (including the money franchise) in a legislative forum could help accomplish this aim. Thus the reversal of CBI could open the way to the integration of democratized finance into a more thoroughly democratized economy.

Making the coordination of fiscal and monetary policy a matter of explicit public contention will serve the same aim. Kalecki argued long ago that one explanation for the hesitance of business representatives to endorse fiscal stimulus despite the economic improvement it ought to bring is their reluctance to endorse subsidizing mass consumption, for "here a 'moral' principle of the highest importance is at stake. The fundamentals of capitalist ethics require that 'You shall earn your bread in sweat'—unless you happen to have private means."[55] QE, and monetary stimulus more broadly, had the effect of reducing the economic and thus the political costs of subordinating fiscal policy to this sort of self-interested moralizing. Central banks' compensatory reaction to the lack of systematic integration of Keynesian insights into fiscal policymaking thus wound up strengthening everyday libertarianism. The goal of ensuring that publicly created money franchises serve authentic public purposes can be reached only if this damaging dynamic is broken. And that end requires the direct subordination of central banks to elected officials.

5

Three Modes of Democratic Participation in Finance

Michael A. McCarthy

Since at least the 2008 financial crash, proposals have circulated that aim to democratize financial flows by subjecting them to democratic processes and public accountability. Politicians in both the Democratic Party in the US and the Labour Party in the UK, less than a decade ago a key source of market reforms, developed parallel plans that called for the creation of a public investment bank and a share levy on firms to fund worker-owned pools of capital that would be subject to democratic allocation.[1] Other plans, such as Fred Block's and Robert Hockett's, democratize finance at other scales. Their credit franchise model aims to democratize finance through local credit unions, whose boards are elected by and responsible to their members and subject to public policy constraints about their lending practices.

Yet few have offered a full account of how their plans will enhance democratic participation and make such democratic processes durable. This is quite possibly the most difficult question facing activists working toward radical forms of financial transformation. That political concerns lie beyond the purview of much of the popular and scholarly discussion is a mistake, in my view. Financialization has transformed politics in rich capitalist democracies, weakening democratic institutions and rearticulating political coalitions.[2] This chapter suggests that unless the democratic politics of reform are confronted clear-eyed and policies are developed that can also weaken the capacity of financial elites to erode newly installed democratic institutions, democratic projects won't be viable. Democratizing finance must not just be workable economically, but also socially and politically. To explore this, I compare several popular progressive plans for democratizing finance. My aim is to assess the degree to which they might enhance or diminish the democratic accountability of finance to the public and weaken the capacities of business or political elites that stand to erode it.

First, I examine three modes of public participation: representative democracy, direct democracy, and deliberative minipublics. Each offers a different approach to mobilizing public participation in the management of finance. Then I turn to a brief description of several plans to democratize finance, including the credit franchise model, public investment banks, sovereign wealth funds, inclusive ownership funds, and bank nationalization. Next I explore the ways in which both the financial and nonfinancial sectors of business crowd out the voice of ordinary citizens in politics. Drawing from the political sociology on business power, I identify two critical mechanisms of corporate political influence, *active engagement* and *structural prominence*, that might be activated to erode and undermine democratic projects.[3] I then ask how the reform proposals might democratically perform once installed. This section focuses on the degree to which each reform does or does not confront the direct and indirect powers of capital that I identify in the first section. In particular, it considers how democratizing finance *itself* might restructure the balance of political forces in society or leave those forces undisturbed. Answering these questions requires us to shift away from purely economistic concerns, such as the allocation of financial assets and market efficiency. Additionally, we need to address questions of power and politics. I argue that for democratizing finance to be viable, it needs to radically curtail the power of finance in politics while it empowers ordinary people in the management of public finance.

Three Modes of Democratic Participation in Finance

Though this short chapter throws up more questions than it can reasonably answer, it suggests that of the five proposals, bank nationalization goes furthest in guarding against the democratic dilemmas likely to beset any democratizing project. Yet even here, and this is key, simple public ownership, if rooted solely in systems of representative democracy, is not likely to empower ordinary working people in decisions about flows of credit. Public ownership alone will likely lead to principal-agent problems that arise from the separation of ownership from control and undemocratic top-down modes of management and decision-making. This section identifies four reasons why representative democracy as a mode of public participation is insufficient: informational asymmetries between the state and the public, the problem of "quiet politics" (that is, in areas of policy-making that occur outside sustained public scrutiny the concerns of elite special interests tend to hold sway), the weakness of actually existing democratic institutions in the US, and finally fiscal constraints on state managers that have historically promoted return-maximizing investing over social investing.

I argue that given these drawbacks to representative forms of democratic participation, even nationalized public finance might only poorly enhance popular control over finance flows. Public ownership may be a necessary but insufficient condition for financial democracy. Therefore, in addition to thinking through the kinds of ownership models suitable, this essay concludes by pointing to the crucial need to develop new models of public activation and engagement in financial governance.

Three modes of public participation

For the most part, global flows of finance are driven by private actors in capitalist markets aiming to maximize returns. Rhetorically democratizing this finance aims to make credit allocation and financial markets accountable to the public. Such an ambition has historically been defined as "socialism" but today might be recast to include "democratic" in the moniker. In Block's words, democratic socialism is "simply the extension of democracy to include the economy" and a "commitment to democratic institutions and democratic norms."[4] In order to realize this rhetoric in practice, any project for democratizing finance would need to be specifically attentive to the kinds of democratic institutions that might be installed to activate and reproduce popular engagement and public influence. New institutions of democracy that mobilize public participation will be core to a project that democratizes finance. In this section I do not discuss actual proposals to democratize finance, but rather focus broadly on how publics might participate. Below I discuss three distinct modes of public participation that might be pursued in a democratizing-finance agenda: representative democracy, direct democracy, and deliberative minipublics. These modes of engagement vary in two dimensions: the degree to which participation is voluntary or mandatory and the degree to which preferences are expressed through representatives or active deliberation.[5]

Representative democracy

Most of the proposals considered in this essay, with the exception of inclusive ownership funds, rely exclusively on representative forms of democracy. Here participation is voluntary; all citizens can opt in or out of participating. And their main means of exercising political voice is in voting during elections, propositions, and referendums. However, representative forms of democratic governance, where the public elects politicians who govern on their behalf, have historically been beset by principal–agent problems. Principal–agent problems arise in situations in which agents are tasked with taking actions that determine some payoff to the principal but there is both an information asymmetry between the principal and the agent, with the latter having more access to information, and an asymmetry in their preferences.[6]

The problem, at its heart, is that separating operational decisions from public oversight and input weakens democratic accountability. In the case of public finance, embedding lending agents in ongoing and direct personal relations with the

Three Modes of Democratic Participation in Finance

primary principals, the public, begins to solve the monitoring and accountability problems. In this way, community members, workers, and users of new credit lines should institutionally be integrated into the decision-making process in a more direct way. First and foremost, this requires significantly enhanced collective financial literacy for middle-income and poor workers and nonexperts. Here, I do not have in mind the sort found in financial self-help books that promote the formation of an "investing subject" attuned to "mad money"–style investing or even the logic of modern portfolio management.[7] Instead, a new popular education for financial literacy needs to be developed that concerns investing *for the social*—not solely for profit. This requires significant state resources for full-time social investment research teams housed in various universities and governments, popular education projects and publications, time off work for workers to participate, and regular conferences and public events, among other initiatives. Broadly, there are two institutional alternatives to representative democracy that might achieve this embedding: *direct democracy* and *deliberative minipublics*.

Direct democracy

Direct democracy subjects decisions to public deliberation, discussion, and direct control—removing the representative. These institutions are akin to the participatory budget experiments, modeled most famously in Porto Alegre, Brazil, and installed in over 1,500 cities worldwide.[8] Participatory budgeting is done by citizens in community and district-level assemblies who gather to deliberate, negotiate, and eventually make decisions about how to allocate public money. First, they develop a diagnosis of their needs (related to everything from sewage to education to health care) and resources, then they hold assemblies to discuss and vote on priorities, and finally they hold a larger-level assembly to make a binding budget. These "schools of democracy" are open to all who wish to attend and therefore operate on a voluntary basis. With respect to public finance, similar forms of direct democracy might be developed in the allocation of credit at different geographic scales—the neighborhood, the city, the region, the nation, and so on. One major drawback of direct democracy is that this mode of public decision-making might be unsustainable because of participation fatigue or other kinds of collective-action problems with respect to actual participation. Because the cost of participation is relatively high in terms of time, in this mode of participation we run the risk of self-selection biases with respect to what individuals come to deliberate.

Deliberative minipublics

Another possibility is the management of financial flows at various scales through representative bodies chosen at random or through a stratified selection from the relevant constituencies. For set mandatory terms, akin to citizen juries, these bodies might serve as trustees for the public with respect to the operational management of public finance. Democratic theorists call such bodies *deliberative minipublics*.[9] It is increasingly understood that democracy requires divisions of cognitive labor where some make judgments on the public's behalf about issues for which most people lack operational knowledge. In all likelihood, we simply cannot know what is best for every policy area at all times or be engaged in enough simultaneous debates to learn.[10] Representative democracy attempts to resolve this dilemma through elections. But because interest groups undermine the democratic process both during and between elections, the result is a less democratic outcome in real terms that runs counter to the aspirations of deliberative democracy. As a matter of civic duty, deliberative minipublics would learn and deliberate about the system of public finance, and take on the role of its operational managers, before passing on their duties to a new group when their term concludes. Such an arrangement has the advantage of being both deliberative and not subject to self-selection biases.

There have been a wide range of experiments in democracy, and these institutional designs are hardly exhaustive.[11] Regardless of the particular design of new democratic institutions to embolden the public in financial reform projects, wider stakeholders must be included both in setting the mandates and in the operational management of the system. For reform to be democratically viable, not only must the power of capital be confronted directly, but also the capacities of ordinary citizens must be greatly enhanced.

Five plans to democratize finance

With greater public control over lending and flows of finance, the reallocation of credit might not only help stabilize financial turbulence but also could redirect capitalist societies toward new forms of social egalitarianism and more ecologically sustainable modes of organizing life. So Hockett's and Block's parallel chapters tread on urgent ground. Taking their views together, democratizing finance is an attempt to push progressive discussion of finance in new directions—beyond simply using the power of the state to pursue regulatory modifications, and instead toward feasible and viable models of finance that are socially allocated and publicly accountable. But in developing a plan for credit franchises, Hockett and Block are not alone in their effort to draw up a proposal that democratizes financial flows. Others circulate, even at the highest levels of politics. These are the creation of a public investment bank, the creation of a sovereign wealth fund, the creation of inclusive ownership funds, and finally the state nationalization of banks "too big to fail." After briefly describing each of these democracy proposals, I will turn to the political sociology of business power to comparatively assess their potential democratic durability against countermobilizations from capital. None alone, I argue, sufficiently curtails the power of business and activates public engagement to make them viable.

Nonprofit credit unions

Block's proposal for democratizing finance rests on Hockett's analysis of the existing financial system in places like the US.

Hockett argues that with respect to its institutional design, "the financial system looks much like a franchise arrangement in which the public is franchisor, while the institutions dispensing its full faith and credit are its franchisees."[12] Contrary to popular lay understandings of banking, Hockett argues that lending is not directly tied to deposited pre-accumulated loanable funds. Instead, accommodation (when a public authority takes on a privately issued debt liability as its own) and monetization (when the beneficiary of accommodation can spend the proceeds of the loan as currency) are operations by which the state enables credit to be generated in an immediately spendable form. Hockett takes this argument to its logical end, suggesting that there are no hard limits to the state's ability to spontaneously generate credit or money. In short, credit creation is ultimately dependent on the power and resources of governments.[13]

Building upon Hockett's public–private franchise model, Block's proposal for financial reform relies on the representative mode of democratizing finance and incrementally creates supplemental nonprofit credit unions governed by state investment guidelines that allocate investment into credit-starved sectors at lower rates of interest. In his view, this would have *two* key results, one allocative and the other political. First, it would significantly improve the distribution of credit, enhancing the economic welfare of working and poor people and certain sectors of business. New nonprofit franchisees would be tasked with allocating credit to credit-starved sectors of the economy, such as infrastructure, clean-energy and energy-saving retrofits, small and medium-sized firms, multifamily housing for middle- and low-income families, and social-entrepreneurship projects. These institutions would supplement the existing ones as a "parallel credit system" to fill the gaps in the credit sector that large-centralized financial institutions are not willing to lend to.[14]

Yet there are also political implications. Block characterizes this proposal as a "real utopia" in the Wrightian sense because a parallel credit system would then help left-wing governments overcome formidable barriers to a democratic transition to socialism. Historically, in periods of attempted democratic transition, resistance from both domestic and foreign companies in the form of disinvestment or capital flight, shifting liquid or productive capital in and out of the domestic market, has led to economic downturns and slowdowns. These political recessions, which result from the exercise of business structural power, erode popular support for socialist agendas, undermining the governments that are trying to advance them. Erik Olin Wright has theorized this as the "transition trough" in his *Envisioning Real Utopias*.[15] These troughs are very deep in transitory strategies that rely exclusively on radical "ruptural" breaks with existing institutions and structures of power. As Wright notes, "Any serious [ruptural] move towards socialism would trigger significant destruction of the incentive and information structures that animated economic coordination under capitalism."[16]

Block's proposal is not a ruptural one, but instead combines Wright's "symbiotic" and "interstitial" transitional paths toward socialism. According to Wright's definition, it is symbiotic because it entails critical elements of class compromise. By supporting certain sectors of business with much-needed capital, Block's proposal aims to avoid a direct confrontation with capitalist class power. But the path is also interstitial because the support of credit unions as franchises makes "relatively small transformations [that] cumulatively generate a qualitative shift in the dynamics and logic of a system."[17] These changes occur within unoccupied spaces in the dominant financial system.[18] It is argued that this supplemental financial system will help pave the way toward a more traversable break with the dominant financial order. This eventual break will still generate a transition trough, albeit one more shallow than the ruptural path. However, with the franchisee model of finance installed, the severity and duration of the transition trough will be reduced in two ways. Nonprofit credit institutions will have the ability to increase domestic investments to offset domestic investment slowdowns and can also increase their borrowing abroad to offset pressures of capital flight on the currency.

Public investment banking

North Dakota is home to the US's only public bank, but in recent years the idea of installing others has achieved greater popularity. Though most legislation is at the municipal level, some have argued for a national investment bank. Like Block's plan, a public bank does not replace existing financial institutions but rather supplements them with financial services provided by the government. And in most plans the basic governance design relies on representative democracy. Supporters argue that the public provisioning of banking goods and services might fill gaps in the market for plain vanilla banking; offer lower-costing debt to local, state, and federal governments; allocate credit to small businesses at lower interest rates; and invest in infrastructure. Many banks have moved away from low-cost financial services to more high-profit activities, leaving a significant percentage of poorer workers without financial services.[19] Nearly 27 percent of the American population in 2015 was unbanked or underbanked, pushed into high-cost forms of borrowing to survive. These include payday loans, check cashing, money orders, pawnshops, international remittances, and auto loan titles.[20] Mehrsa Baradaran proposes a public banking option situated in the United States Postal Service (USPS), where there is already a working infrastructure in place.[21] In the US, there is a post office in every zip code and 5.5 times the number of branches as Wells Fargo, the largest bank branch network.

Thomas Herndon and Mark Paul argue that the USPS model would be restricted from direct competition with private banks, and that direct public–private competition in the provisioning of financial services could be a powerful lever for financial regulation.[22] As a possible solution, they argue that a new public bank should be created that instead partners with the USPS to take advantage of its infrastructural resources. In their proposal, the public bank would be set up as a government corporation instead of an agency, avoiding the congressional appropriations process and able to generate its own revenue to cover costs. Herndon and Paul suggest that it would also help regulate the private financial

Three Modes of Democratic Participation in Finance

system though competition. Predatory lenders that charge exorbitant fees and interest rates would need to change their practices to be competitive, and the government could limit access to an online financial services marketplace to only those firms that accept robust consumer protection standards.

The above public banking option, much like Block's nonprofit franchises, is geared toward fixing an allocative market failure, filling gaps in credit-starved sectors. But public banking might also be geared toward industrial policy by investing in ways that shape the direction of economic development to deal with large-scale social problems. Block and Matthew Keller, and Mariana Mazzucato, have pointed to the critical role played by state investment in the development of new technologies.[23] To confront inequality, climate change, and demographic change, public banks might invest in areas of uncertainty in order to nurture new lines of technology for broader social purposes. With the recent upsurge of the left in electoral politics, this idea has even found its way onto party platforms. The centerpiece of the Labour Party's industrial strategy in the UK is a national investment bank. Over ten years, the bank would raise and manage a £250 billion fund, with the primary aim of reallocating 60 percent of energy to renewables and zero-carbon sources; doing so would increase research and development to 3 percent of GDP by 2030.[24] In addition to this core objective, the bank would serve to coordinate a network of regional development banks that would fill gaps in the credit market in much the same way that Block's franchises do.

Sovereign wealth funds

Another set of proposals calls for the establishment of sovereign wealth funds.[25] More than fifty countries have established one; together they hold over $7 trillion in assets.[26] About half of these assets are held by Middle Eastern funds, large and notable examples being those of Saudi Arabia, Kuwait, and United Arab Emirates. But the largest fund is Norway's, which holds an average of 1.3 percent of every publicly listed company in the world. The country's oil fund was founded in 1990 as a vehicle to invest surplus profits from the state-run oil company. By 2017 it had grown massively, holding nearly 8,500 billion kroner. Today it has over $1 trillion in assets.

How sovereign wealth funds allocate their investments is largely political and again typically based on a representative form of democracy. However, in societies with authoritarian states, such as Saudi Arabia, the funds shouldn't be considered institutions that democratize finance to any degree. Quite the opposite—they might even be working to centralize control of asset allocation into fewer hands. But in societies with functioning institutions of representative democracy, there has been some public input into how these funds are managed and their financial assets allocated. We can imagine deeper modes of democratic control of these public funds as well. But with respect to transparency, political accountability, and the adoption of responsible investment standards for actually existing sovereign wealth funds, the two that stand out are Norway's and New Zealand's. Norway's fund in particular has taken a role in actively disinvesting from products that it has deemed socially harmful, such as tobacco, nuclear arms and cluster weapons, and coal. Furthermore, with mixed success, the fund occasionally uses shareholder voices to try to insert its hand into corporate governance decisions. But the monetary costs of these stances are small; the fund is primarily governed by the profit incentive, and thus is heavily constrained by the global financial markets in which it is invested.[27]

By the estimation of the People's Policy Project, a similar fund could be established in the US to create a more egalitarian distribution of wealth. They argue that the government can bring assets into the fund through a combination of voluntary contributions, ring-fencing existing assets (transferring existing state assets into it), levies (taxes and fees on consumption, payroll, and capital), leveraged purchases (government could borrow at low interest rates to invest in the fund and orient itself toward investing aimed at higher rates), and monetary seigniorage (the Federal Reserve could create new money to buy assets in the fund).[28] Similar to proposals for a public bank, the project argues that the fund should be set up as a state-owned corporation through the Treasury Department, which would appoint its board members, chairs, and auditor. The treasury would create rules and mandates, and the corporation would manage and follow those rules in the day-to-day. Asset allocation of the fund itself, as well as ownership rights and voting as a shareholder, would be decided through Congress and issued as directives to the corporation through the Treasury. The critical outcome of this plan is the distribution of a universal basic dividend from the returns on the fund's portfolio. Every qualifying citizen would be given one nontransferable share in the fund that would entitle them to that dividend.[29]

Inclusive ownership funds

Under 2018 plans announced by the Jeremy Corbyn–led Labour Party in the UK and the Bernie Sanders campaign in the US, all private companies employing more than 250 people would be compelled to adopt an inclusive ownership fund, which allocates shares of the firm to their workers and increases labor's power in governance decisions.[30] Here, the democratization of finance operates within firms to reallocate streams of finance generated within nonfinancial and financial enterprises alike. Within a decade of adoption of the Labour Party plan, every eligible company would be required to allocate 10 percent of its equity into the worker's fund. The *Financial Times* describes this as "one of the most interventionist business policies put forward by a mainstream political party in the UK for a generation."[31] The former shadow chancellor of labour, John McDonnell, has said that "what this will ensure is that in large companies, in addition to rewarding workers with wages, they will reward them with shares that will go into a pool that will allow them to have an ownership role."[32] Though their shares would build over time, workers would not be able to cash them in or trade them, as with the share plans promoted by Margaret Thatcher in the 1980s.

In addition to giving workers a direct stake in a firm's profits and how those profits are used, these funds promise a crucial form of workplace democracy as well. In theory, with their ownership stake workers will have the ability to directly influence the daily management and broad direction of the firm. In addition, according to Labour, workers would receive about £5 billion a year in dividends by the fifth year of the plan's operation. However, the dividends received by particular workers would be capped at £500 per year, with the rest distributed to a public fund that would be used to pay for welfare benefits and a renewal of decaying public services. This would counter the possibility of rising sector- or firm-based economic inequality between workers. Labour calculated at the time that 10.7 million workers—approximately 40 percent of the private sector workforce—would initially be covered by the plan.

Distinct from sovereign wealth funds, which are established at the level of a country and accountable to representative democratic processes—the inclusive ownership funds would be established at the firm level as a means toward industrial democracy. To the extent that the public outside those firms are stakeholders in their decisions, they would not be participants in decision-making. This also contrasts with Sweden's experiment with the wage earner funds in the 1970s, which were going to be established at the sectoral level. Commonly called the Meidner Plan, the wage earner funds were to be installed by a gradual transfer of the ownership of Swedish companies away from private shareholders to funds that would be administered by labor unions. To avoid paying a hefty tax on their profits, companies would issue new company stock to the relevant sectoral fund. As somewhat distinct from sovereign wealth funds or inclusive ownership funds, the Meidner Plan was oriented around the goal of socializing capital itself. In his 1978 book *Employee Investment Funds*, Rudolf Meidner suggested that with an average profit margin of 15 percent a year the funds would have a majority ownership of Swedish firms within twenty-five years. Through the exercise of shareholder rights, this would effectively give workers control over the firms. Many of the plan's most ambitious features were drastically rolled back and it was eventually terminated entirely, largely due to resistance from Swedish capital.[33]

Three Modes of Democratic Participation in Finance

Bank nationalization

The final financial reform on offer is to eliminate private financial institutions "too big to fail" entirely by converting them into public ones.[34] There has been a massive concentration of financial resources into a handful of institutions over the last few decades. In 1990, the top ten banks in the US controlled 25 percent of total bank assets. On the eve of the crisis in 2007, the top ten banks owned 60 percent.[35] Subjecting these assets to state control, and therefore representative democracy, enters entirely new terrain in places like the United Kingdom and the United States, which, unlike France, Japan, or Germany, lack a robust tradition of public ownership of finance.

Proposals for nationalized banking tend to rely on representative forms of democracy. And as with every proposal under consideration, so much depends on the nature of the political mandate. Much like others, a nationalized sector could fill gaps in credit markets by granting more opportunity for small and medium enterprises to become financed and might provide credit for green initiatives and technologies, education, health, and housing. It might also underwrite government bonds issued for important social purposes. Their financing, in combination with the public's claims on any profit generated through them, could generate the resources necessary to restore public provisioning of goods across several areas of social need to become the basis for a Green New Deal or other large-scale public projects. In contrast to credit franchises and public investment banks, which would supplement the existing milieu of capitalist financial institutions, these public banks would operate within this milieu and would compete with and perhaps replace these institutions.

While new investment practices are adopted, others, such as predatory lending and risky speculation on exotic financial derivatives, could be eliminated.[36] Nationalizing banks too big to fail might be part and parcel of a general reversal of financialization itself, as public finance would also help rein in financial markets by imposing pricing and trading-volume regulations on them. Furthermore, much like the mission-oriented banks discussed above, the provision of higher-quality banking services with enough market share could promote a dynamic of a "race to the top" in the quality and cost of financial services provided.[37] Currently, large banks allocate their most risky activities through wholly or partially owned subsidiaries such as hedge funds and private equity funds. Public ownership over these institutions could entail the partial elimination of this "shadow banking system."[38] These activities often fall outside the regulated banking system, involving little transparency and weak or no fiduciary, leverage, or capital requirements.[39]

Threats to democracy in public finance

Exploring questions about the democratic viability of these proposals is particularly important with respect both to the mechanisms of democratic engagement they rely on and to their capacity to remain durable against business efforts at retrenchment. The latter is particularly important given the outsized role of business power in formal democratic institutions. There are two key ways in which business power is exercised in capitalist democracies. The first is through active engagement, which refers to the direct ways in which businesses influence politics with campaign donations, lobbying, and interpersonal connections with state managers and policymakers. Second, however, businesses influence politics indirectly through their structural prominence. This refers to the way a business or sector's position in the economy and control over key investment decisions matter to policymakers.[40]

Much of the research on the political power of finance focuses on the direct ways financial institutions influence politics. In the twelve months of the 2017–18 election cycle in the US, banks and financial interests spent $719 million on campaign contributions and lobbying to influence policy, far more than of any other sector of industry identified by the Center for Responsive Politics.[41] Sixty percent of these contributions went to Republicans, while the remainder went to Democrats. Financial firms and banks actively engage in politics, directly intervening where they can, and expending significant organizational resources to anticipate and change regulatory rules and decisions before policymakers take action on their own. Andrew Hindmoor and Josh McGeechan show how lobbying efforts of US banks led both to regulatory changes and to the policy embrace by lawmakers of the idea that they were too big to fail.[42] Drawing from comparative data, they demonstrate that the financial sectors in both London and New York are able to remain one step ahead of regulators in a "game of regulatory arbitrage."[43] In their view, states simply don't have "the administrative or regulatory capacity to tame finance." And since 2008, financial industry spending has exceeded spending levels prior to the crisis. This might help explain why, in 2017, the House majority rolled back key parts of the Dodd-Frank Act and the Senate weakened rules that guarded against discrimination in lending and that allowed consumers to sue financial companies that broke the law.

Because it is indirect, structural prominence offers far more challenges to researchers.[44] In general, it refers to the position in the economy of a firm, a sector, or capital, and how that position bears on the decisions and capacities of policymakers. This means that it is often anticipated by political actors, requiring the researcher to delve into the somewhat murky area of policymakers' perceptions of their action environments.[45] The early work on structural power considered the role of business in politics broadly. Lindblom and Block famously argued that the power of business in capitalist societies, in contrast to that of elected officials and other organized interest groups, lies in their ability to make crucial decisions about the production and distribution of goods and services.[46] In market systems, private investment choices have far-reaching public implications. As a result, states are dependent on firms to invest in ways that promote growth and employment. Despite this insight, attention to structural power strangely fell from view in the 1990s and 2000s, criticized by some as too abstract. Much of the work concerned the structural power of capitalists qua a class themselves; few, however, considered how that power varied.

But as Hacker and Pierson note, "the structural power of capital is variable, not constant."[47] Only recently have scholars redirected their attention back to structural power with respect to its mechanisms and variability across cases. In their study of bank bailouts in the US and the UK, Pepper Culpepper and Raphael Reinke identify two types—automatic structural power occurs when governments anticipate and respond to business, while strategic structural power occurs when businesses take a disinvestment action to achieve an aim.[48]

The relative weight of the private sector in the economy has been the fundamental measure of the structural power of capital. However, one can employ a similar methodology to consider the relative size of a particular industry or even a particular firm. Sectors with greater structural prominence contribute toward a larger share of the economy, might generate significant employment, and typically have multiple linkages to other sectors.[49] For finance to be durably democratized, as part of its installment any financial reform project must confront both of these sources of political power. If the active engagement and structural prominence of financial interests in politics isn't significantly curtailed, the resulting arrangement will only be weakly democratic. We should presume that financial interests will draw upon their sources of power to roll back popular influence and gains. I now turn to a discussion of several proposals for financial reform, after which I will return to the question of finance's power.

Active engagement and structural prominence in practice

Given our discussion of active engagement and structural prominence, a viable plan to democratize finance would not only activate public participation in decisions but also weaken the private interest groups that currently play a disproportionately large role in policymaking. For now, let's table the questions of the feasibility and desirability of implementing the above democratizing-finance projects. Here I want to take up another issue—to what degree would these reforms put in place

Three Modes of Democratic Participation in Finance

institutions that would make them democratically durable and run in ways that more genuinely reflect popular will than the sectoral business interests that already hold greater power in capitalist democracies?

With the important exception of bank nationalization, each plan to democratize finance leaves the financial sector as is to remain actively engaged in the democratic process. To the extent that corporate financial institutions will be weakened, this will largely be *relative to* the growing power of the new public ones that supplement them. That being said, an inclusive ownership fund and a sovereign wealth fund do offer two distinct routes to weakening the efficacy of active engagement on the part of financial institutions. The Labour Party's inclusive ownership funds would not significantly alter the prominence of London's financial sector in the economy, but they might change the orientation of nonfinancial and financial firms with respect to both their corporate governance and how they approach their own particular involvement in politics. As workers gain a greater share of, and greater voice in, the firms they work for this might lead to a different governance orientation, even if the profit motive still imposes hard limits on what is possible. But this route to taking on the active engagement of business in democracy is not without significant roadblocks. At minimum, for workers to use their voice to redirect corporate governance depends heavily on their own level of political engagement, the extent of rank-and-file democracy, and their degree of financial literacy.

Bank nationalization goes even further than inclusive ownership funds, sovereign wealth funds, credit union franchises, and national investment banks to limit finance's active engagement in democratic politics. Challenging the property rights of financiers by establishing public ownership over too-big-to-fail banks in combination with active public control of those banks directly negates their organizational power as private entities. Surely, the needs of public banks and the influence of their personnel would still impact policymakers. But the public ownership and control of banks that Sanders's "Too Big to Fail, Too Big to Exist Act" deems too big to fail would swiftly undercut the power of finance capital's direct influence on politics.[50] US banking is highly monopolized and concentrated.[51] And the ownership of publicly traded banks is also concentrated in just a few asset management firms such as BlackRock, Vanguard, Fidelity, Berkshire Hathaway, Wellington, and State Street.[52] Making these banks public would also erode the capacities of these asset management and mutual fund corporations for direct leverage in politics, even if just marginally.

Leaving aside the question of finance's active engagement in politics, the deep structural dependencies that currently exist between the state and the financial sector will certainly persist if that sector is left unrestructured. To the extent that the proposals for financial reform other than nationalization will alter the structural prominence of financial institutions, they will do so only by relatively slowly filling in new niches in the market. National investment banks, credit union franchises, sovereign wealth funds, and inclusive ownership funds are, after all, each *parallel financial institutions* that at worst would only operate in the interstices of the existing profit-oriented system. While the structural prominence of finance might not be undermined in the short run by these parallel institutions, how might the political strategies that finance capital, as well as nonfinance capital, employs be affected by these reforms?

Capital strikes (withholding investment) and capital flight (moving liquid or physical assets elsewhere) both lie at the core of the exercise and threat of structural power.[53] Even the threat or hint can be enough to get policymakers to act on the behalf of business.[54] The classic socialist solution to guard against such an indirect mechanism of business influence in politics and the economy more generally is capital controls. But supplemental forms of public finance that can be strategically allocated to offset disinvestment might also run counter to capital strikes or flight. New pools of public finance could be mobilized to offset the social costs of business exercising their structural power. So, though supplemental public finance doesn't directly undermine the structural power of finance, it is at least theoretically possible that it could be allocated to do so indirectly.

Three Modes of Democratic Participation in Finance

In the case of sovereign wealth funds, as we have seen, Norway's oil fund is both the largest and the most progressively oriented. With respect to capacity, with over $1 trillion in assets, it appears that it could offer a line of investing defense against capital flight and financial disinvestment. There are two distinct ways the fund might be used to weaken the exercise of Norwegian capital's structural power. First it could allocate finance into areas that are being disinvested from. Second, it could use the shareholders' voice in companies in which it owns a large share to help shape corporate governance decisions in the public interest. Yet reality hardly matches the theory here. By design, Norway's oil fund was set up not as a means to alter the balance of class power but rather to generate state profits. The allocation of investments in its portfolio largely reflects this. The fund's assets are channeled in ways largely driven by political mandates to achieve competitive rates of return, not to allocate resources in ways that best promote the social good—even if these profits are in part used by the state to fund public programs. Disinvestment has been carried out in select cases; since 2006 the oil fund has disinvested from coal, oil, nuclear weapons, and cluster munitions. But it is largely incapable of being mobilized in ways that exert influence over Norway's domestic capital. Unlike Norway's smaller Folketrygdfondet, the sovereign wealth fund is not domestically invested to any significant degree. To offset the greater risk of more localized economic crises, it is diversified and primarily invested in international financial markets.

The fundamental issue is that leaving capitalist financial institutions intact and private fails to confront their basic source of structural power in politics: their control over the allocation of finance. With the sole exception of nationalization, in each of the democratization plans finance's economic power remains highly concentrated in a small number of institutions. As a result, profit-oriented financial firms will retain substantial power as their share of the financial market won't be undermined, at least in the short term, by the supplemental financial institutions in each of the reforms. Most working people aren't credit-starved, they are rather credit-saturated—and as a result heavily in debt to these companies. These dependencies give financial institutions significant leverage over the electorate and politics. Reform proposals that aim to undermine this structural prominence over the long term with plans that gradually erode it, as the credit union franchises, inclusive ownership funds, and sovereign wealth funds do, face the potential backlash of disinvestment and political recessions in the shorter term.

This raises a critical concern. If the gradual installation of non-profit financial institutions, inclusive ownership funds, national investment banks, and sovereign wealth funds did begin to weaken the overall structural prominence of finance capital, then capital would likely intervene to undermine their installation before they were widespread enough to sufficiently weaken private financial institutions. Weakening the class power of business has been a great historical motivator for its reactionary movements, and these reforms will undoubtedly motivate such a reaction even if the institutions they create fill gaps in the credit market rather than explicitly undermining the profits of financial firms. Such an immediate class reaction has already been hinted at by business even as these ideas circulate far away from real legislative debate. With respect to the establishment of inclusive ownership funds, the director general of the Confederation of British Industry, Carolyn Fairbairn, warned on BBC Radio 4's *Today* program, "Take steps like this and we will set the clock back, investment will flee our country and, whatever Labour says about this, the outcome will be one that reduces pay in people's pockets."[55]

Fairbairn's promise of disinvestment raises concerns about the temporality of reform. If plans to democratize finance are gradualist in their implementation, any social power they might afford to poor and middle-income workers will likely only result once they have *matured*. With the exception of inclusive ownership funds and bank nationalization, other plans implicitly accept Block's warning about the need to "avoid pursuing reforms that challenged the power of big business directly."[56] These proposals aim to enact financial democracy behind the backs of the large and centralized financial institutions themselves. But as the state

Three Modes of Democratic Participation in Finance

changes capital flows, firms will anticipate the danger this poses, not only to their bottom line but in some cases to their very organizational survival. It is hard to imagine a scenario where large financial firms simply let this happen when they have the means to intervene to bring it to a halt. Financial and nonfinancial firms alike will recognize this *well before* gradual implementation comes close to being complete and the balance of class power has shifted in favor of the public.

This again suggests that the path that directly confronts financial power, bank nationalization, might also be the most *democratically* viable. What is crucial, however, is developing the political and social power to make this break with the dominant model of finance possible in the first place. This points to the importance of developing organizational power for working people both outside and inside the state prior to such a large-scale transformation. How to achieve such a shift in the balance of class forces, the question of feasibility, is beyond the scope of this chapter. But it will certainly require large-scale organization in the workplace, in the community, and in formal political institutions. Democratizing finance won't be the means to that organization; it will be the result of it.

Pitfalls of representative democracy in democratizing finance

Both the active engagement of banks in politics and their structural prominence in the economy result from their private control and allocation of investments. State takeover and public ownership might appear as the simple solution to this problem, but even here thorny problems remain that might stagger the project of democratizing finance. In short, publicly owned financial institutions will not necessarily be public in their orientation. In this section, I explore the democratic pitfalls of forms of public ownership that rely exclusively on representative democracy.

In *The Unseen Revolution*, Peter Drucker argued that "if 'Socialism' is defined as 'ownership of the means of production by the workers'—and this is both the orthodox and only rigorous definition—then the United States is the first truly 'Socialist' country."[57] Drucker came to this conclusion because of the widespread dispersal of stock holding in the US by the mid-1970s. Through their pension funds, workers own a significant share of American capital. By the time Drucker was writing, nearly 25 percent of all US corporate equities were held in the pension funds of American workers.[58] But the field of corporate governance casts serious doubt on Drucker's view. Simply put, ownership need not equal control.[59] Though the actual degree of stock dispersal across the population has been subject to considerable disagreement, there is no doubt in the debate itself that not only do owners not necessarily have control, but indeed managers (or those with daily operational control of firms) might also have a lack of accountability to the owners.[60] As a result, managers might direct corporate strategies in ways that run contrary to what the owners might prefer.

The question of the separation of ownership and control helped generate a large body of research on principal–agent problems—not only in economic relationships but in political processes of representation as well. Therefore, governance design is a critical question in the project of democratizing finance. Some proposals develop explicit mechanisms and means for ordinary workers to more directly control investment allocation, while others rely more heavily on representative democracy. The People's Policy Project's proposal for a sovereign wealth fund puts governance decisions solely in electoral politics and formal political institutions, which leaves popular participation limited to voting for elected officials. The fund would be managed by a state-owned enterprise under the Treasury Department. The Treasury would be responsible for creating the rules, mandates, and directives that guide the fund's operation, but the employees of the state-owned enterprise would be responsible for day-to-day operations. Block's credit franchise model, which encourages credit unions to invest in areas where there is an established social need, with state subsidies or guaranteed rates of return, ultimately rests on a similar form of representative democracy. Because they are credit unions, they will be organized as cooperatives, with each member having a vote to elect the board leadership. But at the same time, in their role as franchises of the state, membership decisions about what to do with state franchise investments would be driven by directives established by Congress that would lay out clear lending guidelines. Somewhat distinctly, the National Investment Bank proposed by John McDonnell in the UK would have a two-tier board: a supervisory board including representatives from business, labor, and local government that sets an overall strategy within parameters set by government policy, and an operating board responsible for day-to-day management and decisions.[61] And finally, the inclusive ownership funds would be owned collectively by the workers of a firm—and would give the workers voting rights in the governance questions of how the firms allocate streams of income.

Reform proposals that rely on government control alone democratize finance in a distinctly *representational* form—this is the model of governance either explicit or implicit in most nationalization proposals as well. In this mode of participation, the state enforces guidelines on public finance that presumably reflect the will of the electorate. However, there are four interrelated reasons why representative state institutions of public finance would not be durably capable of reproducing active engagement and influence from the public: information problems between the state and the public, the problem of "quiet politics," the weakness of actually existing democratic institutions, and resource constraints on state managers.

First, democracy in public finance run by state representatives is beset by informational disadvantages that the public confronts when it comes to developing opinions on financial policy. The public faces significant collective-action problems with respect to both political participation and collecting relevant information on the issues, especially ones as inaccessible to nonexperts as policy concerning investment and credit allocation. In a representative democracy, there is also no clear way for the population to monitor what the government does, especially in its administration of programs and the development of policies that are often off the radar of the popular press. Even in the ideal representative democracy, if an elected official or party fails in its tasks, they get voted out in the next election cycle. Yet given these information asymmetries, the public will likely face deep disadvantages in their ability to adequately assess the performance of policymakers in their management of public finance. *A simple state-centric solution like nationalization does not circumvent this problem.*

Second, research in political sociology demonstrates that the practice of representative democracy is far less democratic than the theory—much happens without the public's knowledge or input. It is in these areas of "quiet politics" that elite and business group influence creeps back in and has more leverage over the decisions of policymakers.[62] Therefore, even in a well-functioning representative democracy, where people understand the issues and vote, if deliberation and decision-making are left to state managers who act as trustees of the public interest, special interests will likely hold greater sway in the policy arenas subject to less popular scrutiny between elections.

This is compounded by the third and related issue, the deep weakness of the actually existing institutions of representative democracy with respect to their democratic accountability. Though problems of disproportionate elite interest cut across the capitalist world, American democracy is particularly insulated from the preferences of average voters. Even in cases when the public does have a strong preference in a policy area, where lack of information is not the concern, as above, research suggests that these preferences have at best a weak relationship to actual policy outcomes. Martin Gilens and Benjamin Page show that policy change in the US isn't responsive at all to low- and middle-income voters' policy opinions—but is instead responsive to the members of the economic elite.[63] The opinion of ordinary voters appears "to have only a minuscule, near-zero, statistically non-significant impact upon public policy."[64] Together, these problems should cast significant doubt on any state-centric reform proposal that doesn't specifically include mechanisms that empower the disenfranchised. Therefore, the degree to which a government-run public finance project is democratized should, in significant

Three Modes of Democratic Participation in Finance

ways, reflect the democratization of the state itself. Proposals that depend on implementation by the US Congress are at high risk of being commandeered by the special interests that *already* operate most successfully on the institutional terrain of the state.

Fourth, and finally, since the 2008 crash, federal, state, and local governments have faced ongoing and deepening fiscal crises imposing tough constraints on their budgets.[65] If left unchecked, public sector bureaucrats tasked with administering the sovereign wealth fund, the nonprofit franchise system, public investment banks, or a nationalized banking sector should be expected to favor modifications and criteria that push their operation and allocation of assets in a direction that prioritizes accumulation over the social good in order to enrich the public purse. This potential for neoliberal tinkering with democratization plans in ways that undermine their social objectives is a significant risk in a context of weak democratic accountability. In all likelihood, targeted investment strategies will show losses relative to more profit-oriented alternatives. Firms are bound by the law of competition, where cost cutting and generating negative externalities are crucial components of profitability. Capitalists fight vigorously against labor, environment, and work standards at every level because they cut into their bottom line. Organizing investment around social goals *necessarily* subordinates profits to values that society agrees are more important. Bureaucrats and experts in charge of managing public pools of finance, more concerned with their own jobs and the survivability of their programs, will themselves likely favor investments that perform better economically. If the market imposes constraints on the public sector more generally, as the state manages public finance it will confront parallel constraints and challenges.

As stated at the beginning, this chapter poses more questions and concerns than it can adequately resolve. But my hope is that it is not simply a wet blanket; these concerns point us in a direction for thinking through the details of an adequately *democratic* financial system. To be democratically robust and durable, that system would need to simultaneously activate and reproduce popular engagement in governance decisions and weaken the capacities of finance to engage in de-democratizing forms of political retrenchment. I have suggested that leaving dominant financial entities intact while developing democratic alternatives in the interstices of the financial system will likely lead to a democratizing-finance project vulnerable to an antidemocratic business offensive. But nationalization is no silver bullet. If developed in a way that simply relies on representative democracy as the core mechanism of public engagement, it will also likely fail along democratic lines because of principal–agent problems between the state and society. Deliberative and mandatory forms of public participation, as we find in proposals for deliberative minipublics, are areas to explore more fully as both researchers and practitioners muddle through various institutional designs. A key question for scholars and activists building alternatives is how to install, and build to last, new institutions of democracy that can make public finance accountable to the popular will.

III. ALTERNATIVE FINANCIAL VISIONS

6

"A Modern Financial Tool Kit"

Lessons from Adolf A. Berle for a More Democratic Financial System

Sarah Quinn, Mark Igra, and Selen Güler

> The Wall Street banking system is doing exactly what one would expect it to do—no less and no more. If anything real is to be accomplished along these lines, the foundation has to be laid for a capital credit system that really works.
>
> Adolf A. Berle Jr., 1938

Adolf A. Berle Jr. was one of the twentieth century's great theorists of corporate power and democratic accountability.[1] At the close of the 1930s, he circulated two memoranda that asked readers to rethink the national allocation of long-term credit. The memoranda culminated in a proposal for a "modern financial tool kit" made up of (1) a public works finance corporation, (2) loan guarantees for small businesses, and (3) a new "banking system for capital and credit" to be developed by a government committee. Berle's memos provide few details about how these ideas should actually be designed and implemented, but they do elaborate on the necessity for bold reform. Berle rejected the idea that banking necessarily had to be a for-profit enterprise. On the contrary, because public institutions made banking and credit possible, banks should pursue the public good, not private profit.

This chapter recovers Berle's program for banking reforms and puts that plan in conversation with the writings of Robert Hockett and Fred Block in this volume. To establish the importance of focusing on Berle's plans, and to provide useful context for understanding his arguments and goals, the chapter opens with a brief biography of Berle and a refresher on *The Modern Corporation and Private Property*, his classic book cowritten with Gardiner Means. This is followed by an overview of the immediate context in which Berle writes about banking reform, which includes an overview of other proposals for banking reform that proliferated during the late New Deal. These other proposals informed Berle's work, and Berle's work can be read as one expression of these more general debates. We then present summaries of his proposals—two memoranda prepared in 1938 and 1939 for members of the Temporary National Economic Committee (TNEC).

The paper ends with a discussion of some lessons that can be gained from Berle's work for people interested in democratic and progressive banking reform today. Specifically, we draw three lessons for a theory of democratized finance that are consistent with Berle's work. First, Berle addressed the shortcomings of alternative approaches. In that spirit, we believe that proponents of democratized finance should ring the alarm about private equity's encroachment on public infrastructure. Second, Berle stressed precedents for government action as justifications for further reform. Here we argue for a closer focus on the trillions in loans currently owned or guaranteed via federal credit programs. Third, Berle regularly articulated core principles and essential elements of financial reform. In that tradition, we offer a distillation of the overarching principles that might guide democratic financial reform today. Specifically, we posit three pillars, or primary orienting principles: fair allocation, local and global sustainability, and political accountability.

"A Modern Financial Tool Kit"

Why Berle?

There were many proposals for banking reform circulating in the 1930s, so why focus on Adolf Berle's? We believe that Berle's plan is particularly noteworthy because he was one of the nation's great thinkers of democratic accountability and finance. *The Modern Corporation and Private Property* was a landmark of organizational scholarship that helped establish corporate governance as a field of study.[2] Moreover, Berle paired scholarship with a remarkable career. As a Wall Street lawyer, a member of Roosevelt's brain trust (initially called the "brains trust"), and legal counsel to the Reconstruction Finance Corporation (RFC), Berle held an insider's perspective and exercised influence at the upper echelons of US politics. This section outlines Berle's personal history, intellectual contributions, and political work—all of which help us make sense of the logic and stakes of his modern financial tool kit.

From the social gospel to corporate finance

Adolf Augustus Berle Jr. was born in Boston on January 29, 1895, the second of four children. His mother, Augusta Write, was from a well-off New England family and did missionary work with the Sioux Indians after graduating from Oberlin. Adolf Sr. was a Congregationalist minister ("one of the most controversial and forward-looking clergymen of his day," according to the *New York Times*) and a professor of applied Christianity at Tufts.[3]

A proponent of the social gospel, the Reverend Doctor Berle traveled the nation giving lectures on the importance of efficiency in public school education. The four Berle children were homeschooled year-round according to these theories of child development, which included a belief that children should learn language before mathematics. Adolf Sr. was an autocratic taskmaster, and the children performed accordingly: the two boys started Harvard at the age of fourteen, the two girls started Radcliffe at sixteen.[4] Adolf Jr. passed Harvard's entrance exam when he was twelve, although due to his young age he did not enroll until age fourteen. He went on to earn a BA at eighteen, an MA at nineteen, and a law degree at twenty-one, all from Harvard. Adolf Sr. frequently invoked his children's accomplishments while on the lecture circuit. "Do not say prodigy to me," the senior Berle was quoted as saying, "Prodigies do not come four to a family."[5]

Active in progressive circles, the Berle family socialized with luminaries like Jane Addams, Lillian Wald, and Louis Brandeis. This all had a lasting impact on Adolf Jr. "He entered adulthood," writes journalist Nicholas Lemann, "fully persuaded that taming the power of centralized business was the overwhelming task facing the country."[6] In that spirit, Berle Jr., like his father, saw drastic economic reorganization as a means to social reform.

During his senior year in college, Berle provided research assistance to Edward Channing, who was writing his Pulitzer Prize–winning *History of the United States*. Under Channing's supervision, Berle wrote his master's thesis on Alexander Hamilton's Assumption Act.[7] Also known as the Funding Act of 1790, the act led to the issuance of the first US Treasury securities and allowed the federal government to assume state debts. This work presaged Berle's future proposals to use centralized federal credit as a remedy.

It was partly through his beliefs and partly through his father's guidance that Berle ended up pursuing law.[8] The close relationship between social reform, law, and the economy was established early on in Berle's life. After graduating Harvard, he spent a year in Brandeis's law firm, and then left to join the army near the end of World War I. There, among other things, he served on the committee charged with negotiating the Treaty of Versailles. After the war, he opened a law practice with his brother. The office was located on 70 Pine Street in New York, a block off Wall Street and three short blocks to the Stock Exchange. Berle's work on Wall Street gave him deep insight into corporate finance and the relative position of shareholders in modern firms. In these years, Berle frequently wrote for magazines like *The Nation* and *New Republic*.[9]

In 1927 Adolf married Beatrice Bend Bishop, an heiress, intellectual, and reformer in her own right. First trained as a social worker, Beatrice sometimes taught psychology and sociology at Sarah Lawrence. She later attended medical school while their three children were still at home.[10] The year they married, Berle received a grant from the Social Science Research Center to start work on a study of corporate finance. He subsequently joined the faculty at Columbia Law, which would thereafter serve as the institutional seat of his research. He also hired a graduate student in economics, Gardiner Means, to work on the project.[11] "To their collaboration, Means brought an original and capacious economic intelligence," writes Arthur Schlesinger. "Berle, a few months the senior of the pair, [brought] both the finicky precision of a legal technician and the broad perspectives of a social prophet."[12]

The Modern Corporation and Private Property

Berle's great intellectual triumph –*The Modern Corporation and Private Property*—was also the achievement that opened the door for his future as a statesman. Work on the book began in 1928. Berle and Means oversaw a team of graduate students who amassed statistical data on corporate power and consolidation. Published in 1932, *The Modern Corporation* immediately made waves. An executive at General Motors read an early copy and successfully pressured the publisher's owner (the Corporation Trust Company Commerce Clearing House) to drop the book. Macmillan picked up the title, giving it an even larger distribution than it might have otherwise had.

Reviewers sang its praises. In *New Republic*, socialist economist Stuart Chase called the book "epoch shattering."[13] Preeminent historian Charles Beard called it the most important work on American statecraft since the federalist papers. Berle's protégé John Kenneth Galbraith would later deem it one of the two most important books of the 1930s, alongside John Maynard Keynes's *General Theory of Employment, Interest and Money*.[14]

To understand the book's immediate success, one must take into account the timeliness and relevance of its subject matter. Americans had debated the pros and cons of rising corporate power for decades. The onset of the Great Depression added a fresh sense of urgency to those debates. Economic catastrophe had tarnished the right's preferred "hands-off" stance and created a window of opportunity for the left, but it had its own internal divisions to overcome. Historians sometimes group the crosscutting and shifting tangle of New Deal alliances into two camps. On one side were the antitrusters and anti-monopolists who wanted to break up corporate power. On the other side were planners who sought to harness corporate power.[15] Despite the fact that Berle had worked for Brandeis, the leading proponent of breaking up the power of corporations, Berle himself had moved toward the approach typified by Theodore Roosevelt, one that called for a stronger central government as a force that could counterbalance the accrual of corporate power. Berle believed that corporations were here to stay. The best path forward was to redirect the modern corporation toward a broader civic agenda.

Today *The Modern Corporation* is most famous for its discussion of the separation of corporate ownership from control. The book painstakingly details decades of court decisions that conferred power over corporate resources to the managers, and the subsequent dilution of shareholders' discretionary capacity over the use of corporate property. For Berle and Means, this separation of ownership and control "split the atom" of property rights and destroyed "the very foundation on which the economic order of the past three centuries has rested."[16] These ideas, alongside Ronald Coase's work on transaction costs (published five years later), became the foundation of corporate governance theory. And because the *The Modern Corporation* continued to be read largely from within the field of corporate governance, it was remembered primarily for the things later scholars of corporate governance cared about, namely the idea that shareholders had lost control of the firm. Berle and Means had presaged agency theory, which would work to align the interests of managers with those of the shareholders. Consequently, *The Modern Corporation* is remembered by many as a treatise on shareholder rights.

It is no small irony that the book is known today simply as a defense of shareholders.[17] As scholars like Delia Tsuk and Mark

"A Modern Financial Tool Kit"

Mizruchi have noted, a narrow focus on shareholders betrays the breadth of Berle and Means's critique.[18] Berle and Means pressed readers to rethink the foundations of the modern corporation. The main lesson was that corporations were quasi-governmental entities with so much power, over so many people, that they had become law-creating entities in their own right. Corporations, in other words, were essentially little governments, and undemocratic ones to boot. "There is no great difference between having all industry run by a committee of Commissars and by a small group of Directors," in Berle's words.[19] Recast as governments, it was possible to see corporations as organizations beholden not simply to the needs only of shareholders but also to the needs of workers and consumers.[20]

Berle and Means's endgame was not shareholders' rights. It was civic accountability for the modern corporation.

Berle and FDR

While Berle and Means's larger critique is often overlooked today, that was not the case when it was published. Columbia political scientist Raymond Moley passed the book along to then governor and presidential candidate Franklin Delano Roosevelt (FDR), and Moley invited Berle to prepare materials on "credit and corporations."[21] Berle had reservations. He had been a progressive Republican and an active member of the party until 1928. Moley assured Berle that it was his technical expertise, not political support, that the brains trust needed.[22] Assuaged, Berle signed up. He would become a central player. Notably, together Adolf and Beatrice wrote Roosevelt's Commonwealth Club speech, which became famous for its early articulation of New Deal principles.[23]

With FDR's electoral victory, *The Modern Corporation* became the "economic bible" of the new administration.[24] Berle rejected FDR's offer to chair the Federal Trade Commission, believing that he could be more influential as an informal adviser. This also freed up Berle to serve as adviser to New York's legendary mayor Fiorello La Guardia.[25] Berle did, however, accept a position as legal counsel to the RFC. That appointment ended in 1933, but Berle remained friendly with its powerful president, Jesse Jones.[26] Berle participated in politics throughout his life as an adviser, appointee, fund-raiser, and organizer. After 1937, when an inheritance from Beatrice's family gave their family new financial security, Berle retired from law. In 1938, he accepted a position as assistant secretary of state for Latin affairs. Founder and leader of the New York Liberal Party, Berle backed strong government but campaigned vigorously against anyone known for communist sympathies. He died of a stroke in 1971.

"A short, intense, small-boned man with the energy of a dynamo," wrote the *New York Times* in his obituary, "Mr. Berle had a brilliant mind, and, according to some New Dealers whom he rubbed the wrong way, he knew it."[27] Caustic and combative, he was "one of Washington's most disliked figures," and peers disparagingly referred to him as a Little Atlas or The Brain.[28] "Berle had had a whirlwind career as an infant prodigy in Harvard College and Law School," Moley's memoir quips. "Someone has been so unkind as to suggest that he continued to be an infant long after he had ceased to be a prodigy."[29] Moley then softens the blow by enumerating Berle's formidable talents: "But I always found that the slightly youthful cockiness and brashness to which this strained epigram referred was more than compensated for by the toughness of his mind, his quickness, his energy, and his ability to organize material well."

How does this background inform a reading of Berle's banking proposals? At base, Berle's personal history shows that his proposals are the work of a prominent intellectual with a deep well of knowledge of the nation's political terrain. Beyond that, this background situates his banking plans as part of a larger project of corporate accountability. Berle worked on Wall Street. He was a proud liberal and staunch anticommunist. He was no socialist. But raised on the social gospel, influenced by luminaries like Brandeis and Wald, Berle saw in the evolution of capitalism an array of possibilities for corporations to serve the public good, provided that they were guided by higher principles and subject to government oversight. Berle believed that the right kind of management could yield "a collectivism without communism" in which a capitalist economy ultimately served not individual profit but "the national life as a whole."[30]

The larger context for the proposals: New Deal banking reforms

Most people are well aware of the economic reforms put into law during the New Deal: the implementation of deposit insurance, the separation of commercial and investment banking through Glass-Steagall, the formation of the Securities and Exchange Commission (SEC), the restructuring of the Federal Reserve. Less well known are the plethora of additional proposals that circulated at the time. If we look specifically at the latter half of the 1930s, when Berle set forth his ideas for a modern financial tool kit, it becomes clear that his efforts were emblematic of a larger set of ongoing debates. "The country needs and, unless I mistake its temper, the country demands bold, persistent experimentation," Roosevelt said in his 1932 speech at Oglethorpe University. "It is common sense to take a method and try it: If it fails, admit it frankly and try another. But above all, try something."[31] Encouraged by FDR, emboldened by crisis, Berle's work on financial reform unfolded in an environment that proved fertile ground for the cross-pollination of policy ideas.

Berle's earlier work on credit reform

Berle's early work on banking reform started before FDR was in the Oval Office. In May of 1932, six months before Roosevelt's election, Berle and Louis Faulkner, of the Bank of New York and Trust Company, presented Roosevelt with a comprehensive overview of the economic crisis and recommended policies that became central New Deal programs. In addition to reiterating *The Modern Corporation*'s warnings, the Berle-Faulkner proposal (and other early work for Roosevelt) emphasized two things: first, that the economic system should be managed to provide people with stable employment and a livable wage; second, that the credit system and social insurance could be tools for ensuring economic stability.[32]

Berle and Faulkner based their recommendations on the principle that "as a matter of sound economics and decent humanity, an economic policy of the government ought to be adopted towards the restoration of individual safety."[33] In Berle's view, Hoover, who preached individualism as a rationale for limiting government assistance to struggling Americans, misunderstood the term. To Berle, a "far truer individualism" viewed economic security as a necessary condition for individuals to thrive.[34] For this reason, Berle rejected alternative New Deal proposals that would save corporations but leave individuals to fend for themselves.[35]

Banking reform was key to fixing the economy. With deposits withdrawn at a rate of $100 million each week over the prior year, Berle and Faulkner homed in on the need to ensure depositor confidence in order to prevent bank failures. The idea of protecting depositors had long circulated around Congress. It was finally achieved with the creation of the Federal Deposit Insurance Corporation (FDIC).[36] Berle and Faulkner also proposed farm credit support systems that were enacted with the creation of the Home Owners' Loan Corporation (HOLC) and the Farm Credit Association. The proposal further backed the expansion of the RFC, old age pensions (Social Security) and unemployment insurance.

The 1932 proposals presaged Berle's later proposals for a modern financial tool kit. Berle and Faulkner recommended that low-interest, guaranteed loans be provided to companies that committed to maintaining employment levels, particularly for projects benefiting their communities. For longer-run stability, Berle and Faulkner called for a federal board which could monitor security sales, a function that would be fulfilled by the SEC, and "could exercise a real control over undue expansion of groups of credit instruments, where issue of these reached a point threatening the safety of the financial structure."[37] This last goal was not addressed until the 2008 financial crisis prompted the creation of the Financial Stability Oversight Council as a component of the Dodd-Frank reforms.[38]

Other New Deal proposals

Berle's more developed prescriptions for a modern financial tool kit drew from and consolidated many ideas that were debated at the time. His proposals stood out not for their novelty, but for their comprehensiveness, and for their explicit discussion of motivating principles. Table 1 contains a summary of several plans in circulation during the late New Deal, including that of

Table 1. Types of New Deal banking reforms, 1938–39

Targeted solutions	
Mead (S. 1482, 1939)	Mandated RFC insurance for small-business lending up to $100,000 for seven years.
Mead (S. 2343, 1939)	RFC guarantees up to 90 percent of $1 million loans up to ten years in duration.
Pepper (S. 3430, 1938)	RFC-insured loans for small business expansion. (Similar to Mead)
Barkley-Steagall (S. 2759, HR 7120, 1939)	RFC will fund $2.7 billion in projects (roads, electrification, railroads) that are off-books due to self-liquidating nature.
Hansen Testimony (1939)	Separate budget for capital expenditures.
Radical reforms	
Pepper (S. 3630, 1938)	Regional industrial banks to bypass investment bankers, Fed, and RFC.
Long (S. 1743, 1939)	Create a new independent Federal Investment Bank Board and Federal Insurance Corporation to fund "independent small business."
Voorhis (H.R. 115, 1939)	Treasury-funded public works at national, state, and local levels.
Voorhis (H.R. 5910, 1939)	Regional banks empowered to lend and invest in equity. Primary investor is RFC.
Voorhis (H.R. 4931, 1939)	Nationalize Fed, allow government to spend without issuing debt, eliminate fractional reserve banking.
Defensive countermeasures	
Fed/Eccles (1939)	Long-term loans via new Federal Industrial Loan Corporation.

Berle's. None of these plans were instituted, with the exception of a limited expansion of RFC small-business lending in the late 1930s. These later New Deal banking reform proposals can generally be categorized into four groups, based on their focus and approach: (1) the small-business reforms, (2) targeted solutions, (3) radical overhauls, and (4) defensive countermeasures.

Targeted solutions

Some reform proposals focused on changing the financial system in ways that were dramatic but sharply defined in scope. Here we focus on two of them: calls for small-business credit provision, and calls for accounting changes.

James Mead, the Democratic junior senator from New York, led the effort to expand small-business credit. In the spring of 1939, Mead proposed a bill that mandated the RFC to offer loans of up to $100,000 for the plant, equipment, or operations. A second bill proposed that the RFC provide a 90 percent guarantee for ten-year loans of up to $1 million.[39] The RFC lent only to businesses that had already been turned down by local bankers. These bills would be a significant expansion. Mead wanted a system for small businesses that filled the "no-man's-land" of private credit for small businesses, much as the Home Owners Loan and Farm Credit Association had done elsewhere.

The hearings on the Mead bills began in late May 1939. They provided a forum for stakeholders—including small-business owners, representatives of the American Banking Association, Jesse Jones, and Marriner Eccles of the Federal Reserve—to weigh in on small-business loan program proposals. Mead's bills received support from establishment figures such as Fed governor Ernest Draper, SEC chairman Jerome Frank, and Commerce Secretary Harry Hopkins.[40] However, they were opposed by bankers, some Democratic senators, and, perhaps most importantly, RFC head Jesse Jones.[41] At his appearance before the committee in June 1939, Jones strongly resisted any financing mechanism beyond the existing capabilities of the Federal Reserve and the RFC. Jones noted that the Federal Reserve had authority to make business loans, but the volume was low, indicating that the market was working. With regard to the RFC's loan program, Jones told the committee, "Any deserving borrower who can furnish security that will reasonably assure repayment of his loan can have a loan if he will apply to the RFC for it, and on very generous terms, provided the loan will serve a useful purpose and is consistent with the law."[42] The decision as to who was a deserving borrower, what counted for security, and what constituted a "useful purpose" would be left with the RFC. Jones, who in fact had no desire to extend the RFC's reach into small-business loans, did reluctantly oversee an expansion of small-business loans in the post-1938 period, perhaps as a way to prove his assertion of the liberalness of the RFC's loan standards.[43]

Another type of forward-looking but targeted reform concerned the accounting standards used in the federal budget. We can see this in the remarks of Alvin Hansen, a Keynesian economist from Harvard. Hansen suggested that the government consider separating the budget into an operating budget and a capital budget. Accounting for capital expenditures separately, as a business would, might allow the government to allocate costs and depreciation over a period of years. This would prevent the incursion of an immediate lump sum charge, and make it easier for the government to spend money or issue loans outside the already off-budget RFC. Hansen thought that the severity of the economic depression heightened the need for separate budgets.

Opponents of capital budget reform saw the proposal as a threat to small government. This critique is exemplified by Lehman Brothers economist Alexander Sachs, who was keenly read and followed by Roosevelt.[44] While acknowledging the need for federal spending on things like regional economic development projects, Sachs argued that big government was the main threat to democracy. Capital budgeting would make the government seem smaller than it actually was. Better for the state to look larger to the public, lest people decide it had plenty of room to grow.

The Roosevelt administration tried to get around the lack of a capital budget by moving more government programs—for railroads, rural electrification, toll roads, and other capital projects—off-budget. With the support of the administration, Kentucky senator Alben Barkley and Alabama representative Henry Steagall sponsored a bill that would allow the off-budget RFC to issue bonds on behalf of agencies like the Department of Agriculture and the Public Roads Administration.[45] Though Jones, Morgenthau, and Eccles all spoke in support of the bill, it did not receive universal support from Democrats, and Republicans denounced the bill as "Socialism by stealth" that enabled pork barrel politics and constituted a form of "subterfuge to raise the legal debt limit." The House declined to bring the legislation to a full vote.[46]

Radical overhauls

Unlike more focused changes to extend credit to small businesses or to reform government accounting rules, more radical reformers envisioned a system-wide transformation. We see this with California congressman Jerry Voorhis's bill proposing a public works finance corporation. Voorhis, like Berle, was an adherent of the social gospel. Voorhis felt that the government should not have to take on any debt at all to create money, writing, "Why in Heaven's name cannot the United States Treasury with greater reserves than any bank possesses, buy the bonds of the Housing Authority, the P.W.A., or of a State or county by the same process of credit creation that the banks now employ?"[47] After reintroducing his bill in 1939, Voorhis approvingly quoted Berle's plans (discussed below) as an argument for funding his proposed public works finance corporation, but had a larger agenda of nationalizing the Federal Reserve, allowing the Treasury to fund programs without issuing debt, and eliminating fractional reserve banking. Roosevelt agreed to the Fed nationalization plan for a period of roughly two hours until Fed chairman Eccles intervened. Later Voorhis would go on to be the first victim of Richard Nixon's no-holds-barred red-baiting approach to politics, losing his seat in Nixon's first campaign after allegations of supporting communism.[48]

Florida senator Claude Pepper's plan for regional industrial banks was similarly bold in its approach: it would create a system of regional industrial banks, one of which would be owned by the Treasury.[49] Each bank would begin working with a capital stock of $100 million. The stock of each could later be increased up to $1 trillion with a possibility of their acquisition by the public. Treasury ownership of the banks meant that lending policy would be constrained by neither the independent Federal Reserve nor the conservative standards of Jones's RFC. In hearings for the Mead bill, Pepper said he introduced the bill because "investment bankers are not interested in the little fellow ever, and in the second place, they are interested in the big fellow only when they can quickly dispose of his security issue at a profit to themselves."[50] The regional industrial banks would be Treasury-owned banks that could invest in equities as well as long-term loans, both of which were difficult to come by. Neither the Pepper nor the Voorhis plan went anywhere in Congress.[51]

Defensive countermeasures

Proposals for incremental change of existing institutions were supported by Jones and Federal Reserve governor Marriner Eccles. In 1939, as the Mead bill was created, and around the time that Berle would propose the creation of a new system of credit banks, Eccles proposed the formation of a new industrial loan corporation from *within the Federal Reserve System*. Eccles further suggested that his proposal might be incorporated into the Mead bill, even though it was fundamentally incompatible with Mead's RFC-based approach. Making his case, Eccles offered a critique of Mead's plan: he argued that it would not entice banks to lend because of the potential 10 percent loss on insured loans and the limits imposed on loan interest rates. Instead, Eccles offered a counterproposal that would keep authority centered in the Federal Reserve. In this approach, the Fed's existing business-lending powers would be replaced with a new corporation operating out of the Fed's existing regional banks and overseen by the Fed Board of Governors. Eccles claimed that his plan would offer commercial and industrial enterprises funds on a "sound but liberal basis, for long periods of time if that were necessary and desirable."[52]

Make no mistake, the Eccles program was a defensive maneuver. Though Eccles clearly preferred his plan to the Mead plans, he also cautioned against its implementation. "I do not believe that this or any other similar loan plan which has been or might be offered," Eccles explained, "however desirable, as an improvement in the existing mechanism for facilitating the flow of funds for small business, will or can in itself be material in bringing about a substantial business improvement."[53] It is no coincidence that both Eccles and Jones resisted substantial legislation to modify the credit system. The Federal Reserve Board had already suggested a long-term congressional study of the banking system, but Eccles was afraid of a rushed, piecemeal approach to reform. At an interdepartmental meeting a few short months before the Mead bill was introduced, Eccles told Jones and other senior banking officials, "As a practical matter, I know damn well that no such committee should develop legislation."[54] For his part, Jones concluded that no bank reform legislation was needed, and no congressional study of the banking system was even necessary.[55]

In this context of the above policy proposals, Berle's own approach to reform stood out for its articulation of a coherent rationale and motivating philosophy. Berle's integration of principles from law, economics, and social change would make his outlook more inclusive than more defensive or narrowly targeted reforms. His careful promotion of government involvement in cases of national interest, without socialist affiliations, would distinguish Berle's plan from the more radical proposals.

The immediate context for the Berle proposals

The Temporary National Economic Committee (TNEC) provided the immediate context for Berle's own proposals for banking reform in 1938 and 1939. The TNEC itself was a response to the recession of 1937–38. Between May 1937 and June 1938 real GDP dropped by 10 percent, unemployment hit 20 percent, and industrial production fell by 32 percent.[56] Antitrusters like Leon Henderson (an economics professor from Swarthmore) had angled for years for a stronger response to the concentration of corporate power. Now those antitrusters pressed their case. Historian Ellis Hawley summarizes their argument: "American capitalism had been sustained from the beginning by federal intervention, by such expedients as the public land grants, wartime spending, protective tariffs, and deficit financing. If this were true, it seemed obvious that the government would have to intervene again."[57] With arguments for a federal answer to the antitrust question, Hawley concluded that the TNEC was an "escape mechanism" for FDR, because an investigation was the least controversial way for him to address the divisive matter.[58] While it was convened by Congress to investigate monopolies, in the New Deal historiography the TNEC is best known for the role it ended up playing in helping to popularize Keynesianism.

When considering Berle's proposals for the TNEC, it is necessary to keep in mind the particular historical moment. This was late in the New Deal. Budget hawks like Treasury Secretary Morgenthau nearly talked FDR into killing the RFC before the recession, and it seemed like they might do so again; they wanted to use its funds to balance the budget, a goal FDR publicly espoused in 1938.[59] We know in retrospect that World War II would soon cause a surge in RFC activities, but Berle had good reason to believe that even a surviving RFC would not be as progressive as he would like. Consider the matter of lending to small business, an unmet need frequently discussed in these years. The RFC began lending money to businesses in 1934, and within four years lent $500 million through 9,000 loans, often via partnerships (sometimes private banks that provided part of the capital; sometimes the RFC offered to purchase loans at a later date, effectively using put options to spur private lending).[60] These RFC business loans overwhelmingly focused on manufacturing and medium-sized firms, and Jesse Jones, the powerful head of the RFC, resisted Berle's calls for more lending to small borrowers.[61] The RFC also made no loans to hospitals because Jones felt that hospitals should be supported by their local communities.[62] While Berle and Jones were friendly, the memoranda suggest Berle's willingness to work around Jones's RFC. This was part of the policy backdrop for Berle's proposals.

We should also keep the timing in mind when considering Berle's political clout. At forty-three, Berle was embarking on his career as a diplomat as assistant secretary of state. He had passed the high point of his policy influence. The period historians refer to as the "Second New Deal" (a push starting in 1935 best known for the Works Progress Administration, Social Security, and the National Labor Relations Act) brought into prominence a new wave of brain trusters, a group that included Berle's longtime nemesis Felix Frankfurter, who hewed to a Brandeisian strategy of breaking up corporate power. Berle now moved within a more crowded field of experts, and he did so at a time when the New Deal was losing steam.

The twelve-member TNEC, made up of congressmen and agency heads, was something of a microcosm of the larger divisions of the entire New Deal. The planners set against the anti-monopolists, who were set against the defenders of market competition in turn. Berle sat in the planning camp, which had already lost some big battles by 1938.[63] For Berle and the other planners, the TNEC provided a fresh opportunity to realize their vision, provided they could neutralize the anti-monopolists.

As soon as the TNEC convened, Berle drafted a memorandum, "Investigation of Business Organization and Practices." The memo was promptly leaked, and its publisher later reported that government agencies were "flooded with requests" for copies. In his personal papers, Berle filed "The Investigation of Business Organization and Practice" alongside his larger plan for banking reform, titled "A Banking System for Capital and Capital Credit." Berle's own files therefore indicate that we should treat the two memos as a set.[64]

"A Modern Financial Tool Kit"

Banking and the big picture

Berle's memo "The Investigation of Business Organization and Practice" reads as an economic primer for TNEC members. Its rhetoric reflects Berle's efforts to position himself relative to other New Dealers. On the one hand, he stresses his progressive bona fides by privileging the well-being of workers and consumers relative to corporate profits. On the other hand, Berle sets himself apart from those further to the left by stressing the protection of individual liberties, and openly rejecting socialism as a desirable path forward.

As a kind of primer, the memo covers a good deal of ground. It opens with a discussion of the role of the government in the economy, and then details how differently sized companies have different levels of productivity, different sorts of advantages, and different patterns of innovation. Berle next addresses the matter of concentrated corporate power, and urges the committee members not to focus on property ownership but on control (or "power") that is exercised through board interlocks, lines of credit, patent licenses and restrictions, and supply chains. Berle recommends that when evaluating industries, the TNEC members consider not just profits but the interests of consumers, labor, and managers. Finally, Berle entreats the committee to make explicit the principles behind its recommendations, warning that the failure to do so leaves a regulation vulnerable to misinterpretation or regulatory capture.[65] He valued both transparency and democratic oversight.

The memo repeatedly pushes back against the antitrusters. Berle argues against a uniform approach to the economy.[66] Any solution should fit the structure of a specific industry: unfettered competition, cartelization, quasi-governmental enterprise, or public ownership should all be viable options, depending on the context. Berle warns that small businesses are not necessarily competitive or humane, but are often just more localized monopolies.[67] Moreover, small businesses could not efficiently produce many of the products that consumers desired. While not necessarily or uniformly beneficial ("it is not clear that the standard of living would decrease if they [consumers] stopped wanting cigarettes or canned soups or cosmetics"), Berle felt that these industrial goods should nevertheless be provided: "people are entitled to want what they actually do want"; telling people otherwise "becomes tyranny."[68] Cartelization may be appropriate where "planning of output is inherently necessary," which includes motors, oil, and possibly copper and textiles.[69] It is dangerous, Berle states, to break up large business when resulting unchecked competition would be wholly destabilizing. "You cannot gamble with the economic safety of a large district simply in the hope that the expansion of inventory will lower price."[70]

While making these arguments, Berle makes a set of rhetorical moves of particular note:

- **Guiding principles.** For the TNEC, Berle proposes a three-part test to evaluate an industry: (1) Is there an adequate supply of goods based on the normal standards of the market and apparent need? (2) Can a maximum number of people make a living and support their families out of poverty? (3) Is this all accomplished "with due regard for the liberty and self-development of the individual?"
- **Need for government action.** Berle builds a case for a more active government in the economy. Large corporations might be necessary for certain markets, but it does not follow that we can trust corporations to be fair or efficient. The size of the modern corporation means that it can "outrun the moral and mental stature" of managers, and what seems like efficiency may actually be the result of large corporations' capacity to impose externalities. Corporate efficiency, Berle notes, "may merely mean a plant which has succeeded in unloading the maximum possible amount of obligations on the community."[71] A truly efficient corporation is one that provides an adequate supply of goods and adequate employment without imposing externalities.
- **Precedents for government action.** The memo shows that it is not private efforts alone, but a unity of public and private

initiative, that allows markets to thrive. Berle lists various ways the government supports business. Patents and trademarks subsidize industry by effectively granting monopolies (as with utilities). Tariffs and price controls protect businesses. Large purchases (like wartime purchases from Bethlehem Steel) boost sales. The memo lists other indirect forms of support and subsidy: public infrastructure, like roads, without which many private businesses could not exist; health efforts that drive down insurance rates; poor relief, which is a subsidy insofar as it reduces labor costs. If the full scope of government support for business was recognized, "A slightly different view of 'private initiative' would probably emerge from such a picture."[72]

- **Metrics of success**. How should the government go about building a better economy? On the first page of the first memorandum, Berle advocates for the government to use a "triple income statement" to evaluate the industrial system's impact not just on investors but also for labor and consumers: Does the industry provide steady work for decent pay? Is the output useful and distributed at a reasonable price? And does the industry provide a decent work life for laborers, such as to mitigate disruption due to innovation? How this would actually be calculated goes unsaid. What matters for Berle is the idea that such a technique could guide the TNEC's evaluation of different industries.

Berle closes the memo with a high-level view of an ambitious program to use the control provided by corporate licensing to provide more and better goods, jobs, and access to capital. This process likely entails different tactics for different industries. It is in this section that Berle broaches the subject of a system of capital credit banks backed by a capital reserve bank. He further elaborated these ideas in the middle of 1939, with a memorandum for the TNEC entitled "A Banking System for Capital and Capital Credit." It is to this second memorandum that we now turn.

A banking system for capital and capital credit

"A Banking System for Capital and Capital Credit" provides a deeper dive into finance for members of the TNEC tasked with an investigation of investment banking. Berle considered this twenty-page memorandum a "general guy-wire."[73] Like the previous paper, it offers guiding principles rather than detailed instructions for policy design.

Berle begins with a diagnosis of the problem at hand. The United States has the skill, drive, and natural resources required for a thriving economy, Berle writes, so a failure to deliver on full employment must be due to some sort of "malorganization." Berle blames the financial system. It does not work and must "be supplemented by vast amounts of Federal credit which make up in some measure, but inadequately, for difficulties in the existing system of private finance." While the rise of central banking has modernized the field of short-term credit, long-term capital markets have not followed suit. The bond business, for instance, is much the same as it was at the time of Napoleonic Wars and the British East India Company. "We have no really modern system of long-term finance," he laments.[74] But why shouldn't the government now do for long-term economic development what the Federal Reserve did for short-term credit? Part of the problem is that Americans have neglected new economic theories. In addition to discussing Keynes, Berle spends time discussing the work of Chicago institutional economist (and first president of Brookings) Harold Moulton. Moulton's "discovery," Berle summarized, was "that a large part of what had been assumed to be 'savings'— that is, the money destined for long-term investment—was not different from any other kind of created bank credit." Long-term investment could be stimulated by "properly controlled banking operations." Just as there is no need to allow banks to collapse in times of crisis, there is no need to stop investing in capital assets during downturns, provided that there is underused capacity.[75]

Berle specifically identifies four main underlying causes for financial malorganization. First is "the restricted base of national enterprise." The rise of totalitarianism has led to nationalized markets, and this in turn hurt American exports. The second underlying cause is the rise of "needed social services" caused by rapid economic growth. Rapid economic expansion has elevated social needs beyond the market's ability to meet them. This includes a need for infrastructure, like bridges. It also includes a sense of relative poverty that has increased people's wants ("Whether the needs are logical or psychological, they are real enough"[76]), and social ills that arise from rapid changes like urbanization (which increase the need for hospitals, for example). Private finance is unable and unwilling to meet many of those needs.

"The Fears of Capital and Capital Groups" is the third underlying cause of financial disorganization. Here Berle observes that when investors become afraid of economic loss during downturns, they hoard capital. In this context, investors complain that additional government intervention or any additional taxation will further scare them away from the market. Berle acknowledges this, but with limited patience for threats of capital flight or hoarding. "There is something in all these contentions, but probably all have been exaggerated entirely out of measure … Prophesies of complete stoppage or complete disaster have been made whenever any reform has been undertaken; and they have usually proved unfounded once there is acceptance of reform."[77] Investors might threaten to exit the market when faced with an expansion of state power, but that does not mean they actually will.

The fourth and final underlying cause of financial disorganization is a failure of market-making for public goods, which Berle calls a "Need for a Causative Mechanism." For Berle, there is a set of needs that are social, rather than commercial, that banks neglect due to a combination of profit motive and regulatory constraints (read: Glass-Steagall). In these cases, government must take on a more active role and provide capital to spur businessmen into action. Long-term capital has stagnated, and is in desperate need of "new processes, new products, new developments, and new methods."[78] A new system of capital credit banking can help with this.

The solution: a modern financial tool kit

The second half of the memo discusses solutions. Here the argument culminates with three recommendations for future TNEC action:

1. A bill for a public works finance corporation. This would use Federal Reserve privileges to ease the issuance of credit for both federal and local infrastructure projects. It would be off-budget and provide low interest rates for nonprofits.
2. A bill for small-business loan insurance. This would allow small businesses to more effectively compete with large businesses.
3. A committee to investigate policies for capital credit banks for underserved public and private enterprise.

Together, these three steps make up a "modern financial tool kit" that would allow the capital system to fully employ the productive capacity of the United States. These are not "a panacea," Berle writes, but "tools so that initiative and ideas can go to work."[79] Berle offers few details for each individual proposal, perhaps because he thinks the centerpiece—the system for credit banks—should be designed by a TNEC subcommittee. Later congressional testimony indicates that others believed that if Berle's new banking system was indeed put into place, the need for the other proposals would be obviated.[80]

Berle posits many possible ways for a system of capital credit banks to work: banks could take deposits or issue bonds; the entities could be part of an entirely new or existing system; a plan could be organized on a national or regional basis, or be created by functionally dividing up different banks (e.g., into a manufacturing specialist, a transport specialist, etc.). No matter the approach, a breadth of customers could be served: individuals, companies, municipalities, and semipublic authorities. No matter the approach, certain "essential" goals must be met. A new system should provide (1) cash for investment in (2) commercial and noncommercial wealth (like public infrastructure, low-cost

"A Modern Financial Tool Kit"

housing, and hospitals) that has (3) flexible interest rates over time, and (4) selective interest rates (that is, rates that vary based on the social value of the investment), but (5) not offer too much credit (investments should be limited to really productive things) and (6) not be too inflationary; in fact, at multiple points he returns to the idea that the banks must somehow be connected to the Federal Reserve. The system should also (7) serve public needs and never be "cut off merely through private motives."[81]

Lessons from the second memo

Berle's second memo makes six points that we believe are worth stressing. First, Berle defends nonprofit banking. Berle states that a bank's ability to make a profit is created by a government-granted ability to create currency by lending based on fractional reserves. Berle likens the ability to make profits from a government-granted privilege to "tax-farmers'" rights to keep a cut of what they are authorized to collect. Because they are dependent on a government privilege, banks need not maximize profits. Their main task is "to keep an even flow of capital constriction and to see that the country is well served."[82] While a new system could possibly be made up of private entities with well-paid managers, there need not be a return to shareholders.

Second, Berle argues against charging high interest on loans for public infrastructure. Because the new system should prompt the creation of public wealth, higher interest rates should only be given to for-profit enterprises. When the "community as a whole is paying" for public goods and nonprofits, the interest rate should be a reserve to cover losses. The only reason for a high interest rate in that case would be to discourage overbuilding. As long as the amortization rate is set so that the loan is paid off within the life of the asset (making the loan "self-liquidating"), the system will be sound.

Third, Berle stresses that finance has political ramifications. Frequently mentioning the rise of totalitarianism, Berle paints his plan as a preventive measure. "Either we are on the eve of a change in our financial system; or we are on the eve of a change in our social system," he warns.[83] That said, Berle offers no guarantees. It may be that the US will become socialist; if so, the banking reforms he proposes will still be able to work. And he acknowledges that none of this may matter if there is another world war.

Fourth, Berle distances himself from supporters of nationalization. "I am frankly in favor of public ownership of certain forms of wealth," he asserts.[84] But here he is circumspect. The government should only control industries that produce relatively uniform public goods. He notes that state efforts to fund production, depending on how it is organized, could lead to a kind of "drift" where over time the government effectively controls most of the productive capacity of the nation, because it has funded that capacity.[85] His solution is therefore to have a system of capital credit banks that are nonprofit and nonpolitical, managed by professionals tasked with promoting the public good.[86]

Fifth, Berle calls for democratic accountability in financial systems. For the most part, Berle rejects the idea that his proposal is particularly divisive: businesspeople simply want long-term credit, and will not care much about how that is arranged. That said, Berle sees his proposal as radical in its willingness to transform power over economic development from private hands to public oversight. He writes:

> Control over economic expansion today lies chiefly in certain groups mainly allied with the investment banking operation. Development of capital credit banking undoubtedly does shift that control. New centers are set up; centers which should be more responsible to the public, and carried on by groups which, by their nature, assume greater responsibility for maintaining a continuous economic flow.[87]

Here Berle comes to the crux of the matter: in the age of the large modern corporation, some relatively small and powerful group is going to control the nation's flow of long-term credit. Who will that group be, and what principles will they follow?

Sixth, Berle regularly anticipates potential complications. To manage the threat of corruption, have an independent board of

"A Modern Financial Tool Kit"

governors run the new system. To manage the threat of inflation, give the Federal Reserve oversight. Berle observes that bankers are trained to focus not on the nation's capital needs but on high returns; his answer is to pull employees from nonprofit, savings, and mutual companies. And to prevent patronage politics, Berle suggests that managers of the new banking system be barred "from political connection or office."[88]

In all, Berle's memoranda for the TNEC is the work of a liberal policymaker taking care to distance himself from socialism while making a full-throated call for a mixed economy. Berle believed a market must be evaluated holistically, with the well-being of workers and consumers placed alongside the accrual of profits. Finance was a crucial component of this vision. Later, testifying to Congress on these matters, Berle stated his point even more succinctly, echoing a common theme of the time: "I think the economic system is our servant and not our master, or, rather, ought to be."[89] Nonprofit long-term banking must serve the public interest.

What happened to all these ideas? Our research uncovered vague references to Berle's proposals being "out of touch with the temper of the times."[90] In retrospect, we know that the New Deal's most energetic days were already over. FDR had more trouble getting many proposals through by this time. Republicans had forged an alliance with southern Democrats to push back against expanded labor rights, starting a process of diluting its great accomplishments that would go on for years.[91] The general history of the TNEC and New Deal indicates that some combination of war and shifting interests washed out the debate about banking.

Three lessons for financial reform today

While Berle's memoranda offer few details about actual policy design, they can nevertheless be mined for inspiration and insight. In the space we have remaining, we would like to highlight three themes, all in the spirit of Berle's vision, that we believe are especially promising.

Sound the alarm on private equity

Berle was never afraid to attack his competition. His call to action was not just grounded in what is currently going wrong, but in what could be even worse. In the context of the TNEC, this meant calling out the dangers of inaction (a totalitarian turn) and the dangers of wrong action (antitrusters' "gamble" with industries).

This strategy, we believe, is especially important when it comes to the encroachment of private equity on public infrastructure. America's infrastructure desperately needs capital, and political gridlock has thwarted traditional on-budget solutions. In the absence of a sudden and dramatic shift in political climate, something must give. If proponents of democratic finance do not provide Congress with a viable democratic solution to infrastructure finance, private equity firms will gladly help implement an antidemocratic alternative, one that puts for-profit firms in charge of the nation's most essential shared resources.

The privatization of public infrastructure has already started and can get much worse. Partnerships with private equity grant crucial decision-making capacities to a group of private firms that pride themselves on predatory resource extraction.[92] Private equity knows that elected officials do not want to raise taxes or be held accountable for debacles like Boston's Big Dig.[93] Privatization offers an alternative, one that can be readily sold to a public primed to believe that market efficiency will always save costs, and to a public primed to dismiss warning signs—like the neoliberal austerity measures that ended up poisoning the people of Flint—as entirely irrelevant.

All of this means that if we do not want public infrastructure turned into for-profit enterprises, where elites keep all the profits while the public retains socialized risks, we must develop and defend a viable democratic alternative, and soon.

"A Modern Financial Tool Kit"

Consider the federal credit programs

On what grounds does the government have the right to participate in credit allocation? Berle answers this by drawing on precedent. He reminds readers that the federal government already supports industry and banking, a reminder that is both pragmatic (businesses regularly need help) and moral (societies get to make claims on profits that the public has facilitated). Hockett and Block make the same move in their essays in this book, and not just with Hockett's argument about banking as a government franchise; both Hockett and Block point out that the government has already entered the allocation business, through the RFC and farm and home loan systems. Such historical precedents matter, but we should not focus on them at the expense of a full account of what is happening today. We do not need to reach into our past for a justification for these plans, because the federal government today is extensively involved in the business of credit allocation.

Federal credit support did not end with the RFC, so much as it was reorganized into a decentralized system. In 1963, the House surveyed federal credit agencies and found that the government contained seventy-four separate credit aid programs, fifty-one of which issued loans directly, which together had amassed $30 billion in assets, and insured or guaranteed another $70 billion. While this system was highly concentrated at its core—three-quarters of guarantees originated in the FHA and VA—it was also sprawling. The resulting report noted that "the credit programs extended to every segment of the American economy—financial institutions, agriculture, business, private housing, State and local government, international trade, and individual households."[94] Through the credit programs, the federal government bolstered nearly every sector of the economy and provided extensive backing to core industries: first agriculture, then housing, then education. These programs have been pivotal institution builders. The Farm Loan Act promoted the use of the long-term amortizing mortgage. The Export–Import bank boosted certain kinds of overseas lending.[95] The Small Business Administration backed the early venture capital industry.[96] The US federal government in

2018 owned $1.4 trillion in direct loans, and guaranteed another $2.6 trillion, reaching a total of $4 trillion through hundreds of credit programs.[97] Numbers are larger if you include currently off-budget entities like Fannie Mae. In times of crisis, government support ramps up. In 2009 a web of guarantees and supports meant that in a worst-case scenario, the US federal government was on the hook for $23.7 trillion—the equivalent of 150 percent of that year's GDP.[98]

A firmer grounding in the credit programs—both their current operations and their long history—supports the claim that what is new about Block's and Hockett's proposals is not the fact of government involvement in credit allocation, but simply the principles that direct it.

A statement of principles

Berle did not assume that the principles of good economic governance were self-evident or self-sustaining. Instead, he articulated essential points, often by listing them. Such lists could be doubly useful for policymakers: first as a kind of compass to guide program design, and second as a yardstick to gauge results. Block's chapter similarly offers a list of organizational priorities when he explains why financial reform should be nonprofit, decentralized, and specialized. Building on this, we ask more generally, what are the core principles of democratic finance itself?

With Berle's work in mind, and taking into consideration the arguments proposed by Hockett and Block anchoring the democratic-finance agenda, we propose that the principles of democratic finance can be reasonably summarized as consisting of three pillars: allocation, sustainability, and accountability.

a **Fair allocation.** This category concerns the overall distribution of access to credit and financial services. This includes, as McCarthy writes in his chapter, "popular access" to credit and financial services. This category also includes, as Berle emphasizes, the extent to which credit is allocated in accordance with civic priorities.

"A Modern Financial Tool Kit"

When it comes to enterprise, fair allocation means that viable public works projects and small businesses can compete with larger firms for capital. When it comes to families, democratic allocation means that financial services and resources are not hoarded by privileged groups, so the poor are left unbanked, or only able to access credit on exploitative terms. Given the legacy of racial discrimination in US credit markets, this will require taking steps to actively redress the legacy of previous lending regimes in redlined and underbanked communities.[99] When it comes to federal credit, democratic allocation means a reasonably close coupling of risks and profits so that private firms cannot capture years of profits and then externalize catastrophic losses.

b **Local and global sustainability**. By sustainability, we mean a financial system that promotes short- and long-term stability on the connected levels of the family, the nation, and the planet. This presumes a financial system that is internally stable, which is to say, able to avoid spinning off into extreme booms and busts.

For families, sustainable credit is provided through banking terms that are not extractive and exploitative, which is to say via contracts that support the growth, instead of the destruction, of family finances. An example of this can be found with the nonprofit Beneficial State Bank, which has shown that low-interest rates on auto loans for the working poor can result in default rates of 3 to 4 percent rather than the 30 or 40 percent default rates of their competitors.[100] Over decades, innovations in adjustable-rate contracts and risk-based pricing have shifted interest rate and prepayment risks from corporations onto families and small borrowers. A more sustainable financial system will shift more market risks back into the hands of organizations with resources and expertise that enable them to pool and manage such risks.

For the nation, financial sustainability means many things. Berle saw in his capital credit banks a potential countercyclical mechanism for dampening the boom and bust cycles in coordination with the Fed.[101] In an even broader sense, sustainability means anticipating and addressing long-term social and environmental needs. This includes, but is not limited to, infrastructure development.

Internal stability means that the financial system is well regulated, with safeguards against regulatory arbitrage, predatory competition, and rampant speculation. Internal stability facilitates, but does not ensure, other facets of stability; a financial system can stay afloat without meeting civic priorities. Robust systems of accountability, which ensure against destabilizing corruption and fraud, reinforce the principle of stability.

c **Political accountability.** This category concerns the process by which decisions are made about financial markets, as Michael A. McCarthy's chapter explains. For this we ask, can citizen groups monitor, make claims against, and hold accountable the management of our financial system? Are protections in place to minimize corruption, political patronage, and information asymmetries?

We should rightly celebrate the heyday of the RFC, but also not forget that it spent its last years mired in accusations of kickbacks and insider dealings, subject to a series of congressional investigations before Eisenhower wound it up in 1954.[102] We can do better than the RFC when it comes to oversight. Berle provides some ideas here. To encourage a more civic-minded form of banking, for example, he anticipates staffing needs, and suggests recruiting from nonprofits, savings, and mutuals.

There are good reasons to believe that establishing democratic accountability will require special attention to off-budget and partnership-based programs. As Greta Krippner notes, elected officials may go to great lengths to avoid political responsibility for economic outcomes.[103] Similarly, in other work Sarah Quinn studied federal credit programs and found that government officials repeatedly traded oversight and control for off-budget status.[104] Time and again, elected officials are not just pulled by powerful financial interests into conceding authority and power; they actively *push away* responsibility for the economy. All of this complicates the matter of oversight and control. As Block notes, we will likely need to adapt structures already in place in quasi-governmental reserve banks, where the boards of governors provide oversight.

Berle provides some guidance here as well. Consider his proposal for the TNEC to use a triple income statement to evaluate the success of an industry. We might take a page from his book, and develop metrics that can be used by third parties to evaluate socially responsible financial soundness.

Whether or not fair allocation, sustainability, and accountability are the best ways to summarize the animating principles of democratized finance, the core point here is that there is something to be gained by clearly articulating such guidelines. When it comes down to the nitty-gritty work of policy design and implementation, it will be useful to have such statements available to guide the way and measure our progress.

Conclusion

Berle's proposal to the TNEC was one among many that circulated at the time. Progressives in the late 1930s turned to federal finance to help an economy awash in unutilized private capital but also deeply troubled. Some proposals narrowly focused on small-business lending. Others offered radical reimaginings of the financial system, or conservative countermeasures designed to undermine more dramatic overhauls. Berle's proposal for a modern financial tool kit is worthy of consideration, therefore, not because it was an isolated call for reform, but rather because it was a vision of American finance steeped in the great debates of its time. Through Berle's memos, we gain insight into a lively era of policy reform, insight that is filtered through the interpretive lens of one of the nation's great theorists of democracy and capitalism.

Many points raised by Hockett and Block in their essays find resounding support in Berle's memoranda. Some of the resonances are clear and striking, like debunked myths about the supposed autonomy and efficiency of the private sector; the assertion that government-granted privileges are the basis for banking profits; calls for a public works finance corporation; attention to the needs of small business; and, above all, the insistence that banking serve a larger civic purpose. Berle even offers support for the notion that such a banking system would transition into a new socialist era, although he flatly rejects the desirability of doing so.

Today we can look to Berle not just for specific ideas—the three-part test to evaluate an industry, selective interest rates for public goods, the barring of directors of government banks from political office—but also for more ideas about how to approach questions of finance. In that spirit, this chapter has drawn three principles to guide an ongoing approach to banking reform. First, in the spirit of Berle's pugnaciousness, we call on today's reformers to be bold in their critiques of counterproposals. With this in mind, we reject the encroachment of private equity into the management of public resources. Our second lesson concerns precedents for government action; here we call attention to the trillions in loans currently owned or guaranteed via federal credit programs as justification for further reform. The third and final lesson concerns Berle's focus on core principles. In that spirit, we posit three principles of democratic finance: fair allocation, local and global sustainability, and political accountability.

Above all, Berle's memos reveal that one of the nation's great thinkers of corporate power and democratic accountability saw banks as public goods that should anticipate and meet a broad range of needs. By that logic, there is no more reason for finance to be subject to wild fluctuations, high profits, and the whims of speculators than our roadways, our energy markets, or our water supply. In fact, there is no need for banks to be profit centers at all when it comes to core social needs. In key domains, interest rates can be set by the needs of the group, not by the tastes of investors. Ultimately, the memos are highly consistent with the notion of banking as a public utility proposed by Hockett and Block at the start of this volume, and the memos offer strong support for a new and more democratic approach to finance.

7

Democratizing Finance or Democratizing Money?

Mary Mellor

The proposal to democratize finance by extending the critique of finance to money demands a radical critique of money.[1] This critique is important because of the way theories of money influence public policy. When the welfare needs of people, or suggestions for new public services or infrastructure, are put forward, they are routinely met by the politically disabling question "where is the money to come from?" This is a more fundamental question than "how will this be financed?" Finance implies the reallocation of already existing money. Where that money comes from in the first place is rarely addressed. Who or what has the power to create and circulate money? Who controls the money supply?

Robert Hockett's chapter gives us the answer in relation to finance. He carefully builds a picture of the intricate relation between the banks and the state. The seemingly autonomous banking and financial sector is shown clearly to be dependent on state monetary authority. Block goes on to suggest ways in which finance can be treated more as a utility administered by nonprofit structures such as cooperatives, state banks, and credit unions. Although the development of social and public utility banking is an important step, money can also be seen as a utility, a public resource[2]—and, as the 2007–8 crisis showed, a public responsibility.

The claim that public expenditure cannot be afforded because there is no money is based on a number of myths,[3] the two key ones being that money is essentially scarce and that it is generated exclusively by the market. As will be explained below, neither is true. Hockett's article clearly demonstrates that the complex system of bank lending and, increasingly, shadow bank lending relies on the backstop of publicly generated money or, more precisely, publicly generated confidence in the money system.

Modern theorists of money have challenged the view of money as essentially limited.[4] In place of the mythic image of money's originating as scarce gold, contemporary theories see it as a social and political construct that can take a variety of forms and can be represented by as little as a keystroke. Moreover, money is not a passive actor in economic processes. It is not a mere reflection of underlying economic activity. Who gets access to money determines who has money with which to invest, consume, or speculate. Such access involves power not only over the circulation of money but also over its creation in the first place. For this reason, although it is important to make the case for the democratization of finance in relation to public and private credit and investment, the ability to create and circulate money in the first instance also needs to be the focus of democratic debate.

This chapter aims to challenge the mythic assertion of the right of the market to control the creation and circulation of money and to reclaim money as a public resource. The case for democratizing money is based on the argument that what should be the sovereign power to create money has been captured by privatized finance. Exposing the contradictions of a privatized, bank-led money supply based on debt, and recognizing that the sovereign power to create money still exists, could provide a radical response to the claim that there is no money for progressive social spending.

Creating money

In the case of a public currency (pound, euro, dollar), the power to create money rests with two agents: the state (or its equivalent)

Democratizing Finance or Democratizing Money?

and the banks. States have the sovereign power of a formal monopoly over the creation of the public currency. This power may reside with the treasury or a central bank. Alternatively, states can nominate an external public agency, as in the case of eurozone countries, or adopt another state's currency, such as the dollar. Despite their formal power to create money, contemporary capitalist states are constrained by the self-imposed political injunction that states should not "print money." In theory, this leaves only one source of new money: the market via the banks. Particularly under neoliberal ideology, the market sector is seen as creating wealth through "making" money. Central to the making of money is bank lending, which embodies another myth: that banks are merely intermediaries between savers and borrowers.

However, it is increasingly recognized, even by banking authorities, that banks create new money in the course of making loans; they are not merely recycling existing money.[5] In doing so, banks are effectively privatizing or, in Hockett's terms, franchising the sovereign power to create money. The resulting balance of power over money between state and bank/market goes to the heart of modern politics. If the state retains the sovereign power to create the public currency, it has, for good or ill, control of the direction of economic priorities. If money is seen as emanating from the market, then state spending is limited to what the market considers it can "afford." The direction of the economy also then rests, for good or ill, with market priorities.

The market's monetary dominance in modern economies was evident in the 2007–8 crisis. The financial crisis of the collapse of lending was supercharged by the threat of a collapse of the money supply. The fear of governments was not the failure of private investment but that the ATM machines would run dry, and that was because there is relatively little tangible currency (notes and coin) in circulation. In Britain it is only 3 percent of the total, the remaining 97 percent being composed of bank accounts. Bank lending had become a major source of new money.[6] John Kenneth Galbraith noted as long ago as 1975 that "the process by which banks create money is so simple that the mind is repelled. Where something so important is involved, a deeper mystery seems only decent."[7] Even states, the traditional authority governing money, had become major borrowers.

The difference between money creation by the state and money creation by the banks is that banks only create new money by lending whereas states can create new money by spending directly into the economy. The democratization of lending, for example through public or social banks, is important. But there are also areas where lending would be inappropriate, including social and environmental needs that at present lie outside the public and private monetary framework. Unlike finance for investment, such allocations of money would not generate a monetary return (although there may be many social or environmental benefits). These would not be suitable areas for a money system based on debt, even with democratic input.

From an ecofeminist perspective I would argue that what is needed is a money system that puts the needs of ecological sustainability and social provisioning first, not last. This shift will require, among other critical factors, substantial changes in how money is created and used and by whom. To achieve those aims we must challenge conventional thinking about money, particularly the myth-laden neoliberal approach to public money that I have described as "handbag economics."

A critique of handbag economics

In capitalist economies the balance of power over money has tipped decisively toward the market. Particularly under neoliberalism, the state is derided as wasting the (private) taxpayer's money. Similarly, the sovereign power to create money for direct use, condemned as "printing money," is seen as having inevitable inflationary consequences. The public economy is feminized by a handbag economics that sees the public sector as equivalent to a household that has to live within its means. As markets are deemed to be the source of all wealth, public spending is seen as a drain on market funds. This zero-sum view assumes that more public spending must mean less money in the market sector.

Democratizing Finance or Democratizing Money?

Rulers and states have certainly misused and abused the power to create money. However, the focus of the neoliberal onslaught has not been corrupt rulers but the public spending of welfare states. It is an attack on the ability of people to provide services for one another without a market imperative. This capture and hobbling of the public economy has been enabled by economic myths that promote private and market structures over public structures in the evolution of money.

The core myth is that the origin of money lies in the market. The critical moment of money's birth is seen as the invention of coinage, which enabled market exchange to emerge from non-money barter. This myth is entirely false. There is no historical evidence of widespread barter-based economies, and coinage has a much more complex social and political history. Far from being a product of markets, coinage was created and controlled by rulers following its invention around 600 BCE, 2,000 years before the emergence of market economies.

For much of its history, rather than enabling markets, coinage played a central role in the growth of empires, particularly of Greece and Rome. Individual coinages were associated with centers of power because control over the creation and circulation of money confers seigniorage, the benefits of the use of that money. Central to the use of money by rulers is the sovereign power to tax. Rather than rely on the traditional receipt of tribute in kind, a ruler could pay for goods and services with money that could later be reclaimed through taxation. As I will explain below, this link between publicly issued money and taxation still exists today.

Another damaging aspect of the myth of the market origin of money is the assumption that the original and ideal form of money was created through the adoption of a valued commodity: precious metal. Seeing money as made of something scarce and valuable (gold, silver) suggests that money should be desirable in itself, an embodiment of intrinsic value. It also leads to the assumption that money is necessarily scarce.

Even if the claim that money was originally made of precious metal were true, it is certainly not the case today. Modern money clearly demonstrates that it is valueless in itself (base metal, paper, electronic information). It exists by fiat, that is, by authority alone. There is no "natural" shortage of any of these media. The existence of fiat money enables us to see that the idea that money is essentially precious and in short supply is purely ideological. What fueled the market and the growth of capitalism was not the invention of gold coin but the proliferation of bank-issued debt. The problem with trying to connect an ideological conception of money as gold to the emerging fiat money was illustrated by the prolonged attempt to rein in the banking sector by restricting the issue of banknotes to levels of state reserves of precious metal. The aim to maintain what became known as the gold standard was not finally abandoned until the 1970s.

The emergence of bank-created money

Precious metal money could never have fueled the development of markets and capitalism because of its natural limits. If capitalism was to monetize and marketize increasing sectors of society, it needed a flexible and expanding medium. This it found in commercial paper, a private network of credit–debt promises that linked investors, producers, traders, and consumers. These promises were periodically "cleared" by setting total commitments against one another. When that process was completed, relatively little formal currency was needed to settle any outstanding debts.

A crucial step in the history of modern banking and modern money was taken when what had previously been privately issued commercial money became the public currency. Formed in 1694 to make private loans to the state, the Bank of England issued those loans as private Bank of England credit notes, backed by a "promise to pay" taken to be in precious metal. Eventually the note itself became the designated public currency: the pound note. Thus the Bank of England, private until 1946, began its balancing act like all central banks, as banker/money creator to

Democratizing Finance or Democratizing Money?

the state and banker to the banks. Today, although central banks are widely recognized as lenders of last resort for the banks, they are not generally seen as money creators of last resort. The implications of the way modern central banks combine their role as the backstop for bank-generated money with the sovereign power to create and control money are hardly recognized, let alone addressed.

In the same way that public currency banknotes evolved from privately issued patterns of credit and debt, bank accounts have gradually been acknowledged as creating new public currency. Bank accounts were originally seen as merely credit balances, not "real" money, but that position no longer holds in a digital age. As increasingly recognized by major institutions such as the US Federal Reserve, the Bank of England, and the International Monetary Fund, and long argued by heterodox monetary theorists, banks do not merely act as a link between savers and borrowers; they create money. When banks make loans they do not debit existing accounts; they create new deposits of previously nonexistent money that the borrowers undertake to repay (as shown in Figure 1).

Within the banking circuit, money is created, lent, and returned. What is important about this circuit is that there is a larger arrow for repayment, as the need to repay with interest means that more money must be returned than is lent.

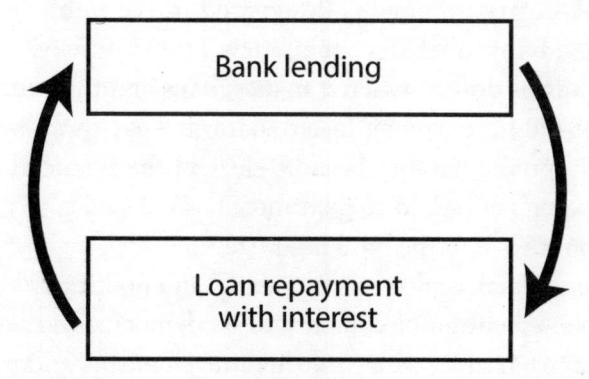

Figure 1. The banking circuit of money

Bank-created money is crisis-ridden

A public money supply that relies on debt is socially, ecologically, economically, and politically unsustainable. It is socially unsustainable because creating money as debt exacerbates inequality. Money flows to those most able to pay back loans with interest. Favoring the more creditworthy borrower and the most profitable use of money does not necessarily fund the services and products people need. Bank lending is socially exclusionary because it locks out the poor, forcing them to go to more exploitative moneylenders.

Creating money through debt is ecologically unsustainable because it drives economic expansion. If loans are to be repaid with interest, there must be growth of some form. Debt-based money does not necessarily cause ecological damage (it could just bid up the price of existing assets), but there is certainly no basis for degrowth or even a steady-state economy.

Bank-created money is economically unsustainable because basing the money supply on debt will eventually lead to crisis when governments, businesses, and citizens cannot or simply will not take on any more debt. This tendency to crisis leads to the political unsustainability of privatizing the public money supply as bank lending. Whereas the decision about who gets the loans is considered a private matter, the liability for the money created by those loans is very much a public matter. That is because the new bank-created money is designated in the public currency. The HSBC bank does not create new HSBC money; it creates new pounds or dollars when it makes loans and thus adds to the supply of public currency in circulation. That the new money becomes a public liability became clear in the financial crisis of 2007–8 when states had to guarantee bank deposits to maintain public confidence in the banking system.

For these social, ecological, economic, and political reasons, the bank money-creation circuit should be democratized and made publicly accountable, with its current mechanisms and privileges exposed. Bank lending must be seen as a public matter. The need is not just to democratize finance but to challenge the source and

Democratizing Finance or Democratizing Money?

use of the money supply. Banks have become a major source of new money, and the problem is that it can emerge only as debt. The alternative is to reclaim the sovereign power to create money that can be circulated free of debt, that is, spent directly into circulation.

As described above, neoliberalism, which has influenced so much of contemporary thinking about money, is adamant that the public sector must not create ("print") money. As a result, public expenditure must be limited to what the market can "afford." Money, in this view, is a limited resource that the market ensures will be used efficiently. The 2007–8 financial crisis has fundamentally undermined this neoliberal dogma. The banking sector mismanaged its role as a source of money so badly that states had to step in and provide unlimited monetary backing to rescue it. The public monetary economy was revealed as the ultimate backstop for the banks. It became clear that the banks were creating a public resource, the public currency, which has to be underwritten by the state. Bank lending could no longer be seen as a private, commercial activity.

Following the crisis, the very evident public creation of money revealed the inherently political nature of money. When other fiscal and monetary solutions appeared unable to refloat damaged economies, central banks resorted to the explicit creation of money out of thin air. Under what was described rather obscurely as "quantitative easing," vast amounts of newly created electronic money were used to rescue financial institutions. There was no question of the new money's being borrowed from anywhere. It was a clear demonstration of the sovereign power to create money. Radical voices quickly asked why, if the central bank could create money out of thin air to rescue the banks, they could not create new money to rescue the people.

Unfortunately, the dominance of neoliberal ideology was so strong that center-left politicians could not be seen to advocate printing money for public purposes. Nor was there a demand to cancel the government debt held by financial institutions that was being bought up with the new publicly created money. In Britain, where more than £400 billion was spent mostly on buying up government debt, that debt stayed on the books. A Tory-led coalition and subsequent Tory government used the high level of public debt as an excuse for a harsh program of austerity. To escape such reactionary politics, a radical alternative theory of money is needed.

Rethinking money

Money can be seen as the agent of the overconsumption and exploitation of people and the planet, but it is difficult to envision how goods and services could be produced and circulated without a money-like mechanism. It is how money is created and circulated in modern market economies, not money itself, that is the source of the imbalance in our relationship with one another and with nature. The primary aim of the capitalist market economy is not the provision of essential goods and services for the people but the investment of money, labor, and resources in activities that channel more money (profit) to the owners of capital. The result is a two-step economy: people have to work to secure an income in order to pay for the basic goods and services they need to survive. And because work is necessary for survival, and the market determines its purpose and availability, people can end up in jobs that are harmful to themselves, others, and the environment.

The existence of money does not entail the existence of a market. Some form of money has existed in most, if not all, human societies, including pre-market and pre-state communities. The money-thing, whatever form it takes, simply provides a recognized unit of measurement that can compare relative value and, in most cases, also transfer that value. The value can relate to money prices in the market, but it can also measure the size of a gift, the level of a fine for a misdemeanor, or an assessment of need. Equating money with coinage, as is commonly done, confuses form with function. It implies that money embodies value when it simply represents value. The money-thing can take the form of something with use value (cattle, grain), something with social value (a special stone, shells), a medium that has little or no value (paper, wood, base metal), or even something with no physical form (bank transfers, verbal promises). The unit of value may be either tangible (sheep, beads) or intangible (pound, dollar, euro).

Money, in other words, is a social and political construct. Using money does not intrinsically encourage human exploitation or ecological destruction. It is capitalist ideology that puts monetary gain above social and ecological concerns, and it is the private, bank-issued money system that leaves us with a pernicious cycle of debt and growth. Money could encourage socially and ecologically sustainable production and consumption, but only if it ceased to be a creature of the market and was reclaimed as a social and public representation of value. A focus on capitalist markets also ignores many other important sources of value: unpaid domestic labor, community, conviviality, and ecological resilience. There is an obvious desire in some quarters simply to protect these areas from commodification, but doing that alone would leave the rest of the system intact.

What is needed is an approach to money that embodies a social and public role. Rather than prioritize wealth creation as the accumulation of money and assets, the aim would be to create "wellth," that is, well-being for all. This approach would see money being created and circulated in the social and public economy through the exercise of sovereign power and seigniorage (the benefit of first use of that money). Public money would be spent to achieve social purposes before flowing into the market sector, against the converse view that money is created and circulated in the market sector before being taxed out into the public sector. The case for seeing money as a public resource is not that states should create money; it is that they do. It has already been accepted by leading monetary authorities that banks create the public money supply when they lend. The equivalent case can be made for the public sector: that it creates money when it spends. What is needed is to recognize that the money supply is created through a public money circuit as well as a bank lending circuit.

The public circuit of money

As shown in Figure 2, money flows out from the state and back in through taxation and other payments. The dynamic of the circuit is conventionally seen as state income driving state expenditure. It is also assumed that the ultimate source of state income is the market sector. I would argue that both assumptions are incorrect.

States do not tax and then spend; they spend first and tax later. The larger arrow in Figure 2 representing public expenditure also indicates that the state may circulate more money than it reclaims. Unlike in the bank-lending circuit in which the bank always wants more money back than is lent, in the public circuit the money reclaimed through taxation can be less than the amount spent. This is because the public sector can exercise the sovereign power to create money free of debt. Publicly generated money can also be directly spent into the public or private economy.

The failure to recognize the existence of publicly created money reflects assumptions about the dynamics of the public money circuit. If it is assumed that taxation drives public spending, the money-creating effect of state spending will be ignored. However, the evidence that public expenditure comes first is quite straightforward. States do not have a piggy bank full of collected taxes when they spend. Budgets are allocated on the expectation that the money spent will be returned as taxes in the same way as

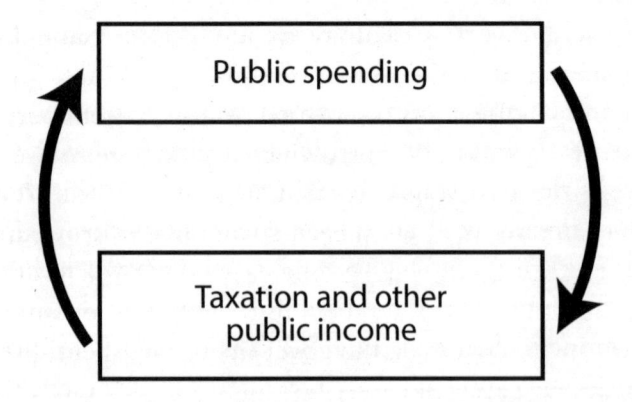

Figure 2. The public circuit of money

banks assume that their loans will be returned. If states did have piggy banks there would never be a deficit: they could only spend what they had in the pot.

The logic of handbag economics would also imply that, as the money to fund public spending comes from the market "wealth-creating" sector, that is the only sector that is taxed. However, the market is not the only source of state income. Public sector employees and organizations also pay their taxes, arguably more reliably than private sector employees. Whereas it could be argued that taxes raised from the market sector draw on privately created money and therefore can be seen as prior to state spending, the same cannot be true for taxation of actors in the public sector. For this sector, public funding must come first; otherwise individuals and organizations would have no money with which to pay their taxes.

Governments expand the money supply when they spend in the same way that banks expand the money supply when they lend. By the same token, repayment of bank loans and payment of taxes reduce the money supply. The overall impact and balance between public expenditure and public income becomes clear only after the expenditures have occurred. The political choice at that point is what to do with any "deficit," that is, a surplus of public expenditure over income. If there are no inflationary pressures, the extra money created by state expenditures could be left to flow around the economy. In times of recession this would be a sensible strategy.

Instead, under the ideology of handbag economics, it is demanded that public expenditure must be balanced by public income. Any deficit must be covered by government borrowing. This is a strange form of borrowing, as it does not raise money to spend. The existence of deficit/surplus expenditure means that the money has already been spent. The borrowed money cannot be used for further public expenditure. What the loan to the government does is return to the public economy money equal to the extra money the government has spent. In return, the lender has a financial asset, a state promise to repay the loan with interest.

Handbag economics treats government deficit as if it were an overdraft at the bank. However, public sector borrowing is not an overdraft. When a private individual or company overdraws at the bank, they are spending the bank's money. States, when they spend extra money, are not spending someone else's money. The sovereign power to create money means that no other institution is liable for state spending. There is no need for the state to borrow from the private sector to cover its surplus spending. As the money has already been spent, borrowing is merely a way to recover that money. Progressive taxation is another way the same end could be achieved. However, the demand that states should borrow to "balance the books" means that state deficits become compounded into a national debt of the public sector to the owners of money as capital.

The "balance" in question is not between tax and spending within the public circuit, as claimed by handbag economics, but between the public circuit and the market sector to avoid inflationary pressure. It is a case not of balancing public expenditure with tax income but of adjusting tax income to control how much publicly spent money flows out into the market. That does not mean that states can create unlimited amounts of money any more than banks can create unlimited amounts of debt. Both are constrained by the level of real labor and material conditions. However, the ability of states to create money is an important resource for the public economy.

Money as a public resource

Identifying the two circuits of money, bank and state, challenges the existing distinction between fiscal and monetary activity. The conventional view is that monetary activities govern the money supply and should be independent of public policy. Fiscal activities are concerned with tax and spending of money already in circulation. However, I argue that both bank lending and public spending are creating and allocating a public resource: money. Rather than the banking system being the support mechanism

Democratizing Finance or Democratizing Money?

for public spending, the state is the backstop for the banks, as the 2007–8 crisis showed. Privately created money became a public liability. If it is to be a public liability, money should be reclaimed as a public resource. Control of the money supply and, more generally, the monetary system confers a tremendous amount of power. In the absence of recognition that the public circuit of money exists, monetary power over the public economy has been left with the privatized banking sector.

The ideology of market supremacy is used to undermine the principles of the welfare state and its concern for public well-being. Instead of a burden on the (private) taxpayer, public spending should be seen as the people creating and allocating money to provide goods and services for themselves—that is, a public economy based on money as a public resource. Money can represent social and public value, not just commercial and private value. And rather than only being a mechanism for profit-driven exchange, money can be a tool for creating "wellth"—the provision of goods and services that people actually use, and guaranteeing everyone a right to livelihood.

However, although the power to create the public resource that is money cannot be left to the privatized banking sector, can we trust the state with it? Neoliberals warn of the dangers of state intervention in a market-based system. Proponents of social and local economies likewise harbor suspicions of the state, particularly its distant and opaque bureaucratic apparatuses. Many states have proved to be inefficient, corrupt, and autocratic. However, without an expanded role for the state, many people will continue to fall through the gaps in the market and voluntary sectors. What is needed is a public money system that is robustly democratic. We cannot assume that public authorities will use money wisely unless they are subject to democratically determined mandates and effective public scrutiny. Exclusive control of the money supply must not simply be put in the hands of the government in power or the state apparatus and left unchecked. Public management of the creation and allocation of money must be transparent and accountable.

Democratizing money

The democratization of money would require the development of public platforms to open up a debate about the public and private creation and circulation of money. The democratic process must apply to both the banking and the public sector. Banks' money creation through lending is of public concern because the money created is a public liability. As pointed out, a debt-based money supply also leads to social, ecological, economic, and political problems.

Should banks be prevented from lending money at all? Should they lend money only from existing accounts? There is certainly a case for curtailing bank lending. In earlier eras, particularly following the Great Depression, banks were regulated and restricted. The structure of banking is also important. Should banking be seen as a utility under social or public ownership? Should banks be able to make grants as well as loans? Accountability and transparency are also vital. At a minimum it is necessary to know to whom the banks are lending and for what purpose. Activities could be curtailed, such as lending for speculation rather than providing working capital for the provision of goods and services.

Shifting economic priorities from a search for profits to the provisioning of social needs would put the main focus of the economy on the social and public sectors rather than on the market. That focus emphasizes money creation through public budgeting rather than bank lending. Public budgeting could include the provision of a basic income—a monetary allocation to each individual as a matter of rights, supplemented by additional payment based on need—and collective expenditures on public services and infrastructure. Public expenditure could be through direct spending of money created free of debt. The limitation on such spending would be not what the market deems it can afford but actual resources and labor capacity. There is no reason to assume that the private market would make better use of these resources than the public or social economy.

Exercising the public's right to create, spend, and oversee the public resource of money requires a wide range of democratic decision-making and entails a mixture of strategic and participatory processes.

Strategic decision-making

The first debate at the national or regional strategic level would need to address the overall balance of the economy as between the public and commercial sectors. How will control of the capacity to create money be distributed between them? Will the state reclaim all the power to create the public currency, or will banks continue to lend new money on a commercial basis? Should the banking sector be treated as a utility and be socialized or nationalized, remain private but regulated, or be totally private and unregulated? A linked debate would need to decide the principles for investment. Should it be based on an allocation of publicly generated money as a grant or a loan, or should it be a commercial loan or a transfer of existing money from private investors? Recognizing that money is a public resource and a public liability, we can hope that its use in the commercial sector would be based on ecologically sustainable and socially just principles.

As with any government budget, specific strategies would need to be put forward, such as the level of any basic income or proposals for spending on public services and infrastructure. Proposals would need to be laid out about measures to address the redistribution of income and wealth, whether to tax resource use or land, or which other expenditures should be taxed. The allocation of money between administrative and economic centers, regions, and localities would need to be democratically determined. Which decisions should be devolved?

Given the complexity of the process set out here, these budgets and the corresponding allocations would need to be set for at least a five-year period, with a modest margin for interim adjustments. Adoption of a participatory and transparent approach to decision-making would militate against domination by any particular group or body. The setting of long-term budgets would ensure that governments could not, simply for political gains, substantially amend proposed money creation or expenditure levels during the run-up to elections.

Participatory budgeting

The top-down strategic proposals would be augmented by a system of participatory budgeting. Citizens and user–producer forums would identify specific public expenditure needs and provide input into local, regional, and national budgets. The starting point for these discussions would be existing levels of expenditure and their adequacy. It could be argued that such participation would require highly developed financial literacy. People may not be able to address such complex areas effectively. However, evidence exists that participatory approaches to budgeting are already well established. The best-known example is that of Porto Alegre, Brazil. An initiative of the Brazilian Workers' Party, the system of participatory budgeting was launched in 1989 in which grassroots assemblies of citizens determined public spending priorities. The assemblies then elected budget delegates to put these proposals forward to higher levels of decision-making. Since that time, more than 2,000 examples of participatory budgeting have been explored or established in all parts of the globe. However, participation must not just be about how to spend a given amount of money; a people's budget would determine how big the public economy should be.

Participatory monitoring and evaluation

Another important focus of democratic participation would be the enhancement of public spending oversight. All organizations that received a direct or indirect allocation of public money would need to have clear mechanisms in place for democratic accountability and transparency. Interested citizens along with workers and user groups would monitor their expenditures and business practices on a regular basis. Such monitoring would minimize the possibility for abuses, such as over-leveraging of the financial sector or waste and corruption in the public or private sector.

Managing money

Any proposal for democratizing money will be met by the claim that public money creation would be inflationary. This claim ignores the fact that bank-created money is equally inflationary, as the cycle of debt-led booms and slumps shows. All money systems need careful managing. Because the implementation of a democratic money system would almost certainly result in a massive increase in public expenditure, a phase-in would be prudent. Even with a phase-in, the additional money flowing into the market sector could increase the threat of inflation in the short term. Reconceptualizing the role of taxation offers a way to obviate the problem.

As I have said earlier, the need to "balance" the public budget should be in relation not to the income from taxation but to the balance between the level of public spending and the amount of money any continuing market sector can absorb. The role of taxation in this model is not fiscal; it is a monetary instrument. Taxation does not "raise" the money for public spending; it retrieves money already spent, as would any fees and charges for public services. Taxation follows rather than precedes public expenditure, retrieving publicly created money from circulation in amounts sufficient to keep inflation in the market sector in check. If the public sector is much larger than the private sector, taxes might have to be quite high. Far from the claim that high levels of public expenditure are a drain on the (private) "taxpayer" and the money in "his" pocket, high levels of public expenditure put the money into her pocket in the first place.

While levels of budgets and basic incomes can be determined through an open, democratic process, assessing the impact of public expenditure on the commercial sector would require technical expertise. This situation is no different from what we see today: experts in monetary policy try to anticipate and then propose actions to address inflationary pressure, usually by adjusting key interest rates. As is the case today, estimating the impact of public expenditures would be a hit-or-miss process, but a necessary one nonetheless. A committee of experts would make an assessment of the amount of public money the commercial sector could absorb without too great a rate of inflation and, correspondingly, the overall level of taxation required.

However, the expert inflation assessors would have no role in determining how much the total level of public expenditure would be or how the required taxes would be applied. That is where the public would come in, debating questions of what amount to spend and whom, what, and how to tax.

Reclaiming money as a sovereign power

All modern currencies are "fiat money," created out of nothing, their value sustained by public trust and state authority. So why are states and their citizens shackled in debt? Why can the people not simply create the money they need free of debt? Why can that money not be circulated in a nonprofit social or public sector? Why base the principles that govern our economic system on the butcher, the baker, the candlestick maker, and the hidden hand of the market rather than the doctor, the teacher, the care worker, the artist, and the not-so-hidden hand of a solidarity economy? As these questions make clear, freeing ourselves of misconceptions about money opens the door to new possibilities for driving a transition to a just and sustainable economy.[8]

A democratic public money system would enable a one-step economy in which individuals no longer have to undertake socially or ecologically harmful work in order to secure an income. Participation in the market would no longer be essential, as money would reflect an entitlement to livelihood, not just the market value assigned to work. Paid work would continue, but it would focus on democratically determined priorities. Caring for each other and for the planet and building a just society, not financial speculation and resource extraction, would be recognized as the real sources of wealth. New metrics would track and guide progress, with a shift from gross domestic product to a notion of gross domestic provisioning that measures overall wellth, that is, well-being.

The term "provisioning" is broader than the concept "economy." It would include currently unpaid work, the resilience of the natural world, and the vibrancy of conviviality. Priorities for the allocation of money would put provisioning over profit and be attuned to the interplay between meeting human needs and protecting the environment. Work that is currently unpaid or underpaid could be recognized, such as care for the elderly. Although today this responsibility tends to fall on the shoulders of women as unpaid or underpaid work, it could become a major source of meaningful work and societal wealth.

Exercising the sovereign power to create and circulate money to provide services and a livelihood would mean much less need for the private accumulation of wealth, which in turn would enable a shift toward social equity through taxation of existing wealth. Since there would be less need for investment vehicles such as private pensions, public money could be created and used to purchase natural resources and utilities currently in private hands, bringing them back under public control.

Reorganizing the economy around publicly created money is not utopian. It simply requires recognizing and reorienting what exists, and what underpins our money system today. In the wake of the financial crisis of 2007–8, the sovereign power to create public money was made clear when governments used it to rescue the banks and other large businesses, such as auto manufacturers and insurance companies. Let it now be used to provision the people.

8

Democratizing Investment

Lenore Palladino

Americans have trillions of dollars invested in public and private companies, and the stock market continues its upward climb, even in the midst of a historic economic crisis. Yet stock ownership is highly unequal: the wealthiest 10 percent of American households possess 88 percent of all corporate equity and mutual fund ownership (excepting pension entitlements), and there is a large and persistent racial wealth gap.[1] Access to investment opportunities and shareholder payments is a key driver of the increasing wealth disparity, along with housing, income, access to banking, and other assets. The principal role of the government in today's capital markets is to ensure disclosure of corporate activity, a procedural form of regulation, with little public policy focused on creating access to capital markets for those locked out. Part of the Real Utopian project of creating a democratic financial system should be reimagining the role of the government in the private capital markets. This chapter proposes the creation of a "public investment platform" to use innovative financial technologies to create a public option for participation in the capital markets, and a "public investment account" to universalize access to investment opportunities.[2]

US financial history has shown the power of the government to structure financial markets, and as Robert Hockett's work in this volume demonstrates, private financial entities are best understood as franchisees harnessing the public's permission to create credit and wealth.[3] Capital markets are governed by public policies that submerge the role of the public in structuring them and enable an inequitable accumulation of wealth. To democratize finance, new policies are required to democratize participation in investment, and careful attention must be paid to claims of "democratization" that replicate existing hierarchies of wealth and power.

Today's capital markets require a sum of available funds to invest, generally restrict the non-wealthy from investing in private companies, and provide little opportunity for small businesses to seek equity investment. It is nearly impossible for an average American to buy a small equity stake in a local business and virtually no market for them to do so. The non-wealthy cannot invest in the pizza shop downtown and instead must invest in large public companies, usually by purchasing stock through a Wall Street–based fund aggregator, which earns fees through its intermediation activities. Wealthy, or "accredited," investors can invest privately, mainly in large companies or start-ups that have managed to gain access to venture capital. While securities laws were put in place with the intention of protecting the non-wealthy investor from the predation that befell them before the Great Depression, the result has been that the wealth assets of the majority of Americans who hold equities at all are concentrated in large pools of institutional capital that invest in large businesses.

This means that America's businesses have unequal access to capital. Large publicly traded companies have the best access to bank loans and equity investment. Locally owned small businesses are crucial job creators and are key to regional prosperity and competition (though jobs at larger firms tend to have higher wages and better benefits). Crucial economic activities are currently constrained by the financial sector, such as small businesses, care provision, infrastructure, and clean energy, and small loans for small businesses are more difficult to access than large loans for large businesses.

The financial sector is rapidly changing: new financial technologies (fintech), the blockchain, and cryptocurrency are ushering in new possibilities along with new risks. New players outside the traditional regulated system emerge and new ways of doing business become mainstream, even inside traditional financial entities. "Fintech" refers either to new uses of technology within regulated banking institutions or to new types of financial companies that are not regulated as banks, which engage in loans or other types of financial transactions with the public. "Cryptocurrency" refers to the invention of non-government-backed money, stored electronically, which uses a non-bank open and distributed ledger, known as a blockchain. In other words, "money" is not issued by a government in the form of central bank notes, and records of transactions are no longer stored inside financial institutions.

These new technologies open up the potential for a radically different approach to financial participation due to lowered transaction costs and the nearly costless transmission of information. Some have claimed that the rise of financial technology will lead to the private "democratization" of investment. Investment and lending today can be conducted from one's smartphone, and loans can be taken out over a peer-to-peer platform, though both are still intermediated by a large financial institution. The mid-twenty-first-century financial institutions may be far more decentralized in terms of access through technology than today's mega-firms, but this shift could happen without any deeper structural change; the concentrations of power could morph in form but not in function. The physical requirements for a place to make a transaction are gone, and there are new possibilities to scale. Technology has disrupted the regulatory supervision and oversight of single institutions and the system as a whole.[4] This disintermediation has profound implications for the provision of financial services in coming decades.

This chapter asks, what if new innovations in distributed technologies allowed instead for *public* facilitation of new opportunities for wealth appreciation and a rebalancing of power within capital markets? This chapter takes up the charge from Erik Olin Wright: "What institutional designs for a more democratic and egalitarian finance system can be instituted in the present that plausibly prefigure a radically democratic economy beyond capitalism?"[5] In the twenty-first century, what kind of public institutional structure would allow all people to truly participate in wealth creation without opening them up to undue amounts of risk, and could be established in the short term with sufficient political will? As a corollary, what structure would allow for funding the types of businesses that too often lose out in today's Wall Street–driven economy—small businesses, business for social needs, and worker-owned businesses?

The argument proceeds as follows. First, I outline the current conditions of the financial sector and the limits on wealth accumulation for the majority of the population. In this section I also consider the investor protection components of our securities laws. Second, I propose two major areas of policy intervention: the public investment platform and the public investment account.

Wealth inequality in capital markets

Participation in capital markets is deeply unequal: there is a wealthy elite who own the majority of shares, and middle-class investing households who have small retirement or investment accounts. These two groups have different purposes for holding shares and different power vis-à-vis the companies they invest in. Small shareholders are primarily invested in large public corporations and own shares indirectly, through an employer retirement account, a mutual fund, or a pension fund. They tend to hold for the long term. Wealthy shareholders invest in both public and private companies, have much higher average holdings, and invest through funds that turn over their holdings much more quickly. This section discusses why there is such significant inequality in capital markets, and then turns to recent public policies that have tried to create new mechanisms for broader participation in capital markets but mainly reinforce existing inequities of access. In the third section, I will propose policies that would makes strides toward democratizing investment.

The vast majority of Americans do not have any significant stake in corporate securities and have been locked out of one of the main drivers of wealth. Nearly 50 percent of American households own some stock, though only 14 percent own stock directly. Some 46 percent of Americans own stock indirectly, though a pension account (46.6 percent), mutual fund (9.8 percent), or trust fund (3.9 percent).[6] It is important to look at the dollar value of total wealth holdings: only 37 percent of households have total stock holdings over $5,000, meaning that 13 percent have holdings between zero and $5,000. Only 25 percent have holdings worth $25,000 or above.[7]

New data from the Federal Reserve's Distributional Financial Accounts gives a quarterly picture of the evolution of wealth inequality.[8] This new data set combines household-level data from the Survey of Consumer Finances with the Federal Reserve's Financial Accounts of the United States to give the distribution of wealth assets and liabilities on a quarterly basis, starting in 1989, between four household wealth quartiles: the top 1 percent; the next 9 percent; the next 40 percent, and the bottom 50 percent. On the one hand, the data show that inequities in corporate shares and mutual funds have been consistent: in 1989, the top 1 percent held 39.1 percent of corporate equity and the top 10 percent combined held 80.3 percent, while the bottom 50 percent held a mere 1.4 percent. By the second quarter of 2020, the top 10 percent held 88.2 percent of corporate equity (and the top 1 percent alone broke 50 percent), while the share held by the bottom 50 percent had fallen to 0.6 percent—a 0.8 percentage-point decline.[9] Approximately one-third of "pension entitlements" are made up of employer-held direct-contribution retirement plans, of which a large portion are equities. For this category, the top 10 percent held 53.5 percent of all wealth, while the bottom 50 percent was limited to 2.9 percent in the second quarter of 2020.

The racial wealth gap is significant in holdings of direct and indirect stock and grows even starker when examining holdings over $10,000. Holdings have stayed nearly constant from 2001 to 2016: 57.5 percent of white households held stock in both

2001 and 2016, while the share of black households holding stock fell four percentage points to 29.7 percent in 2016, and the share of Latino households holding stock fell two percentage points to 26.3 percent. Perhaps more important is the percentage holding stocks with a value of $10,000: in 2016, there was a gap of twenty-eight percentage points between white and black households (42.9 percent to 15.2 percent), and a gap of thirty percentage points between white and Latino households (42.9 percent to 13.1 percent). Considering portfolios above $10,000, these are roughly the same gaps that existed in 2001 (the white–black gap and the white–Latino gap were twenty-eight points in 2001).[10]

The major divide in the securities markets is between public and private investment opportunities. Private investment opportunities are limited to accredited investors; publicly traded securities require heightened disclosure, and private investment is limited in order to protect investors who can take less risk of losing their investment.[11] The Securities and Exchange Commission defines accredited investors by net worth, which means that many investors qualify as "accredited" based on their inherited family wealth rather than any sophistication regarding judgments about investing. At the time of passage of the Securities Act of 1933, Congress was rightfully concerned that the stock market crash of 1929 meant that investors had lost faith in the financial markets. The motivating purpose of the securities laws was to bring confidence back into the market through full disclosure by issuer companies, and by rules around who could invest. For public offerings, conducted on the exchanges, investors were protected through the stringent registration and disclosure requirements. For private offerings, or those exempt from registration, investors would be protected by limiting who could invest and how the offerings would be conducted.[12]

The Securities Act of 1933 and Securities Exchange Act of 1934 were part of the New Deal package of reforms in response to the speculation of the 1920s that led to the Great Depression. Passed after the Pecora hearings, in which Congress brought the misdeeds of bankers into the public record, the new legal framework for equity was intended to minimize the risks for households who wanted to invest in America's growing corporations. Adolf Berle, a key adviser of FDR's, laid out the framework in his 1932 classic *The Modern Corporation and Private Property*, which was meant to insure against management self-enrichment at the expense of shareholders, and settled on disclosure as the best way to balance the entrepreneurial authority of management with the rights of shareholders for companies offering their shares on public markets.[13] As Julia Ott describes in *When Wall Street Met Main Street*, one strand of argument for broadening access to business equity was that "universal investment could bring corporations in line with democratic political traditions."[14] On the other hand, such broadening of access with guardrails was a way to ameliorate more radical public claims on the country's wealth, and as the description above demonstrates, has not resulted in a "shareholders' democracy" of wealth distribution.

The institutional structure of the asset management industry means that household investors receive lesser returns than elite investors.[15] Public pension funds—the retirement investments of public sector workers—have invested massively with hedge funds, but hedge funds are able to charge large and obscure fees that can leave pensioners worse off than if they had never invested in hedge funds at all.[16] Current securities regulation does not require that financial advisers have a fiduciary standard of care for their clients—meaning that advisers can put their own financial gain from selling a particular product before the financial interests of their advisees—which illustrates just how problematic the nature of financial advice can be, when brokers posing as investment advisers can steer clients toward products that earn the adviser extra compensation.[17] The wealthier the household, the more access to private investment opportunities and better investment advice, compounding wealth inequality over time.[18]

New public policies attempt to "democratize" investment

In the last few years, policies have sought to ameliorate many of the problems described above by purporting to open up wealth accumulation potential to non-wealthy individuals through crowdfunding technology and changes to the rules around private placements (equity offerings by businesses that are limited to "accredited" investors, i.e., only wealthy households). "Crowdfunding" refers to fundraising (whether through donations or equity) from large numbers of people who contribute small sums of money. Although the practice itself is not new, "crowdfunding portals," first for donations and then for equity, have proliferated, allowing individuals and businesses to solicit small amounts of funds from large numbers of people through a central platform.

The JOBS Act of 2012 was meant to open up investment to the general public by regulating crowdfunding portals.[19] Crowdfunding portals allow businesses to solicit investment from nonaccredited investors because the portal itself is supposed to serve as a check on speculative opportunities. The purpose of the crowdfunding platforms is to connect potential investors *as individuals* directly with businesses who are approved by the platform. The non-wealthy can invest through the portal, opening up new opportunities, in theory, for investing in private firms. This is a major change from the original division present in the Securities Act of 1933, dividing investment opportunity into publicly traded and private markets. The stated intent of congressional drafters was to keep the general disclosure requirements that undergird the public capital markets while opening up investment on both sides: to businesses who cannot afford the high cost of complying with the rules of the public markets, and to investors whose wealth limits them to the less than 5,000 companies that are publicly traded.

The portal itself lowers or eliminates many of the transaction barriers that stood in the way of connecting small investors and small issuers. However, participation in crowdfunding portals is limited to those who have funds to invest and the resources to find and participate in such portals. The need to find one's way among the multitude of portals that have emerged since the passage of the act means that it is likely that such portals will not substantially increase the number of households participating in investment.

The purpose of the JOBS Act was to spur entrepreneurship and give start-ups a wider pool of potential capital to tap into. All investors, in theory, are now able to invest directly in any private business that sells its securities through a portal. The JOBS Act's crowdfunding provisions create potential risk for a prospective crowdfunding investor, because the new crowdfunding portals do not have the same due diligence experience as the large brokerage houses, and certain disclosure requirements are relaxed for businesses. Small investors who previously had only been able to participate in the public securities market now have an opportunity to participate in private offerings even if they do not meet the definition of an accredited investor. The debate about whether that constitutes an expansion of investor democracy or an increase in the potential for predatory behavior continues among investor advocates. It is unlikely that these recent innovations will make much of a dent in the wealth-inequality statistics described. However, the idea of crowdfunding portals is useful in that they facilitate direct connection between sources and uses of funds, and can do so in a decentralized manner that allows in lower-net-worth households with appropriate risk safeguards in place. It provides the motivation for one of the policies proposed below, with an important difference: the portals should be run in the public interest.

Another type of securities offering that has democratic features is the direct public offering (DPO). Direct public offerings allow for investment by local investors (limited to within a particular state, in most cases) directly in a business without going through a public securities exchange or a cumbersome registration process. Direct public offerings can be made through an "intrastate offering exemption," which limits investors to residents of the state where the business is incorporated and conducts at least 80 percent of its business. The exemptions must balance the tensions described above: opening up capital raising to the non-wealthy carries risks of predatory and unscrupulous behavior. Businesses must meet regulatory requirements to conduct a direct public offering dictated at the state level, and must fall within a federal exemption to avoid registering with the SEC. Though some small inroads have been made to popularize the idea of direct public offerings, they remain few and far between.

Still, whether using a DPO or a crowdfunding platform, investing is a wholly private act, notwithstanding light regulation by the state. It is unlikely that these mechanisms will bring the 50 percent of American households who do not participate in the stock market currently into investment participation. It is more likely that some investors diversify their holdings through participation in DPOs or crowdfunding, and that start-up businesses are slightly less reliant on the concentrated capital typically used for new ventures, from venture capital funds or angel capital funds. In order to truly democratize finance, government must facilitate entrance to capital markets for all Americans.

An important caveat: this is emphatically not an argument to simply open up investment in private companies that do not have to meet stringent disclosure requirements to all households. Though such an approach is currently under discussion at the Securities and Exchange Commission, the result of a loosening of admittance to private offerings could increase risk and the potential for fraud to household investors, precisely because there would be no intermediary to screen the offerings. The goal of this chapter is to shift away from the notion that democratization of investment must be driven by the private sector.

One final question is what the impact of "futurist fintech" will be on the evolution of the capital markets, and whether these proposals will make sense if financial markets change dramatically.[20] Advocates of blockchain and cryptocurrency argue that the rise of decentralized ledgers will destroy the central power of financial institutions. Though the blockchain would change the nature of transaction costs and intermediation, there is no reason to think that the blockchain in and of itself, or even broader *decentralization* of financial transactions, would substantially increase either wealth equality or asset building for the majority of householders. Instead, new public policies are required to substantially ameliorate the consistent wealth inequality pervasive in the American financial system.

Access to equity, not access to credit

The underlying normative claim of this proposal is that including more people in the financial markets is in the public interest. Before proceeding to discuss the proposal itself, it is necessary to ask whether that claim is true. The financialization of households has meant an increase in household interaction with the financial markets. Families in the United States purchase equity or take out loans for financial needs across the life cycle, including retirement, home purchases, and education.[21] The rise in debt load and market-based risk has been catastrophic for millions of families, as was put in sharp relief by the home and retirement losses in the financial crisis, the student debt crisis of the 2010s, and the pandemic-driven economic crisis of 2020.

This chapter still contends that *public* expansion of access to democratic investment opportunities, where the benefits accrue to both small businesses and non-wealthy households, is in the public interest. This is not a substitute for such needed policies that would increase public provision of basic social goods, like retirement or higher education. First, and most importantly, the proposal here contemplates *public provision of funds for investment*, which places no debt burden on any household, and can make strides toward ameliorating historical racial and gender wealth gaps. Put simply, even if all the funds are lost, the household would not be in a worse place than it is today. Second, the proposal would *add a public option in the financial markets* to reduce the ability of private financial institutions to extract wealth from the majority of American households. Finally, the proposal would *strengthen opportunities for investment for small businesses*, the types of businesses owned by the non-wealthy and currently suffering from a lack of access to capital.[22]

Increasing concentration of wealth is a global hallmark of the economy in the twenty-first century. As Thomas Piketty points out, wealth has always been concentrated, and the current distribution in the United States and Europe can be thought of more as a return to historical levels of wealth inequality after an aberrant period that resulted from the shocks of two world wars.[23]

There are multiple public policies that must be pursued to begin to counter the inequality in the United States, ranging from wealth taxes and higher marginal tax rates on the upper class, to public investments like the Green New Deal, a jobs guarantee, and the public provision of social goods such as health care and education. There is also a range of options to address the problem of the "unbanked," including postal banking and other mechanisms to widen access to credit and banking services to low-income households.[24] Increasing the wealth assets of the non-wealthy must be coupled with policies that reduce the wealth holdings that are passed along and grow for generations. Though discussing in detail reforms like a global wealth tax and increasing top marginal tax rates are beyond the scope of this chapter, it is unlikely that the reforms proposed here will dent the structures of inequality without deconcentrating wealth at the top.

This chapter focuses on the question of access to wealth assets as a central problem for democratizing finance, without assuming that widening access to credit (or liabilities) would necessarily have positive impacts on inequality. As economist Darrick Hamilton says, "Wealth begets more wealth," as wealth is a transmitter of both possibility and freedom to make one's own choices across generations.[25] Unless all goods and services are publicly provided, skewed access to wealth will continue to lock in race and income divides. Wealth *assets* provide security and income that are not dependent on labor. Liabilities, on the other hand, can either create new economic potential or trap an individual in a cycle of unaffordable debt repayment, as today's student debt crisis makes clear. In the United States, closing the racial wealth gap is not a matter of increasing income potential or even of reducing liabilities. Put simply, the wealth-asset gap for households of color and low-wealth white households is so large that other workarounds will not solve the core distributional challenge. That is why using public tools to grant wealth assets is required—along with other tools that tax the wealth of the upper echelons of households.

Financial assets are far more unequally distributed than nonfinancial assets. In the fourth quarter of 2018, the top 10 percent owned 42.4 percent of nonfinancial assets but 72.2 percent of financial assets. The bottom 50 percent's difference is even more stark: this half of the population owned 15.8 percent of nonfinancial assets (including 13.8 percent of all real estate and 25.3 percent of consumer durables) but only 2.1 percent of financial assets. The starkly unequal distribution of corporate equity and mutual funds (50.9 percent, 35.9 percent, 12.4 percent, and 0.8 percent by wealth quartiles, respectively—top 1 percent, next 9 percent, next 40 percent, and bottom 50 percent) means that addressing this asset category specifically—without requiring households to take on new liabilities—is part of closing the overall wealth gap. Because of the inability of the non-wealthy to access privately held corporate equity, and because most equity of publicly traded companies must be purchased by the non-wealthy out of their labor income, there is no mechanism to reduce inequality in such assets without public intervention.

The risk remains that such assets would not perform well, or even that their prices would fall. Because the proposal also contemplates issuing equity shares in the types of small businesses that have not historically been subject to capital market disclosures, it is impossible to say what kinds of returns such investments may have. Business cycles and macroeconomic risk mean that the future performance of small and medium-sized enterprises is unpredictable; however, small businesses are not prone to the shareholder primacy approach to corporate governance that can drive speculation in stock prices at the expense of long-term business investment.[26] Additionally, part of the purpose of the proposal is also to provide small businesses with alternatives to high-interest loans from big banks and fintech lenders that often take the form of personal debt.[27] After describing the proposals in more detail, I will return to the risks of diversifying investments in small businesses.

Policy proposals

In this section I describe the two policy proposals that can facilitate democratic access to capital markets. The first proposal is that the government should establish a "public investment platform," organized in the public interest, that serves as a crowdfunding platform for small companies offering debt or equity securities, and offers an index fund of publicly traded securities at little to no cost to the public. Access to the public platform can serve as a "public option" for wealth creation. The platform would serve two functions: competing directly with private financial platforms, and directly connecting individuals to lending or investment opportunities. A public option would create true competition for the financial intermediaries that extract wealth. A public platform will go beyond the idea of a new public financial institution and instead be more in line with the direction in which the financial sector is going: decentralized interactions among individuals and entities. A public investment platform will ensure that the same power dynamics do not follow us into the new financial structure. The second proposal is to create a "public investment account," in which Americans are provided with a small sum of capital to use as a wealth-building fund,[28] weighted according to family wealth due to historical inequities.[29] These proposals are also compatible with measures such as nonprofit banks,[30] public or postal banking,[31] or other methods for public engagement in the financial market.

Public policy has historically shaped finance

Public policy is required to set the stage for truly democratic participation in finance. The government should recognize the financial sector—both banking and the capital markets—as constituting a "social infrastructure" that requires public intervention to achieve goals of equity and positive social outcomes. The public utility model of governmental regulation, developed by twentieth-century Progressive Era thinkers and undergoing a revival today, is a useful model for understanding the government's role in finance. It posits that sectors of the economy exhibit characteristics of a social infrastructure when "a good [is] of sufficient social value to be a necessity."[32] Balancing accountability and oversight with efficiency of production, the government should treat the sector to a higher level of regulation to counter the likelihood of a serious aggregation of private power. Essential public goods should be understood not according to the mainstream theory of some non-excludable and non-rival nature, but according to the degree to which the good is socially necessary, such that users may be vulnerable to exploitation and when the good is highly utilized and even necessary "downstream," i.e., throughout the rest of the economy. Put another way, there are some goods and services that only some members of the public have access to, but basic social values of inequality and disparity are not magnified. There are others that have a strong negative social impact if access to them is not broadly shared, and those types of goods should receive special governmental intervention. A public option is simply the state stepping in to directly provide the good or service in order to widen access to it while providing a higher degree of competition in a marketplace.

Is the financial sector—and, in particular, investment activity, as distinct from banking—a public utility? Finance is "a critical service upon which the entire economy depends."[33] The results of private control can be seen in the inequitable access to wealth described above. Depository institutions, money creation, and credit creation are rightfully understood as public utilities. I argue here that investment markets should also be considered a public utility and subject to government interventions, described below, to ensure that this form of "social infrastructure" benefits the public. The issuance of stocks, bonds, and other financial instruments is critical to the development of "downstream" business. The ability to invest in, and benefit from, such assets is magnifying wealth inequality today, and the wealth requirements for accessing private investment opportunities in the first place only replicate the problems. Hockett demonstrates why finance is best understood as a public function. Credit creation is ultimately dependent on the power and resources of governments.[34] This power has been deployed to support the profitability of financial institutions.

Durable wealth creation in the hands of individuals, made possible by the distributed technologies of the twenty-first century, has the potential to structurally reduce the power of the financial sector. Crucial to the creation of a more democratic financial system is recognizing the structural inequities in our current distribution of wealth and designing a new financial system. Wealth creates a financial safety net, and creates opportunity through intergenerational transfers of wealth, which fund further asset-accumulation activities. Investment funds also allow new businesses to grow and thrive. Wealth is important across the life cycle to fund education, down payments on a home, and a secure retirement. The government can provide public funds to rebalance opportunities for wealth with direct provisioning of capital, based on family net worth, and by creating a public intermediary to truly democratize access to investment opportunity.

Government plays a central role in the economy: facilitating public and social goods, creating the rules, and allocating credit to finance productive economic activity. Public policy has contributed to wealth creation and also to the unequal distribution of wealth. The bottom 20 percent of taxpayers receive almost no funds, because the policies are intended to promote asset building that requires some initial set of assets: homeownership, retirement savings, and access to higher education. On the other hand, the government creates access to wealth through intervention in the credit markets by offering incentives and guarantees. There is no similar program to intervene directly in access to the capital markets, i.e., not for some other asset appreciation purpose.

Public options in finance are well grounded in our history, as the government has created new products and procedures when pursuing a social goal. Housing finance is a useful example. Pre–Great Depression, housing finance was a private activity, with higher risks and barriers to obtain any kind of mortgage for borrowers. Once the government engaged directly in the mortgage market as a participant, the presence of the new government-sponsored enterprises set new terms for the "American mortgage" with its fixed rate and full amortization.[35] The government does not directly provide mortgages to consumers, but instead provides an upstream public option that takes advantage of the public ability to assume risk. Similarly, the government can create a platform for investment that does not directly replace national securities exchanges, but instead increases competition for use of household investment funds, both regulating and encouraging small businesses' securities offerings. The proposal elaborated below is complementary to the proposal for a "Fed citizen and resident wallet" proposed by Robert Hockett in this volume, which would effectively end private bank hegemony over transactional services, but would not institute the investment platform access described below.[36]

The public investment platform

New financial technologies allow for the direct connection of individual issuers of equity securities and investors (or in theory between any two counterparties in a financial transaction). The proposal for a public investment platform is to introduce a *public* intermediary that can compete with the intermediaries of the twenty-first century and provide a public option for investment participation for those currently locked out of capital markets—both households and small businesses. This will introduce more competition into the financial space and reduce the concentrated power of investment firms. Though private crowdfunding platforms themselves have been touted as democratizing entities, it is unlikely that platforms, at the scale that they are developing today, will reach the size necessary to provide a counterweight. A truly public platform, utilizing the government's unique ability to absorb risk and conduct economic transactions with economies of scale, should be established.

Public platforms would allow for the true vision of peer-to-peer platforms to be met by creating the capacity and rules for true engagement on both sides of a transaction without a profit-oriented intermediary. Some issuers and investors might pay a transaction fee in order to limit unproductive engagement, and to compensate the government for the due diligence that should be required. But the incentives will be completely different if the government is at the center of the platform rather than a private actor. The establishment of the platform and the index fund (discussed below) would perform a powerful regulatory function by setting a floor for the rate of return that the private sector would match.[37] Just as the US government created the "American mortgage," the public investment platform will create the new standard for index funds that the private asset management industry will emulate, lowering costs and setting a higher bar for transparency in the fee structures and rates of return.[38]

An important feature of the platforms would be screening: the platforms should establish appropriate levels of disclosure and reporting requirements, balancing the need for confidence in due diligence without placing impossibly high barriers to entry on small businesses.[39] The goal of public platforms is not that they take the place of the private exchanges or mutual funds that aggregate wealth, but that they serve as a public option for small investors who currently do not have the opportunity to invest except in the large public companies. Crowdfunding, in theory, gives small, local businesses a way to connect with small, local investors, but to date the platforms focus on start-ups and are too dispersed for a household investor to find or utilize as their main source of building wealth. By creating a public crowdfunding portal,[40] small investors do not have to worry about verifying the platform's accuracy or worry about the fees that it charges.

Households would be able to participate on the platform using their public investment account (discussed below) and an additional percentage of their net wealth. The platform could offer several types of securities. The first would be an index fund of all publicly traded securities. In this way, households would have an option to participate in the public capital markets without paying steep fees to mutual funds or other fund aggregators. Since companies whose securities trade on the national stock exchanges are already subject to extensive disclosure requirements under the Securities Act of 1933 and the Securities Exchange Act of 1934, additional screening by the platform is not necessary. The fund would not engage in any active trading strategies but would be limited to holding a balanced portfolio of all equities publicly traded on US national exchanges. The function of the platform index fund is to create more competition in the market for index funds, and to allow the half of American households who currently hold no stock to enter the securities markets. Because of the economies of scale, and the fact that no active trading strategy is required, costs for the Index Fund should be extremely low, as management is largely administrative.

The second type of securities offered would be those of small issuers; in other words, the types of companies who do not have the resources or need to conduct public offerings, and who might turn to a crowdfunding platform. The platform should offer small-business workshops and training, similar to the Small Business Administration's offerings, to introduce small businesses to the benefits and costs of securities offerings. At the same time, the platform would regulate securities issuance by small companies by conducting due diligence to ensure that bad actors and companies inappropriate for offerings are kept out of the system. Not all small companies should offer securities, and not all those who want to conduct offerings are appropriate risks for household investors. The role of the platform staff would be to increase demand through awareness and training, while at the same time limiting supply by conducting due diligence before companies are allowed onto the platform.

The third type of securities will be a new "small-issuer index fund." The public investment platform should create a diversified mechanism for small investors to purchase equity from all small businesses accredited to sell equity on the platform. Investors should be able to purchase equity directly for particular businesses if they choose to invest in their local community or in a particular sector (described above), but these will necessarily be risky investments, as any single business has a higher risk of low performance than a diversified bundle of equity. Therefore, the creation of an index fund for all small businesses on the platform will allow for investors to focus their capital on small and medium-sized enterprises while remaining diversified. The platform would need to devote resources to the creation of the index fund, but given that there is already a screening process in place for small issuers to offer equity on the platform, the standard for inclusion in the index fund is straightforward. It is crucial for both index funds to be established to create the option for public investment account funds to flow to small businesses without placing undue risk on those who choose not to invest solely in publicly traded companies.

The platform should be open to all households: they should be able to use a small portion of their wealth to invest on the platform.[41] But the platform will not on its own enable access to households who do not have any wealth to invest. In order to truly democratize access to private wealth appreciation, the platform must be paired with a public investment account.

The public investment account

The government should provide every American with a local investment account to be used on the public investment platform upon reaching the age of eighteen. The starting sum should be different depending on the net wealth of the person's family, with a very small grant for individuals with significant family wealth and an exponential increase in the grant moving down the wealth ladder. This proposal is inspired by Darrick Hamilton and William "Sandy" Darity's proposal for "baby bonds" to address the racial wealth gap.[42] Most wealth is transferred through intergenerational and interfamily transfers, and since African Americans have been kept from wealth accumulation by de jure and de facto racist economic conditions, race-blind "universal" wealth-creation policies simply replicate historical conditions. Policies that simply "incentivize" savings are incorrect, because African Americans do save at the same level as white Americans once income is taken into account.[43] Targeted universalist policies, like baby bonds that are allocated to children at birth, which can be used at age eighteen to pay for asset building and vary in amount based on the net wealth of the family, take steps to close the racial wealth gap. This chapter follows their mandate and proposes a policy of targeted universalistic public investment accounts intended to address the racial wealth gap in the same manner.

First, a disclaimer. It is critical that such investment accounts not replace public funds that are allocated for societal needs. In other words, the aim here is definitively not to privatize Social Security and turn it into a private account. The aim is also not to displace the baby bonds account, which is a sum of money to be used for other asset-building activities. This sum is an additional set of funds that should be made available to adults based on family net worth. The public investment account builds upon the baby bonds proposal but differs in two important ways. Like the baby bonds proposal, the sum of capital granted to an individual should be based on their access to family wealth in order to address the denial of economic justice to people of color over generations, starting with chattel slavery, and to redress the stratospheric gains in wealth by a small minority of the population in recent decades.

The account should be available for use only on the public investment platform. There should be no way to withdraw the starting grant until the age of retirement.[44] However, yearly dividends would be paid, increasing the wealth earnings of low-income families, who would freely be able to use the earnings. Individuals can choose whether to simply invest in the index funds, receiving yearly dividends and asset appreciation over time, or to invest in the small businesses conducting offerings on the platforms, or to mix the two. Individuals will need basic financial and investment education in order to be able to make effective decisions. But the importance of the initial grant is recognized in the fact that the key to building wealth is not motivating savings but intergenerational wealth transmission.

A critical consideration is the level and method of initial funding for each account. There have been numerous proposals for public grants of money to households in a wide range of dollar figures. Determining the right starting sum for different tranches of households by wealth would be one of the first major operational design issues. Policymakers should also consider reparations for historical injustices, such as chattel slavery, that directly contribute to wealth inequalities, though such policies may be best instituted separately from this proposal. In terms of funding, there are multiple ways to fund such a proposal that would in and of themselves be useful for the productive economy. One mechanism is more equitable taxation of labor and capital, and financial taxation.[45] Adequate capital and financial taxation could raise hundreds of billions of dollars annually. Another approach draws from modern monetary theory, which claims that sources of funding should not be a limit for social needs. Developing a funding mechanism should be the subject of future research.

Limits of the public investment platform and public investment account

Both the public investment platform and public investment account raise important challenges as well as a range of implementation questions that are part of the rule-making process of any significant policy reform. Here, I focus on the top-level challenges, leaving for further discussion the multiple implementation questions, though no fine line can be drawn cleanly between the two. The first challenge is that the focus is on investment in small businesses through a platform, when small-business investment is a relatively untried form of equity investment. The policy mitigates the unknowns by also offering a publicly run index fund, which comprises traditional corporate equity (which index and how it should be constructed is one of the details that should be dealt with in a rule-making process). Since one of the goals of the policy is to increase small-business access to investment funds, it is unavoidable that a risk is small-business closure or lackluster returns. One of the constant risks of investment is that the business fails and the equity is worthless. A related risk is reliance on the crowdfunding platforms themselves to ensure that the businesses that are offering equity have a reasonable chance of being successful; in other words, that only less economically viable businesses seek to make use of the platform.

Important critiques of the public investment account include that the funds might be better spent, and that placing limits on withdrawal from the accounts undermines the autonomy of non-wealthy households to make their own decisions about their wealth assets. Additionally, technical assistance or access to computer technology would be required to ensure that all households have access to the tools necessary to use their accounts. Another concern is whether thresholds should be constructed such that additional resources are granted to families that have lower net worth, but how many tiers to set up, and how exactly to structure the thresholds, remain crucial considerations. Finally, there are critical issues to consider about how more widespread equity holding should influence corporate governance in order to ensure that such a proposal does not inadvertently strengthen the flawed business ideology of shareholder primacy.

Conclusion

If the public creates the ability of private financial entities to earn profit, the public can create new mechanisms to allow all citizens to partake in such profit.[46] America has a vigorous market for debt and equity securities, but access is highly unequal and contributes to generational racial and class stratification. The public investment platform rebalances the power of large financial institutions to capture the gains from investment and lending activity by creating a public option for people's participation in financial markets. The creation of a public investment account structurally rebalances wealth access that is due to historical wrongs. By reducing our collective dependence on Wall Street institutions over time, the political process will also become increasingly independent of the financial system's power, creating the potential for other deep reforms in our political economy.

The proposals here are meant not to exhaustively develop all operational factors but to motivate consideration of structural reforms that would break the cycle of intergenerational wealth transfer and its attendant political consequences. The

Democratizing Investment

financial system of the mid-twenty-first century will evolve to a more disintermediated network, but unless action is taken the power dynamics within the new framework will follow the power dynamics of today's financial system. Public intervention is required to truly democratize finance.

Concluding Observations

Fred Block

I want to thank all of the contributors to this volume for a constructive and collegial conversation. Debates about finance frequently degenerate into sectarian polemics, and it is critically important to recognize that no person, no approach, no school of thought has a monopoly on wisdom.

My concluding remarks focus on two interconnected issues. The first is the problem of implementation. How might it be possible to assemble a strong enough coalition in support of major reforms that can overcome the inevitable resistance of powerful financial interests? The second is the importance of decentralization in the design of a more democratic financial system.

Implementation

David Woodruff's comment makes several telling points. I agree with his first point that any initiative toward democratizing the financial system must include an explicit reversal of policies that have granted central banks independence from political oversight. Those policies institutionalize the fraudulent claim that the policy choices made by central bankers are somehow purely technical or have nothing to do with politics. The reality is that decisions about how quickly or slowly to expand the supply of

Concluding Observations

money and credit or which institutions to rescue in a crisis have significant consequences for the relative position of borrowers and lenders, employees and employers, and are intensely political. Woodruff is correct that a project of financial reform needs to directly challenge the claim that central bank policies occur outside politics and distributional struggles.

His second point is that any project of financial democratization must contend with the everyday libertarianism that has become widespread in the United States and in other developed nations. A similar point has been made by Margaret Somers, who emphasizes that demands for redistribution of income and wealth are frustrated when opponents resort to market justice—the idea that the way that the market distributes income is fundamentally just.[1] Somers's strategy for challenging claims of market justice is to emphasize the reality of predistribution—that how the market distributes income is already shaped by legal rules and institutional arrangements that enhance the power of certain actors. So, for example, lax enforcement of antitrust measures means that the market distribution of income has been distorted by the exercise of monopoly power and the extraction of monopoly rents.[2]

To be sure, "Down with Unfair Predistribution" is unlikely to be successful as a bumper sticker. But what kinds of mobilizing strategies and rhetoric might make it possible to challenge everyday libertarianism and market justice? When socialist movements first emerged in the last decades of the nineteenth century, they confronted a similar problem because then, as well, the unequal distribution of income and wealth was justified as a natural result of market processes. Marx's account of the creation of surplus value, explained and amplified by many thousands of trade union and socialist agitators, played a critical role in politicizing the distribution of income.

Today, however, the multiplicity of mechanisms through which income is directed toward the 1 percent makes references to surplus value problematic. Mark Zuckerberg's vast fortune, for example, comes not from exploiting the surplus labor of Facebook workers but by using advertising to monetize the leisure activity of hundreds of millions of Facebook users.

A more promising strategy for today might be to insist that an intensification of exploitation and injustice is a result of changes in the economy, most particularly the declining importance of classical commodities.[3] The classical commodities are things that are standardized, available from multiple sources, transferred in one moment in time, and not dependent on any other specific purchases. But purchases of financial services, health services, housing, communication and internet services, and even many manufactured goods no longer fit this model. The things we buy are increasingly customized, available from only a few producers, transferred over long periods of time, and reliant on interoperability with other goods and services.

All of these changes reduce the ability of the consumer to take business elsewhere. Sometimes, there is no elsewhere; only one firm provides a particular good or service in a given geographical area. At other times, one might switch providers, but carrying out a switch would be costly in dollars or in time. In other cases, a switch from one provider to another is unlikely to make a difference because practices that are annoying or harmful to consumers have become an industry standard.

The consequence is that power has accumulated in the hands of firms, so they have less reason to be responsive to customers' needs, whether in pricing or in the quality of the services they provide. This problem is particularly acute in the realm of financial services, where many sectors are dominated by a small number of giant firms. When one adds to the picture that the existence of these giant firms has been supported by government actions, it becomes clear that their profits have nothing to do with market justice and everything to do with raw power.

In fact, tollbooths represent the best metaphor for understanding contemporary markets. Actual tollbooths are fast disappearing, but in the past, there were tollbooths on certain highways every ten or twenty miles and drivers would have to pay a quarter to continue onward. Today, we confront a series of transactional tollbooths. We wake up and take medications, and pay a toll to the pharmaceutical industry. If we are lucky, it might just be a few dollars, but some drugs now cost $1,000 a dose. We turn on the computer and log on to the internet, and we then might pay a toll to Microsoft, to Google, to Amazon, or to Facebook. When we put funds into a pension plan or pay for insurance, we pay a toll to one or another financial entity. While some of these tolls might only be a penny, they add up for the corporate entities because one cent on each of a trillion transactions is worth $10 billion.

Nevertheless, an effective attack on everyday libertarianism and theories of market justice requires more than powerful metaphors and a good rhetorical strategy; it also requires sustained organization and agitation. This is precisely why my proposal for financial reform emphasizes the building of locally based, democratically organized institutions such as credit unions and community banks. In the same way that trade unions have often been able to help their members recognize the distortions of market justice, so these new or revived financial entities would help their members to see more clearly the ways in which the existing financial institutions have been organized to funnel money into the hands of a small elite.

The transition from the present reality of extreme inequalities of income, wealth, and political power to major egalitarian reforms of the political and economic systems is not going to happen overnight or even in four or eight years. It is likely to be a project that takes a generation or even longer. The best historical analogy is that most socialist parties in Europe were still very small in 1880; it took a generation of organizing and institution building for those parties to begin contesting for power by the time of World War I.

In short, I see the task of fundamental financial reform as a protracted process that needs to harness the energy of millions of people to build alternative financial institutions and to gain the expertise required to think through how capital should be allocated to different purposes. Such a process would depend on a number of legislative victories that would help to accelerate the process of expanding these alternative institutions and contracting the role of for-profit financial institutions.

In his chapter, Michael McCarthy argues that nationalization of banks would be more likely to be effective as a strategy for bold financial reform. His view is that if there were an extended period of competition between existing banks and alternative nonprofit financial institutions, the private banks would use their considerable power in the political system to crush the upstarts. Moreover, if a left movement were in a position to win the first legislative victories required for my program to get off the ground, bankers and their allies would likely use all of the tools at their disposal, including capital flight and capital strike, to defeat the initiative. For these reasons, nationalization is much more likely to be successful. When the left has an appropriate opening, it would disarm its financial opponents with one bold stroke that would deprive them of the capacity to resist.

I disagree with McCarthy's assessment for several reasons. First, the process of winning the first set of legislative victories that would create space for the alternative financial institutions to grow assumes a broad political coalition that includes many small businesses, civic leaders, and even some medium-sized and large firms that would benefit from greatly increased investments in infrastructure. With the business community seriously divided, it is unlikely that financial interests would escalate the conflict; they are far more likely to retreat and hope that they will be able to blunt or block the reforms at a later moment. Playing the "long game" has always been a preferred strategy of business interests since they recognize that populist upsurges usually burn out after a few years.

Second, I am assuming that the need for new sources of financing is so great that these alternative institutions would flourish, expand, and gather increasing political support. With that support, they would be more difficult to kill even in periods when the conservative party had regained political control. Even in the US, programs that develop a strong political base have successfully survived numerous efforts to zero them out in presidential budgets.[4]

Third, as these alternative institutions grew, so also would an economy that was not based on profit maximization and that was far more responsive to public needs than the current system. This is the process of eroding capitalism that Erik Olin Wright had in mind. The contrast with McCarthy's vision of a sudden nationalization of banks could not be sharper. The newly nationalized banks would not start out with a wide network of projects to which they could allocate capital. Moreover, they would be staffed with people who had learned banking under the for-profit rules. Even when they were told that they need to use entirely different criteria in making loan decisions, they would likely fall back on the rules that they knew.

In short, nationalization as a strategy assumes that a new socialist economy can be built fairly quickly, so the left party would be in a strong position to win in the next election. But this seems as unrealistic as the old dreams of a revolutionary transformation that would happen from one day to the next. Given the complexity of contemporary economies, it seems far more realistic to imagine the transition occurring only after enough noncapitalist infrastructure was in place so that most people would be effectively protected from a chaotic transition.[5]

Centralization

I have another objection to McCarthy's proposal for bank nationalization that also applies to Robert Hockett's proposal for a National Reconstruction and Development Council to oversee the financial system.[6] Pretty much everybody recognizes that a more democratic financial system requires some kind of mix of centralization and decentralization. Centralization is indispensable because the role of validating credit creation and serving as a lender of last resort has to be exercised by a central authority. Moreover, the central government's control over fiscal and monetary policies has to be mobilized if any broad process of financial reform is to be successful. At the same time, it is recognized that significant decentralization in the allocation of credit is important because those decisions require knowledge of local conditions.

However, there are significant differences as to what the optimal mix of centralization and decentralization might look like. Some are comfortable with a high degree of centralized control, while others prefer a greater emphasis on decentralization with central authorities playing more of a role in coordinating information flows and preventing either too rapid or too slow expansions of credit. In terms of maximizing efficiency in the allocation of capital, strong arguments can be made by both those who prefer centralization and those who prefer decentralization.

But from the point of view of politics, there is a clear danger in centralization. The more leeway central authorities have to decide which projects and which enterprises deserve access to credit at favorable rates, the more power will be vested in their hands. Moreover, this is the kind of technocratic power that is difficult to control through democratic mechanisms. As William Simon emphasizes in his chapter, all those democratic mechanisms have their limitations.

In short, I think both McCarthy and Hockett are not sufficiently attentive to the danger that centralized financial power could ultimately subvert the project of democratizing finance. Whether through nationalizing giant banks or through a National Reconstruction and Development Council, the danger is that a small number of institutions will exert disproportionate control over the flows of capital in the economy.

To be sure, McCarthy understands the limitations of representative democracy as a mechanism to organize a democratized financial system. He argues that there is a need to extend and expand democratic participation in financial decisions, and he suggests that "deliberative minipublics" might serve as a mechanism to assure that those making financial decisions are, in fact, held in check by the people they claim to be serving.

I share his emphasis on deepening democracy and experimenting with new participatory institutions.[7] However, it seems to me unwise to depend on new and unproven democratic innovations to guard against the familiar danger of centralized financial power. This is precisely why I emphasize decentralization in my proposal.

Concluding Observations

The goal is to allow people in towns, cities, and subnational regions to exert as much control as possible over the processes of social and economic development. To be sure, central authorities need to set various standards that protect minorities, the environment, and a broad set of democratic rights. But within those constraints, many of the decisions about the allocation of capital should ultimately be made from the bottom up by citizens engaged in democratic deliberation. Getting to this goal will take time, but it will never happen if most financial decisions continue to be made in centralized institutions.

In short, I conceptualize socialism as a radically democratic society in which democratic decision-making extends to such key economic issues as what should be produced, how employees should be treated, and what levels of equality or inequality will be allowed. Achieving this goal requires that ordinary citizens develop more understanding of economic issues and a greater capacity both to formulate preferences and to be effective political actors.

In recent years, we have seen that institutional changes, including changes in property relations, carried out by state socialist regimes have been reversed in very rapid transitions. Similarly, some of the important egalitarian reforms instituted by social democratic governments have been effectively stripped away by neoliberal politicians. And, of course, societies that had earlier established working democracies have recently experienced a precipitous decline into authoritarianism.

These reversals are a reminder that there are no guarantees; any progress toward greater equality and greater democracy is at risk of being reversed. The best hope for avoiding such reversals is a population that understands the urgency of protecting democratic and egalitarian institutions and that also has the political skills to defeat the opponents of equality and democracy. For this reason, I see a decentralized project of radical financial reform as an indispensable element of socialist strategy.

Notes

Introduction

1. On contentious financial politics in the US, see Julia C. Ott, *When Wall Street Met Main Street* (Cambridge, MA: Harvard University Press, 2011); Christopher W. Shaw, *Money, Power and the People* (Chicago: University of Chicago Press, 2019). See also the chapter by Sarah Quinn, Mark Igra, and Selen Güler in this volume.
2. Fred Block, *The Origins of International Economic Disorder* (Berkeley: University of California Press, 1977).
3. Greta Krippner, *Capitalizing on Crisis* (Cambridge, MA: Harvard University Press, 2011).
4. Barry Eichengreen, *Hall of Mirrors* (New York: Oxford University Press, 2015); Adam Tooze, *Crashed* (New York: Viking, 2018).
5. As Robert Hockett indicates in his chapter, participants in the financial markets have need of safe assets as a foundation for new credit creation. When the US federal deficit declined in the second Clinton administration, collateralized mortgage obligations filled the gap. But some of these mortgage-based bonds turned out to be far riskier than sovereign debt.
6. Efraim Benmelech, "An Empirical Analysis of the Fed's Term Auction Facility," NBER Working Paper No. 18304 (August 2012), nber.org.
7. Andreas Schrimpf, Hyun Song Shin, and Vladyslav Sushko, "Leverage and Margin Spirals in Fixed Income Markets during the COVID-19 Crisis," Bank for International Settlement Bulletin No. 2, April 2, 2020, bis.org.
8. OECD, "Corporate Debt Continues to Pile Up," February 18, 2020, oecd.org.
9. Neil Bhutta, Andrew C. Chang, Lisa J. Dettling, Joanne W. Hsu, and Julia Hewitt, "Disparities in Wealth by Race and Ethnicity in

the 2019 Survey of Consumer Finance," September 28, 2020, federalreserve.gov. See also Lenore Palladino's chapter in this volume.
10. For the history of these disparities, see Mehrsa Baradaran, *The Color of Money* (Cambridge, MA: Harvard University Press, 2017); Keeanga-Yamahtta Taylor, *Race for Profit* (Chapel Hill: University of North Carolina Press, 2019).
11. The best resource on these efforts is the Public Banking Institute.
12. This effort is being led by the Campaign for Postal Banking.
13. For an assessment of Wright's intellectual trajectory and legacy, see the December 2020 issue of *Politics & Society*.
14. Thomas Piketty, *Capital in the Twenty-First Century*, trans. Arthur Goldhammer (Cambridge, MA: Harvard University Press, 2014).
15. A future Real Utopias workshop plans to address this topic. See Isabelle Ferreras, *Firms as Political Entities*, trans. Miranda Richmond Mouillot (New York: Cambridge University Press, 2017).
16. Hockett is certainly not alone in making this argument. It is widely embraced by post-Keynesians and proponents of modern monetary theory. See L. Randall Wray, *Modern Monetary Theory* (New York: Palgrave Macmillan, 2012). Woodruff (in this volume) shows that at times even central bankers come close to acknowledging this reality.
17. Sarah Quinn, *American Bonds: How Credit Markets Shaped a Nation* (Princeton, NJ: Princeton University Press, 2019).

1 Finance without Financiers

1. John Maynard Keynes, *The General Theory of Employment, Interest, and Money* (New York: Harcourt, Brace, 1936), Chapter 24.
2. Thanks to Dan Alpert, Sarah Bloom Raskin, Rana Foroohar, Stephany Griffith-Jones, Michael Kumhof, Paul McCulley, Saule Omarova, Katharina Pistor, and Pavlina Tcherneva. Special thanks to Fred Block and Erik Wright, who have been part of this project since its inception in 2014—as well as to Sam Bowles, Philippe Van Parijs, John Roemer, Hillel Steiner, and others in the September Group, where it proved necessary that same year to formulate arguments whose full elaboration was issued in the first draft of this chapter in 2015. It's been a long road, and worth every inch.
3. Investment banks in the US facilitate transactions between others (brokering), buy and sell investment securities on their own account (dealing), and extend credit to favored clients (underwriting).
4. The Frank Capra allusion is to *It's a Wonderful Life* (1946), the bank-run scene from which is iconic.
5. The resources that one acquires or puts to use with borrowed

funds have, of course, been pre-accumulated. But borrowed funds, which are claims on such resources, need not be pre-accumulated at all. They are generated the moment when spendable credit is extended.

6. More background history can be found in Robert Hockett, "Rousseauvian Money," Cornell Legal Studies Research Paper Series No. 18–48 (2018), papers.ssrn.com.
7. Hyman Minsky once quipped that anyone can issue a currency, the trick being to get it accepted. This, we shall see, is the function of bank lending.
8. See Robert Hockett, "A Fixer-Upper for Finance," *Washington University Law Review* 87 (2010): 1213.
9. I believe it has now become intolerable. See Robert Hockett, "The Capital Commons," *Review of Banking and Financial Law* 39 (2019–20): 345.
10. See again Hockett, "Rousseauvian Money."
11. For example, Fannie Mae or Freddie Mac instruments.
12. There is reason to be skeptical of many such claims. See Robert Hockett and Roy Kreitner, "Just Prices," *Cornell Journal of Law and Public Policy* 27 (2018): 101.
13. Knut Wicksell, originator of the doctrine of "loanable funds," recognized the role played by bank-generated credit money in determining the money supply. Keynes and some of Wicksell's "Austrian" and "Stockholm school" followers never forgot this. Others, alas, did. See Knut Wicksell, *Geldzins und Güterpreise* (Jena: G. Fischer, 1898). Among the non-forgetters, see, e.g., Joseph Schumpeter, *Theorie der wirtschaftlichen Entwicklung* (Leipzig: Verlag von Dunker & Humblot, 1911); John Maynard Keynes, *A Treatise on Money* (London: Macmillan, 1930); Bertil Ohlin, "Notes on the Stockholm Theory of Saving and Investment," *Economic Journal* 47 (1937): 53. Among the forgetters, the most egregious is the author of a widely used textbook. See Gregory Mankiw, *Macroeconomics* (New York: Worth, 2013), 68.
14. For an overview of how the Federal Reserve System maintains interbank lending rates and administers the US payments system, see, e.g., Board of Governors of the Federal Reserve System, *The Federal Reserve System: Purposes and Functions* (Washington, DC: Federal Reserve, 2005).
15. Our present system enabling the decoupling of profitability from productivity constitutes a fly in the ointment here, to which I'll return.
16. This, incidentally, is why the nation's first bank regulator, established with the system of federally chartered banks during the 1860s, is called "the Comptroller of the Currency." See Robert Hockett, "Money's Past Is Fintech's Future: Wildcat Crypto, the

Digital Dollar, and Citizen Central Banking," *Stanford Journal of Blockchain Law and Policy* 2 (2019): 1; also Hockett, "The Capital Commons."

17. By convention, "money markets" are markets in instruments with maturities of one year or less; "capital markets" are markets in instruments with maturities greater than one year.

18. "Base money," also known as the "high-powered money," is conventionally defined as currency and bank reserves. See, e.g., Philip Cagan, "High-Powered Money," NBER Paper No. 1642 (1965), nber.org.

19. See, e.g., SIFMA, statistics page, September 4, 2015, sifma.org. For counterpart global market measures, see, e.g., McKinsey & Company, "Mapping Global Capital Markets 2011," mckinsey.com.

20. While the "safe-asset share" is widely regarded as a cross-temporal constant, its actual *significance* must be considered with care—more care than space permits here. Presumably, it has something to do with how much risk market participants are willing to take absent some publicly provided or endorsed "safe haven" investment supplied in adequate quantity. An important complicating factor here is that, as repo markets ran out of bona fide Treasurys to serve as safe repo collateral in the run-up to 2008 (see below), pressure mounted on publicly sanctioned rating agencies to bestow "safe" status even on *endogenously issued private-label mortgage-related instruments*, which market participants then *treated* as "safe" but which turned out to be anything but. One lesson of 2008 seems to be that only public *issuances* are truly "safe" in the sense sought by traders.

21. The sole partial exception here is the proverbial one that proves the rule: the so-called Black CAPM, which is, tellingly, too unwieldy for financial practitioners to employ. See Fischer Black, Michael C. Jensen, and Myron Scholes, "The Capital Asset Pricing Model: Some Empirical Tests," in *Studies in the Theory of Capital Markets*, ed. Michael Jensen (New York: Praeger, 1972), 79.

22. See, e.g., Michael J. Fleming, "The Benchmark U.S. Treasury Market: Recent Performance and Possible Alternatives," *FRBNY Economic Policy Review*, April 2000, ny.frb.org. Also Jason Kestenbaum, "What If We Paid Off the Debt? The Secret Government Report," *NPR Planet Money*, October 20, 2011, npr.org.

23. See, e.g., Gary B. Gorton and Andrew Metrick, "Securitized Banking and the Run on Repo," NBER Working Paper No. 15223 (August 2009), nber.org.

24. The term was coined by the author's close friend and colleague Paul McCulley, then of PIMCO, at the Fed's annual Jackson Hole conference in 2007. See Paul McCulley, "Teton Reflections," *Global*

Central Bank Focus (PIMCO), September 1, 2007, easysite.common wealth.com, 2.

25. M2 includes the cash and checking deposits that constitute M1, along with "near monies," including savings deposits, time deposits, and money market mutual funds (MMMFs), as discussed further below.

26. See, e.g., Tracy Alloway and Michael MacKenzie, "New York Federal Reserve Takes on Key Role in Repo Market," *Financial Times*, June 19, 2014.

27. Ibid. See also Gary Gorton, *Slapped by the Invisible Hand: The Panic of 2007* (New York: Oxford University Press, 2010).

28. See Section I on Fed bank loan accommodation as a function of the payment-clearing imperative.

29. See Federal Reserve Bank of New York, "Tri-party Repo Infrastructure Reform," newyorkfed.org.

30. Derivatives are contingent claim contracts that confer payouts or other rights in response to changes in a contractually referenced value, typically called "the underlying." There are in general as many kinds of derivative contracts as there are contingencies on which financial market participants see fit to "bet." A widely used basic text, on which the author relied during graduate school, is John C. Hull, *Options, Futures, and Other Derivatives*, 9th ed. (New York: Pearson, 2014).

31. See 12 U.S.C. § 372. Also Federal Reserve Collateral Guidelines, June 3, 2014, 3.

32. In July 2014, the SEC adopted final rules requiring prime institutional MMMFs to use floating net asset value (NAV) for their shares. See 17 C.F.R. § 270.2a-7; US Securities and Exchange Commission, "Money Market Fund Reform: Amendments to Form PF," 79 F.R. 47736 (August 14, 2014).

33. See Binyamin Appelbaum, "The Fed's Policy Mechanics Retool for a Rise in Interest Rates," *New York Times*, September 12, 2015.

34. See, e.g., Hockett, "A Fixer-Upper for Finance."

35. See, e.g., Robert Hockett, "The Macroprudential Turn: From Institutional 'Safety and Soundness' to Systemic 'Financial Stability' in Financial Supervision," *Virginia Law and Business Review* 9 (2014): 201; Robert Hockett, "Practical Guidance on Macroprudential Finance-Regulatory Reform," *Harvard Law School Forum on Corporate Governance and Financial Regulation*, Nov. 22, 2013.

36. See Robert Hockett, "Recursive Collective Action Problems: The Structure of Procyclicality in Financial and Money Markets, Macro-economies, and Formally Similar Contexts," *Journal of Financial Perspectives* 3 (2015): 37.

37. See Robert C. Hockett, "Systemically Significant Prices," *Journal of*

Financial Regulation 2 (2016): 1; also Hockett and Kreitner, "Just Prices."

38. See generally Robert C. Hockett, *Financing the Green New Deal: A Plan of Action and Renewal* (New York: Palgrave Economics, 2020).
39. It also bears some similarity to the Board of National Investments proposed by Keynes in Liberal Industrial Inquiry, *Britain's Industrial Future* (London: E. Benn Limited, 1928).
40. For full elaboration, see Robert Hockett, "An FSOC for Continuous Public Investment: The National Reconstruction and Development Council," *Michigan Business and Entrepreneurial Law Review* 10, no. 1 (2021): 45–66.
41. Ibid. See also Liberal Industrial Inquiry, *Britain's Industrial Future*.
42. TDF is a federal venture capital fund created in 1996 for financing small businesses developing telecommunications technologies. See 47 U.S.C. 614 (2015).
43. The SBA was established in 1953 to facilitate small business formation and growth via the "three Cs" of capital, contracting, and counseling. See "About the SBA," US Small Business Administration, sba.gov.
44. See Robert Hockett, "Spread the Fed: Distributed Central Banking in Pandemic and Beyond," *Virginia Law and Business Review* (forthcoming); Robert Hockett, "The Fed Is a Development Bank—Make It *Our* Development Bank," *Forbes*, September 30, 2020, forbes.com; and Robert Hockett, "Spread the Fed," *Forbes*, May 17, 2020, forbes.com.
45. This is the method employed in Hockett, "The Capital Commons." See also Robert C. Hockett, "White Paper: The Capital Commons: A Plan for 'Building Back Better' and Beyond" (2020), papers.ssrn.com.
46. See again Hockett, "Spread the Fed."
47. Ibid.
48. Another tragically forgotten bit of Fed—and hence our republic's—financial history. And an ironic one at that, given the near obsession with discounting commercial paper as the right way to central-bank on the part of Paul Warburg, the most influential Fed founder. See the brilliant Paul M. Warburg, *The Discount System in Europe* (Washington, DC: GPO, 1910).
49. Hockett, "Spread the Fed." See also Robert Hockett, "Spreading the Fed: From Federal Disintegration through Community QE to Decentralized Central Banking—Part II, Law and Political Economy," August 12, 2020, lpeproject.org; and Robert Hockett, "Spreading the Fed: From Federal Disintegration through Community QE to Decentralized Central Banking—Part I, Law and Political Economy," August 11, 2020, lpeproject.org.

50. Hockett, "Spreading the Fed, Part I"; Hockett, "Spreading the Fed, Part II."
51. Ibid.
52. Ibid.
53. Ibid.
54. Ibid.
55. See Hockett, "The Capital Commons."
56. Ibid.
57. Hockett, "The Capital Commons"; Hockett, "White Paper: The Capital Commons." See also Robert Hockett, "Digital Greenbacks: A Sequenced 'Treasury Direct' and 'Fed Wallet' Plan for the Democratic Digital Dollar," *Journal of Technology Law and Policy* 25, no. 1 (2021); and Robert Hockett, "The Democratic Digital Dollar: A Peer-to-Peer-Savings and Payments Platform for Fully Inclusive State, Local, and National Money and Banking Systems," *Harvard Business Law Review* 10 (2020): 1.
58. Ibid.
59. See Robert Hockett, "Chaka's Windows: Works and Days in the Life of a 'Homeless Entrepreneur'" (2019) (book manuscript, on file with the author).
60. Hockett, "The Capital Commons."
61. Ibid.
62. See, e.g., Robert Hockett, "Open Labor Market Operations," *Challenge* 62 (2019): 33, papers.ssrn.com; and Robert Hockett, "How to Make QE More Helpful—By Fed Shorting of Commodities," *Benzinga*, October 14, 2011, benzinga.com.
63. Hockett, "The Capital Commons."
64. Ibid.
65. See again Hockett, "Money's Past Is Fintech's Future." Also Robert Hockett, "Facebook's Proposed Crypto-Currency—More Pisces Than Libra for Now," *Forbes*, June 20, 2019, forbes.com.
66. Hockett, "The Capital Commons."
67. Ibid.
68. Ibid.
69. Fuller elaboration is available in Hockett, "The Capital Commons."
70. Ibid.
71. Ibid.
72. Ibid. "The business of banking" is a term of art in financial regulatory parlance, connoting those features of a firm's business model that subject it to banking regulatory jurisdiction.
73. Hockett, "The Capital Commons."
74. Ibid.
75. Ibid.
76. Ibid.

77. See Robert Hockett, "The People's Portfolio" (2018) (working paper, on file with the author).
78. Ibid.

2 Financial Democratization and the Transition to Socialism

1. This article has benefited from comments by many colleagues on previous drafts and earlier papers. These include Karl Beitel, Matthew R. Keller, Lucas Kirkpatrick, Jan Kregel, Greta Krippner, Margaret Somers, and Claus Thomasberger. I am also grateful to Robert C. Hockett for his important essay in this volume. My late colleague Erik Olin Wright launched the Real Utopias Project, encouraged me to pursue this topic, and commented on many earlier drafts. However, the usual disclaimer applies: I am solely responsible for the remaining weaknesses in this work. The description of the context for reform relies on the US case, but the strategy could be applied in other developed market economies without major modifications.
2. This article continues lines of argument that I have been developing for some time. The most recent version was "Democratizing Finance," *Politics & Society* 42, no. 1 (2014): 3–28. See also Fred Block, "Capitalism without Class Power," *Politics & Society* 20, no. 3 (1992): 277–303; and Fred Block, *Revising State Theory* (Philadelphia: Temple University Press, 1987).
3. The definition of socialism used here is Polanyian—the subordination of the market to democratic politics. For elaboration, see Fred Block and Margaret Somers, *The Power of Market Fundamentalism* (Cambridge, MA: Harvard University Press, 2014).
4. As will be explained, the interest rate at which loans are available is a critical dimension of credit access.
5. Thomas Piketty, *Capital in the Twenty-First Century*, trans. Arthur Goldhammer (Cambridge, MA: Harvard University Press, 2014). See also Jacob Hacker and Paul Pierson, *Winner-Take-All Politics* (New York: Simon and Schuster, 2010).
6. For clarification of the different ways to democratize, see William H. Simon's essay in this volume, "Economic Democracy and Enterprise Form in Finance."
7. Lenore Palladino's essay in this volume, "Democratizing Investment," addresses this issue of creating a new kind of financial literacy.
8. See Sarah Quinn, *American Bonds: How Credit Markets Shaped a Nation* (Princeton, NJ: Princeton University Press, 2019). See also

Monica Prasad, *The Land of Too Much* (Cambridge, MA: Harvard University Press, 2012), 199–200.

9. See Fred Block, "Breaking with Market Fundamentalism: Toward Domestic and Global Reform," in *Globalization and Beyond*, ed. Jon Shefner and Patricia Fernandez-Kelly (University Park: Pennsylvania State University Press, 2011), 210–27. See also Block, "Democratizing Finance"; and Fred Block, *Capitalism: The Future of an Illusion* (Oakland: University of California Press, 2018).
10. Robert Skidelsky, *John Maynard Keynes*, vol. 3, *Fighting for Freedom, 1937–1946* (New York: Penguin, 2002).
11. Adam Tooze, *Crashed* (New York: Viking, 2018).
12. Yanis Varoufakis, *Adults in the Room* (New York: Farrar, Straus & Giroux, 2017).
13. Karl Polanyi, *The Great Transformation* (Boston: Beacon Press, 2001; first published 1944). See also Sheri Berman, *The Primacy of Politics* (New York: Cambridge University Press, 2006); and Stephanie Mudge, *Leftism Reinvented* (Cambridge, MA: Harvard University Press, 2018).
14. For valuable accounts of conflicts over the meaning of financial democracy in the United States, see Julia Ott, *When Wall Street Met Main Street* (Cambridge, MA: Harvard University Press, 2011); and Christopher Shaw, *Money, Power, and the People* (Chicago: University of Chicago Press, 2019).
15. One of the most important current movements in favor of radical financial reform has been the effort to create a universal currency independent of government through Bitcoin or similar initiatives. This effort has been closely tied to a libertarian ideology and is inherently a utopian project since viable currencies cannot exist without the backing of some kind of governmental entity. However, it is possible that the underlying technology of blockchain could be an element in a democratized financial system.
16. John Maynard Keynes, *The General Theory of Employment, Interest, and Money* (New York: Harcourt, Brace & World, 1964; first published 1936), 353–58.
17. Stamped money seems a plausible alternative to the negative interest rates that have become widespread in Europe and Japan in recent years.
18. In 1919 the Bavarian Soviet Republic enlisted Gesell to redesign the financial system, but the republic lasted less than a month. A slightly more durable link between the two traditions occurred when the Swedish Social Democrats embraced the Meidner Plan, which envisioned workers gaining ownership of the means of production through their pension savings. However, employer resistance ultimately defeated this initiative.

19. Erik Olin Wright, *Envisioning Real Utopias* (London: Verso, 2010). See also Erik Olin Wright, *How to Be an Anticapitalist in the Twenty-First Century* (London: Verso, 2019).
20. Wright, *Envisioning Real Utopias*.
21. General Motors' US employment peaked at over 600,000 in 1979. "A Brief History of General Motors Corp.," manufacturing.net. See also Alexis Madrigal, "Silicon Valley's Big Three vs. Detroit's Golden-Age Big Three," *The Atlantic*, May 24, 2017, theatlantic.com. The main exception to this general trend has been Walmart with its 2.3 million global employees, but it seems clear that there is a slot for only one retailer of this size. Most other large retailers in the United States have been closing stores and reducing employment. For a similar argument, see Herman Mark Schwartz, "Corporate Profit Strategies and U.S. Economic Stagnation," *American Affairs* (Fall 2010): 3–19.
22. Henry Chesbrough, Wim Vanhaverbeke, and Joel West, eds., *Open Innovation* (New York: Oxford University Press, 2006).
23. William Lazonick, *Sustainable Prosperity in the New Economy?* (Kalamazoo, MI: Upjohn, 2009). Some of this is explained by a shift away from the publicly traded corporation as exemplified by the rise of private equity deals that allow owners to escape various reporting requirements specific to publicly traded firms. See Gerald F. Davis, *The Vanishing American Corporation* (Oakland, CA: Berrett-Koehler, 2016).
24. The estimate is from the American Society of Civil Engineers, *2017 Infrastructure Report Card* (2019), infrastructurereportcard.org.
25. See James Gray-Donald et al., *Commercial Real Estate: Unlocking the Energy Efficiency Retrofit Investment Opportunity* (UN Environment Programme Finance Initiative, February 2014), buildup.eu.
26. The total dollar value of bank loans to small businesses in the United States dropped sharply in the 2008–9 economic downturn and has still not returned to the prerecession peak. The decline has been attributed to continuing consolidation in the banking industry. Congressional Research Service, *The Small Business Lending Fund*, April 12, 2019, everycrsreport.com; Karen Gordon Mills and Brayden McCarthy, "The State of Small Business Lending: Credit Access during the Recovery and How Technology May Change the Game," Harvard Business School General Management Unit Working Paper No. 15-004 (July 22, 2014), ssrn.com.
27. See, e.g., Matthew R. Keller and Fred Block, "Explaining the Transformation in the US Innovation System: The Impact of a Small Government Program," *Socio-Economic Review* 11, no. 4 (2013): 629–56.
28. Jacob Hacker, *The Great Risk Shift* (New York: Oxford University Press, 2006).

29. This is the place where microcredit lending can be extremely helpful provided that the loans are at low interest rates. The ability to borrow to cover a family emergency or to purchase equipment for a small business can make a huge difference for a household in poverty.
30. Michael S. Barr, *No Slack: The Financial Lives of Low-Income Americans* (Washington, DC: Brookings Institution, 2012); Lisa Servon, *The Unbanking of America* (New York: Houghton Mifflin Harcourt, 2017).
31. Joint Center for Housing Policy of Harvard University, *America's Rental Housing 2017* (December 14, 2017), jchs.harvard.edu. The problem is particularly acute on the East and West Coasts, but Matthew Desmond shows that even in older Midwestern cities, the lack of affordable housing creates extremes of deprivation for the poor. Matthew Desmond, *Evicted* (New York: Penguin, 2016).
32. Board of Governors of the Federal Reserve System, *Federal Reserve Supervision and Regulation Report*, Figure 8, federalreserve.gov.
33. Brian S. Chen, Samuel G. Hanson, and Jeremy C. Stein, "The Decline of Big-Bank Lending to Small Business: Dynamic Impacts on Local Credit and Labor Markets," NBER Working Paper No. 23843 (September 2017).
34. Hyman Minsky, *Stabilizing an Unstable Economy* (New Haven, CT: Yale University Press, 1986)
35. Polanyi, *The Great Transformation*; Block and Somers, *Market Fundamentalism*.
36. One incentive operates through executive compensation and portfolio growth. The larger the institution's portfolio, the easier it is to justify higher pay for top executives. The second incentive is the possibility of kickbacks through which executives get side payments in exchange for making otherwise unjustifiable loans.
37. Brett Christophers, *Banking across Boundaries* (Chichester: Wiley Blackwell, 2013).
38. Richard Deeg, *Finance Capitalism Unveiled* (Ann Arbor: University of Michigan Press, 1999).
39. Significant differences were analyzed in John Zysman, *Governments, Markets, and Growth: Financial Systems and the Politics of Institutional Change* (Ithaca, NY: Cornell University Press, 1983).
40. David M. Woodruff's chapter in this volume, "To Democratize Finance, Democratize Central Banking," argues that the proposal here is incomplete without also reversing the independence of central banks and subjecting them to greater democratic control. I agree with his point.
41. Quinn, *American Bonds*.

42. William H. Simon, *The Community Economic Development Movement* (Durham, NC: Duke University Press, 2001); Sacha Adorno, "Democratizing Finance: A Conversation with Cliff Rosenthal," Opportunity Finance Network (November 27, 2018), ofn.org.
43. Congressional Research Service, *Small Business Lending Fund*, everycrsreport.com.
44. Thomas Piketty, *Capital and Ideology*, trans. Arthur Goldhammer (Cambridge, MA: Harvard University Press, 2020).
45. Minsky, *Stabilizing an Unstable Economy*.
46. Paul Alan Gompers and Josh Lerner, *The Venture Capital Cycle*, 2nd ed. (Cambridge, MA: MIT Press, 2004).
47. Marc Schneiberg, "Toward an Organizationally Diverse American Capitalism?," *Seattle University Law Review* 34 (2011): 1409–34.
48. Deeg, *Finance Capitalism Unveiled*; Gilles L. Bourgue, Margie Mendell, and Ralph Rouzier, "Solidarity Finance: History of an Emerging Practice," in *Innovation and the Social Economy*, ed. M. J. Bouchard (Toronto: University of Toronto Press, 2013), 180–205.
49. The best source on the public banking movement is the Public Banking Institute, publicbankinginstitute.org.
50. Les Leopold, *The Looting of America* (White River Junction, VT: Chelsea Green, 2009).
51. B corporations, or benefit corporations, are incorporated under state statutes that allow them to prioritize interests beyond profitability. See Jane Collins, *The Politics of Value* (Chicago: University of Chicago Press, 2017), Chapter 3.
52. Wright, *Envisioning Real Utopias*, 311–18.
53. If the government allows the value of the currency to fall sharply, imports, including purchases of capital goods, become significantly more expensive, which will also reduce living standards and deepen the transition trough.
54. This is the definition offered by Polanyi, *The Great Transformation*, 242. See also Fred Block, "Karl Polanyi and Human Freedom," in *Karl Polanyi's Vision of a Socialist Transformation*, ed. Michael Brie and Claus Thomasberger (Montreal: Black Rose, 2018), 168–84.
55. Michael A. McCarthy's chapter in this volume disagrees with this assessment. However, business interests often respond to popular pressure by acquiescing in reforms that they assume can be withdrawn or neutralized when the pressure from mobilized groups dissipates, as it often does. In short, business interests often win by playing the long game. The hypothesis here is that they could be defeated by a social movement that also played the long game.

3 Economic Democracy and Enterprise Form in Finance

1. In this volume, Robert C. Hockett, "Finance without Financiers"; Fred Block, "Financial Democratization and the Transition to Socialism"; Michael A. McCarthy, "Three Modes of Democratic Participation in Finance"; and Lenore Palladino, "Democratizing Investment."
2. Claus Offe and Helmut Wiesenthal, "Two Logics of Collective Action," *Political Power and Social Theory* 1 (1980): 67–115.
3. Henry Hansmann, "When Does Worker Ownership Work? ESOPS, Law Firms, Codetermination, and Economic Democracy," *Yale Law Journal* 99 (1990): 1750–860.
4. See, e.g., Masahiko Aoki, *The Cooperative Game Theory of the Firm* (Oxford: Oxford University Press, 1984).
5. Jeffrey N. Gordon, "The Rise of Independent Directors in the United States, 1950–2005: Of Shareholder Value and Stock Market Prices," *Stanford Law Review* 59, no. 6 (2010): 1465–568.
6. See, e.g., Guy Debelle, "Central Bank Independence in Retrospect," speech at Bank of England "Independence: 20 Years On" conference, London, September 28, 2017, bis.org.
7. Nathan Jensen and Edmund Malesky, *Incentives to Pander: How Politicians Use Corporate Welfare for Political Gain* (Cambridge: Cambridge University Press, 2018).
8. A few states have adopted an innovation that allows "limited" outside equity interests in business corporations. James R. Baarda, "'Outside' Cooperative Equity: Obligations, Tradeoffs, and Fundamental Cooperative Character," conference presentation, NCERA-194 Research on Cooperatives, Annual Meeting, Kansas City, November 2–3, 2004, ageconsearch.umn.edu.
9. A variation on the patron-controlled enterprise form that can be found in some water districts and homeowners' associations distributes control (as well as the economic incidents of participation) in accordance with the value of a member's land or housing unit served by the organization. See Robert Ellickson, "Cities and Homeowner's Associations," *University of Pennsylvania Law Review* 130 (1983): 1519–80. Such arrangements minimize the danger of opportunistic redistribution but at the cost of seriously compromising the democratic character of the enterprise. Some argue that the sacrifice of democracy inhibits the solidarity necessary for effective collaboration.
10. Examples include the plywood cooperatives discussed in K. Berman, *Worker-Owned Plywood Companies: An Economic Analysis* (Pullman: Washington State University Press, 1967), 85–92, 93–98, and the garbage collection cooperatives discussed in R. Russell,

Sharing Ownership in the Workplace (Albany: State University of New York Press, 1985), 100. Sidney and Beatrice Webb argued that successful worker cooperatives would inevitably self-destruct either by selling themselves to outsiders or by bringing in new members as employees. Sidney Webb and Beatrice Webb, "Special Supplement on Co-operative Production and Profit-Sharing," *New Statesman*, February 14, 1914.

11. Henry Hansmann, "Condominium and Cooperative Housing: Transactional Efficiency, Tax Subsidies, and Tenure Choice," *Journal of Legal Studies* 20 (1991): 25–71.
12. *Federalist*, No. 10 (James Madison).
13. Charles M. Haar, *Mastering Boston Harbor: Courts, Dolphins, and Imperiled Waters* (Cambridge, MA: Harvard University Press, 2005), 170.
14. Robert Caro, *The Power Broker: Robert Moses and the Fall of New York* (New York: Knopf, 1974).
15. Technically, there are two types of nonprofits—"public benefit" or charitable nonprofits and "mutual benefit" nonprofits. The latter are more or less equivalent to cooperatives.
16. For a brief general account, see Charles F. Sabel and William H. Simon, "Democratic Experimentalism," in *Searching for Contemporary Legal Thought*, ed. Justin Dessaultels-Stein and Christopher Tomlines (Cambridge: Cambridge University Press, 2017), 477–98. For examples, see Charles F. Sabel and Jonathan Zeitlin, "Learning from Difference: The New Architecture of Experimentalist Governance in the EU," *European Law Journal* 14 (2008): 271–327; Kathleen Noonan, Charles F. Sabel, and William H. Simon, "Legal Accountability in the Service-Based Welfare State," *Law and Social Inquiry* 34 (2009): 523–68.
17. See, e.g., Robert J. Marder, *Effective Peer Review: The Complete Guide to Physician Performance Improvement*, 3rd ed. (Middleton, MA: HcPro, 2013).
18. The governing board of the Joint Commission on the Accreditation of Hospitals, for example, has, in addition to representatives of the American Hospital Association, representatives of the various medical practitioner associations, public members chosen by public officials, and independent members chosen for expertise in particular fields.
19. For an example of a regulatory structure that appears to have dealt with such problems effectively, see Christine Overdevest, "Comparing Forest Certification Schemes: The Example of Ratcheting Standards in the Forest Sector," *Socio-Economic Review* 8 (2010): 47–76.

4 To Democratize Finance, Democratize Central Banking

1. Georg Simmel, *Philosophie des Geldes* (Leipzig: Duncker & Humblot, 1907), Kindle edition; Georg Simmel, *The Philosophy of Money*, ed. David Frisby, trans. Tom Bottomore, David Frisby, and Kaethe Mengelberg, 2nd ed. (London: Routledge, 1990), 184, translation trivially modified.
2. The author thanks the participants of the 2018 Democratizing Finance conference in Madison, Wisconsin, and especially Fred Block, for their helpful comments. The usual disclaimer applies.
3. The notion of "everyday libertarianism" is drawn from Liam B. Murphy and Thomas Nagel, *The Myth of Ownership: Taxes and Justice* (Oxford: Oxford University Press, 2002).
4. Ronen Mandelkern, "Explaining the Striking Similarity in Macroeconomic Policy Responses to the Great Recession: The Institutional Power of Macroeconomic Governance," *Comparative Political Studies* 49, no. 2 (2016): 219–52; Adam Tooze, *Crashed: How a Decade of Financial Crises Changed the World* (London: Allen Lane, 2018).
5. See also Paul M. W. Tucker, *Unelected Power: The Quest for Legitimacy in Central Banking and the Regulatory State* (Princeton, NJ: Princeton University Press, 2018), 534–38.
6. Karl Polanyi, *The Great Transformation: The Political and Economic Origins of Our Time* (Boston: Beacon Press, 2001; first published 1944), 242; Fred Block, "Financial Democratization and the Transition to Socialism," in this volume.
7. Barbara Fried, *The Progressive Assault on Laissez Faire: Robert Hale and the First Law and Economics Movement* (Cambridge, MA: Harvard University Press, 1998).
8. John Rogers Commons, *Legal Foundations of Capitalism* (Madison: University of Wisconsin Press, 1957), 327. For Commons's stomach-turning racism, see John Rogers Commons, *Races and Immigrants in America* (New York: A. M. Kelley, 1907); and Abdallah Zouache, "Race, Competition, and Institutional Change in J. R. Commons," *European Journal of the History of Economic Thought* 24, no. 2 (2017): 341–68.
9. Commons, *Legal Foundations of Capitalism*, 260, 329; on money generally, see 250–61.
10. Ibid., 260.
11. Cf. Erik Olin Wright, "Introduction to the Real Utopias Project on Democratizing Finance," paper prepared for workshop on Democratizing Finance, University of Wisconsin, 2017.
12. In a counterfactual law academy where the critical legal studies movement had retained influence, for instance, Hockett's franchise

approach would likely have reacted to the legal realists whose work the movement sought to popularize.

13. Murphy and Nagel, *The Myth of Ownership*, 34–35. For an incisive survey of arguments against the idea that market incomes are deserved, see Tom Malleson, "Offending the One Percent: Seven Arguments against Distributive Desert," *New Political Science* 38, no. 2 (2016): 178–200.
14. Max Weber, "The Social Psychology of the World Religions," in *From Max Weber*, ed. H. H. Gerth and C. Wright Mills (New York: Oxford University Press, 1946), 271.
15. David M. Woodruff, "Ordoliberalism, Polanyi, and the Theodicy of Markets," in *Ordoliberalism, Law and the Rule of Economics*, ed. Christian Joerges and Josef Hien (Oxford: Hart, 2017), 215–28.
16. Polanyi, *The Great Transformation*, 266–67.
17. Brian Blackstone, "A Vote to Upend Banking as We Know It," *Wall Street Journal*, June 1, 2018; Nico Menzato and Andrea Willimann, "Joseph Huber: Erfinder der Vollgeld-Theorie im Interview," *Blick* (April 29, 2018), blick.ch.
18. Jonathan C. Lewis, "Microloan Sharks," *Stanford Social Innovation Review* 6, no. 3 (2008): 54–59.
19. Fred Block, "Financial Democratization and the Transition to Socialism," paper prepared for Democratizing Finance, a workshop held at the University of Wisconsin, July 2018, 56, ssc.wisc.edu.
20. Lawrence R. Jacobs and Desmond S. King, *Fed Power: How Finance Wins* (New York: Oxford University Press, 2016), 125–26.
21. Ezra Klein, "Could This Time Have Been Different?," *Washington Post*, October 8, 2011.
22. "Rick Santelli's Shout Heard 'Round the World," *CNBC*, February 19, 2009, cnbc.com.
23. Theda Skocpol and Vanessa Williamson, *The Tea Party and the Remaking of Republican Conservatism* (Oxford: Oxford University Press, 2012), 64–68.
24. Frank James, "Obama Confronts 'Tea Party' Santelli, His Accuser, Sort Of," *It's All Politics: Political News from NPR*, September 20, 2010, npr.org.
25. Christopher Adolph, "The Missing Politics of Central Banks," *PS: Political Science and Politics* 51, no. 4 (2018): 739. For the eurozone, see David M. Woodruff, "Governing by Panic: The Politics of the Eurozone Crisis," *Politics & Society* 44, no. 1 (2016): 81–116. On the general pattern, see Mandelkern, "Explaining the Striking Similarity in Macroeconomic Policy Responses."
26. Benjamin Braun, "Speaking to the People? Money, Trust, and Central Bank Legitimacy in the Age of Quantitative Easing," *Review of International Political Economy* 23, no. 6 (2016): 1073–77.

27. Michael McLeay and Amar Radia, "Money Creation in the Modern Economy," *Bank of England Quarterly Bulletin* Q1 (2014): 14–27.
28. Claudio Borio, "On Money, Debt, Trust and Central Banking," speech at the Cato Institute, November 15, 2018, bis.org.
29. Clement Fontan, "Frankfurt's Double Standard: The Politics of the European Central Bank during the Eurozone Crisis," *Cambridge Review of International Affairs* 31, no. 2 (2018): 175–76.
30. Benjamin Braun, "Central Banking and the Infrastructural Power of Finance: The Case of ECB Support for Repo and Securitization Markets," *Socio-Economic Review* 18, no. 2 (April 2020): 395–418; Greta R. Krippner, *Capitalizing on Crisis: The Political Origins of the Rise of Finance* (Cambridge, MA: Harvard University Press, 2011).
31. Eric Rauchway, *The Money Makers: How Roosevelt and Keynes Ended the Depression, Defeated Fascism, and Secured a Prosperous Peace* (New York: Basic Books, 2015); Sebastian Edwards, *American Default: The Untold Story of FDR, the Supreme Court, and the Battle over Gold* (Princeton, NJ: Princeton University Press, 2018).
32. Block, "Financial Democratization and the Transition to Socialism," in this volume.
33. Woodruff, "Governing by Panic."
34. Ibid.
35. Mark Blyth, Eric Lonergan, and Simon Wren-Lewis, "Now the Bank of England Needs to Deliver QE for the People," *Guardian*, May 21, 2015.
36. Cf. Larry Summers, "Central Bank Independence," prepared conference remarks, September 28, 2017, larrysummers.com.
37. Finn E. Kydland and Edward C. Prescott, "Rules Rather Than Discretion: The Inconsistency of Optimal Plans," *Journal of Political Economy* 85, no. 3 (1977): 477–80.
38. Kenneth Rogoff, "The Optimal Degree of Commitment to an Intermediate Monetary Target," *Quarterly Journal of Economics* 100, no. 4 (1985): 1169–89.
39. Thomas J. Sargent and Neil Wallace, "Some Unpleasant Monetarist Arithmetic," *Federal Reserve Bank of Minneapolis Quarterly Review* 5, no. 3 (1981): 7.
40. Olivier Blanchard, "Public Debt and Low Interest Rates," presidential address, American Economic Association Annual Meeting, Atlanta, Georgia, January 4, 2019.
41. Sebastian Dellepiane-Avellaneda, "Gordon Unbound: The Heresthetic of Central Bank Independence in Britain," *British Journal of Political Science* 43, no. 2 (2013): 263–93.
42. Nicholas Sowels, "The Coalition's Economic Policy of Fiscal Austerity and Monetary Experimentation by the Bank of England," *Observatoire de la société britannique* 15 (2014): 165–88.

43. Chris Giles, "People's Quantitative Easing—No Magic," *Financial Times*, August 13, 2015.
44. David M. Woodruff, "Monetary Surrogates and Money's Dual Nature," in *Financial Crises and the Nature of Capitalist Money: Mutual Developments from the Work of Geoffrey Ingham*, ed. Jocelyn Pixley and G. C. Harcourt (London: Palgrave Macmillan, 2013), 101–23; Bruno Théret, "Birth, Life and Death of a Provincial Complementary Currency from Tucuman, Argentina (1985–2003)," in *Monetary Plurality in Local, Regional and Global Economies*, ed. Georgina Gómez (London: Routledge, 2019), 153–87.
45. Woodruff, "Monetary Surrogates and Money's Dual Nature," 121 n.18.
46. Yanis Varoufakis, "The Promise of Fiscal Money," *Project Syndicate*, August 29, 2017, project-syndicate.org.
47. Giselda Vagnoni and Gavin Jones, "Factbox: How Italy's Mini-BOT 'Parallel Currency' Would Work," Reuters, May 25, 2018, uk.reuters.com; Gavin Jones, "5-Star, League Want ECB to Forgive 250 Bln Euros of Italy Debt—Draft," Reuters, May 15, 2018, dailymail.co.uk.
48. Ambrose Evans-Pritchard, "Restricting QE to Break Rebel Defiance in Italy Is a Dangerous Game," *Telegraph*, May 30, 2018, telegraph.co.uk; Luigi Zingales, "It's Time to Choose Democracy over Financial Markets," *Foreign Policy*, May 31, 2018, foreignpolicy.com.
49. Sarah A. Binder and Mark Spindel, *The Myth of Independence: How Congress Governs the Federal Reserve* (Princeton, NJ: Princeton University Press, 2017), 240.
50. See, e.g., ibid., 212–13. For a general analysis, see Philip Keefer and David Stasavage, "The Limits of Delegation: Veto Players, Central Bank Independence, and the Credibility of Monetary Policy," *American Political Science Review* 97, no. 3 (2003): 407–23.
51. For a revealingly obscurantist response to this episode, see Ben S. Bernanke, "Budgetary Sleight-of-Hand," Brookings blog post, November 9, 2015, brookings.edu.
52. Polanyi, *The Great Transformation*, 233.
53. Philip A. Wallach, "A Trillion Dollar Platinum Coin to Fix the Debt Ceiling; Why Not 100 Trillion!?," Brookings blog post, October 26, 2015, brookings.edu.
54. Block, "Financial Democratization and the Transition to Socialism," in this volume.
55. M. Kalecki, "Political Aspects of Full Employment," *Political Quarterly* 14, no. 4 (1943): 326.

5 Three Modes of Democratic Participation in Finance

1. Jim Pickard, "Hand 10% of Equity to Workers, Labour to Tell Major UK Companies," *Financial Times*, September 23, 2018, ft.com; Dylan Matthews, "Bernie Sanders' Most Socialist Idea Yet, Explained," *Vox*, May 29, 2019, vox.com.
2. John W. Cioffi and Martin Höpner, "The Political Paradox of Finance Capitalism: Interests, Preferences, and Center-Left Party Politics in Corporate Governance Reform," *Politics & Society* 34, no. 4 (2006): 463–502; Stefano Pagliari, Lauren M. Phillips, and Kevin L. Young, "The Financialization of Policy Preferences: Financial Asset Ownership, Regulation and Crisis Management," *Socio-Economic Review* 18, no. 3 (July 2018): 655–80.
3. Other mechanisms could be included here as well. Another, which Benjamin Braun has recently described as infrastructural power, could be also explored. Benjamin Braun, "Central Banking and the Infrastructural Power of Finance: The Case of ECB Support for Repo and Securitization Markets," *Socio-Economic Review* 18, no. 2 (2020): 395–418. This form of financial power entails the logistical entanglements that happen between government and private sector actors, the latter of whom the former depend on for enacting policies.
4. Fred Block, "Financial Democratization and the Transition to Socialism," in this volume, p. 112.
5. This scheme for understanding democratic participation is highly simplified. Archon Fung's work on "the democracy cube" includes a gradational scale for both dimensions and also offers up a third dimension on the authority and power of democratic participants. Archon Fung, "Varieties of Participation in Complex Governance," *Public Administration Review* 66, no. 1 (2006): 66–75. A fuller exploration of the kinds of democratic institutions that would best democratize financial flows would need a more finely grained analysis along the lines that Fung offers. Here, however, I use these distinctions mainly as a heuristic to understand democratic participation in public finance in very broad terms.
6. Susan P. Shapiro, "Agency Theory," *Annual Review of Sociology* 31 (2005): 263–84.
7. Randy Martin, *Financialization of Everyday Life* (Philadelphia: Temple University Press, 2002); Rob Aitken, *Performing Capital: Toward a Cultural Economy of Popular and Global Finance* (New York: Palgrave Macmillan, 2007).
8. G. Baiocchi and E. Ganuza, "Participatory Budgeting as if Emancipation Mattered," *Politics & Society* 42, no. 1 (2014): 29–50.
9. Mark E. Warren and John Gastil, "Can Deliberative Minipublics

Address the Cognitive Challenges of Democratic Citizenship?," *Journal of Politics* 77, no. 2 (2015): 562–74.
10. David M. Estlund, *Democratic Authority: A Philosophical Framework* (Princeton, NJ: Princeton University Press, 2007).
11. Jane Mansbridge, "Rethinking Representation," *American Political Science Review* 97, no. 4 (2003): 515–26; Fung, "Varieties of Participation"; John Gastil, "The Lessons and Limitations of Experiments in Democratic Deliberation," *Annual Review of Law and Social Science* 14 (2018): 271–91.
12. Hockett, "Finance without Financiers," this volume, 79.
13. Ibid.
14. Block, "Financial Democratization and the Transition to Socialism," this volume, 84.
15. Erik Olin Wright, *Envisioning Real Utopias* (London: Verso, 2010), 311–18.
16. Ibid., 315.
17. Ibid., 321.
18. Ibid., 322.
19. Mehrsa Baradaran, *How the Other Half Banks: Exclusion, Exploitation, and the Threat to Democracy* (Cambridge, MA: Harvard University Press, 2015).
20. Thomas Herndon and Mark Paul, "A Public Banking Option: As a Mode of Regulation for Financial Services in the United States," Roosevelt Institute, 2018, rooseveltinstitute.org.
21. Baradaran, *How the Other Half Banks*.
22. Herndon and Paul, "A Public Banking Option."
23. Fred Block and Matthew Keller, "Where Do Innovations Come From? Transformations in the US Economy, 1970–2006," *Socio-Economic Review* 7, no. 3 (2009): 459–83; Mariana Mazzucato, *The Entrepreneurial State: Debunking Public vs Private Sector Myths* (New York: Anthem Press, 2013).
24. Robin Blackburn, "The Corbyn Project: Public Capital and Labour's New Deal," *New Left Review* 111 (2018): 5–32.
25. Angela Cummine, *Citizens' Wealth: Why (and How) Sovereign Funds Should Be Managed by the People for the People* (New Haven, CT: Yale University Press, 2016). While Cummine uses "citizen's wealth fund" and Bruenig and Lansley use the phrase "social wealth fund," "sovereign wealth fund" is the standard in the literature and financial press. Matt Bruenig, "Social Wealth Fund for America," People's Policy Project, 2018, peoplespolicyproject.org; Stewart Lansley, *A Sharing Economy: How Social Wealth Funds Can Reduce Inequality and Help Balance the Books* (Bristol: Policy Press, 2016).
26. Patrick Mathurin, "Sovereign Wealth Funds Search for New Investments," *Financial Times*, August 18, 2018, ft.com.

27. *Financial Times*, "More Ethical Dilemmas for Norway's Oil Fund," March 8, 2018, ft.com.
28. Bruenig, "Social Wealth Fund."
29. Ibid.
30. Tom Kibasi, "Prosperity and Justice: A Plan for the New Economy. The Final Report of the IPPR Commission on Economic Justice," Institute for Public Policy Research, 2018, ippr.org.
31. Pickard, "Hand 10% of Equity to Workers."
32. Toby Helm, "McDonnell: Labour Will Give Power to Workers through 'Ownership Funds,'" *Guardian*, September 8, 2018.
33. Jonas Pontusson, *The Limits of Social Democracy: Investment Politics in Sweden* (Ithaca, NY: Cornell University Press, 1992); Philip Whyman, "Post-Keynesianism, Socialization of Investment and Swedish Wage-Earner Funds," *Cambridge Journal of Economics* 30, no. 1 (2006): 49–68.
34. Nationalized banking is distinct from banking as a public utility in two ways. First, public utilities rely on joint public–private ownership and therefore remain constrained by competition and the profit motive. Second, they are not subject to close day-to-day public management. Gerald Epstein, "The David Gordon Memorial Lecture. Finance without Financiers: Prospects for Radical Change in Financial Governance," *Review of Radical Political Economics* 42, no. 3 (2010): 293–306.
35. Fred Mosley, "The Bailout of the 'Too-Big-to-Fail' Banks: Never Again," in *The Handbook of the Political Economy of Financial Crisis*, ed. Martin H. Wolfson and Gerald Epstein (New York: Oxford University Press, 2013), 644.
36. Costas Lapavitsas, *Profiting without Producing: How Finance Exploits Us All* (London: Verso, 2013).
37. Gerald Epstein, Dominique Plihon, Adriano Giannola, and Christian Weller, "Finance without Financiers," *Papeles de Europa* 19 (2009): 170.
38. Mosley, "Bailout of the 'Too-Big-to-Fail' Banks," 645.
39. Gerald Epstein and Juan Antonio Montecino, "Banking from Financial Crisis to Dodd-Frank: Five Years On, How Much Has Changed?," PERI working paper, 2015.
40. Robert R. Alford and Roger Friedland, *Powers of Theory: Capitalism, the State, and Democracy* (Cambridge: Cambridge University Press, 1985); Kevin Young, "Not by Structure Alone: Power, Prominence, and Agency in American Finance," *Business and Politics* 17, no. 3 (2015): 445.
41. Americans for Financial Reform, "Wall Street Money in Washington," 2018, ourfinancialsecurity.org.
42. Andrew Hindmoor and Josh McGeechan, "Luck, Systematic Luck,

and Business Power: Lucky All the Way Down or Trying Hard to Get What It Wants without Trying," *Political Studies* 61, no. 4 (2013): 834–49.
43. Stephen Bell and Andrew Hindmoor, "The Ideational Shaping of State Power and Capacity: Winning Battles but Losing the War over Bank Reform in the US and UK," *Government and Opposition* 49, no. 3 (2014): 357.
44. Pepper D. Culpepper and Raphael Reinke, "Structural Power and Bank Bailouts in the United Kingdom and the United States," *Politics & Society* 42, no. 4 (2014): 427–54.
45. Stephanie Mudge, "For a First-Person Political Economy: A Comment on Michael McCarthy's Dismantling Solidarity," *Critical Sociology* 45, no. 4–5 (2019): 757–61; Michael A. McCarthy, "The Capitalist Welfare State and Its Causes: A Response," *Critical Sociology* 45, no. 4–5 (2019): 767–72.
46. Charles Lindblom, *Politics and Markets: The World's Political Economic System* (New York: Basic Books, 1977); Fred Block, "The Ruling Class Does Not Rule: Notes on a Marxist Theory of the State," *Socialist Revolution* 33 (1977): 6–28.
47. Jacob S. Hacker and Paul Pierson, "Business Power and Social Policy: Employers and the Formation of the American Welfare State," *Politics & Society* 30, no. 2 (2002): 282.
48. Culpepper and Reinke, "Structural Power and Bank Bailouts."
49. Tasha Fairfield, "Structural Power in Comparative Political Economy: Perspectives from Policy Formulation in Latin America," *Business and Politics* 17, no. 3 (2015): 411–41.
50. The Sanders proposal does not nationalize but rather breaks up any financial institution with total exposure of greater than 3 percent of GDP ($584.5 billion). It also requires insurance companies with more than $50 billion in assets (such as AIG) to report total exposure to the US government and regularly report on the status of financially significant institutions to Congress. US Congress, "Too Big to Fail, Too Big to Exist," 115th Congress, 2nd Session, introduced October 3, 2018, sanders.senate.gov. In Sanders's proposal, J.P. Morgan Chase, Citigroup, Wells Fargo, Goldman Sachs, Bank of America, and Morgan Stanley would each be broken up. These six institutions have more than $10 trillion in assets and account for more than 54 percent of GDP. They have a total exposure that exceeds 68 percent of GDP.
51. Ibid.
52. José Azar, Sahil Raina, and Martin C. Schmalz, "Ultimate Ownership and Bank Competition," 2016, ssrn.com.
53. Block, "The Ruling Class Does Not Rule."
54. Kevin A. Young, Tarun Banjeree, and Michael Schwartz, "Capital

Strikes as a Corporate Political Strategy: The Structural Power of Business in the Obama Era," *Politics & Society* 46, no. 1 (2018): 2–28.

55. Rajeev Syal, "Employees to Be Handed Stakes in Firms under Labour Plan," *Guardian*, September 23, 2018, theguardian.com.
56. Block, "Financial Democratization and the Transition to Socialism," this volume, 113.
57. Peter Drucker, *The Unseen Revolution* (New York: Butterworth-Heinemann, 1976), 1.
58. Michael A. McCarthy, *Dismantling Solidarity: Capitalist Politics and American Pensions since the New Deal* (Ithaca, NY: Cornell University Press, 2017). Today the non-elite hold financial assets in many different ways: mutual funds, 401(k)s, online individual stock and bond trading services like E-Trade, and other personal investment vehicles. In the postwar period, many American thinkers viewed this, wrongly in my view, as a democratization of American capitalism and finance. Taking this view, one could argue that the scope of American financial democracy has indeed been deepened since Drucker wrote. The proportion of households in the US with stock ownership increased from 20 percent in 1983 to 52 percent in 2001. Gerald Davis, *Managed by Markets: How Financed Reshaped America* (New York: Oxford Press, 2009), 213.
59. Adolf A. Berle and Gardiner C. Means, *The Modern Corporation and Private Property* (New York: Transaction Publishers, 1932).
60. For a critique of Berle and Means, see Maurice Zeitlin, "Corporate Ownership and Control: The Large Corporation and the Capitalist Class," *American Journal of Sociology* 79, no. 5 (1974): 1073–119.
61. UK Labour Party, *A National Investment Bank for Britain: Putting Dynamism into Our Industrial Strategy*, report to the shadow chancellor of the exchequer and shadow secretary for business, energy and industrial strategy on implementation, 2017, labour.org.uk.
62. Pepper D. Culpepper, *Quiet Politics* (Cambridge: Cambridge University Press, 2012).
63. Martin Gilens and Benjamin I. Page, "Testing Theories of American Politics: Elites, Interest Groups, and Average Citizens," *Perspectives on Politics* 12, no. 3 (2014): 564–81; Martin Gilens, *Affluence and Influence* (Princeton, NJ: Princeton University Press, 2012).
64. Gilens and Page, "Testing Theories of American Politics," 575.
65. Wolfgang Streeck, *Buying Time* (London: Verso, 2014).

6 "A Modern Financial Tool Kit"

1. We thank the editors and members of the Democratizing Finance conference (Madison, 2018) for helpful feedback. Please direct communications to Sarah Quinn (slquinn@uw.edu), associate professor of sociology, University of Washington, 211 Savery Hall, Seattle, WA, 98195.
2. Adolf A. Berle and Gardiner C. Means, *The Modern Corporation and Private Property* (New Brunswick, NJ: Transaction Publishers, 2009).
3. Albin Krebs, "Adolf A. Berle Dies at 76: Lawyer, Economist, Liberal Leader Aided Presidents," *New York Times*, February 19, 1971; Nicholas Lemann, *Transaction Man: The Rise of the Deal and the Decline of the American Dream* (Farrar, Straus & Giroux, 2019); Jordan A. Schwarz, *Liberal: Adolf A. Berle and the Vision of an American Era* (New York: Free Press, 1987).
4. John McCarten, "Atlas with Ideas," *New Yorker*, January 16, 1943, 23–24.
5. "New Education Is Need. Increased Intelligence and Ability to Think Is Plea," *Morning Oregonian*, June 26, 1912.
6. Lemann, *Transaction Man*, 32.
7. Elliot A. Rosen, *Hoover, Roosevelt, and the Brains Trust* (New York: Columbia University Press, 1977), 198.
8. Ibid.
9. Lemann, *Transaction Man*, 28.
10. For more on Beatrice, see McCarten, "Atlas with Ideas"; and Lemann, *Transaction Man*.
11. Dalia Tsuk, "From Pluralism to Individualism: Berle and Means and 20th-Century American Legal Thought," *Law and Social Inquiry* 30, no. 1 (2005): 179–224.
12. Arthur M. Schlesinger Jr., *The Crisis of the Old Order: 1919–1933, The Age of Roosevelt, Volume I*, Kindle ed. (New York: Houghton Mifflin Harcourt, 2003), 3001.
13. On the publication history of the book, see Robert Hessen, "The Modern Corporation and Private Property: A Reappraisal," *Journal of Law and Economics* 26, no. 2 (1983), Stuart Chase quoted at 273.
14. On Charles Beard's and John Kenneth Galbraith's take on Berle and Means, see Hessen, "The Modern Corporation and Private Property." On John Kenneth Galbraith and Berle, see Lemann, *Transaction Man*.
15. On Berle and the two camps, see Lemann, *Transaction Man*; and Tsuk, "From Pluralism to Individualism." For the New Deal political infighting, see Ellis Wayne Hawley, *The New Deal and the*

Problem of Monopoly: A Study in Economic Ambivalence (New York: Fordham University Press, 1995).
16. Berle and Means, *The Modern Corporation and Private Property*, 8.
17. For a critique, see Hessen, "The Modern Corporation and Private Property." Hessen argues that Berle and Means overstate the difference between property rights of the corporation and other forms of comingled property, and understate the degree of separate ownership and control in other forms of enterprise. For a rejoinder, see Tsuk, "From Pluralism to Individualism": critiques of Berle and Means often work by limiting the contribution to principal–agency dynamics that flow from the separation of ownership and control, and neglect the broader argument about the accumulation of corporate power.
18. As a legal scholar, Delia Tsuk reminds us that Berle and Means were advancing a long-standing progressive legal approach that saw property rights as a social institution secured through state power. Tsuk, "From Pluralism to Individualism"; see also Mark S. Mizruchi, "Berle and Means Revisited: The Governance and Power of Large U.S. Corporations," *Theory and Society* 33, no. 5 (2004); Elisabeth S. Clemens, "The Problem of the Corporation: Liberalism and the Large Organization," in *The Oxford Handbook of Sociology and Organizational Studies: Classical Foundations*, ed. Paul Adler (Oxford: Oxford University Press, 2009), 535–58.
19. Berle quoted in Schlesinger, *The Crisis of the Old Order*, 3050.
20. Richard S. Kirkendall, "A. A. Berle, Jr. Student of the Corporation 1917–1932," *Business History Review* 35, no. 1 (1961); Tsuk, "From Pluralism to Individualism."
21. Raymond Moley, *After Seven Years* (New York: Harper & Brothers, 1939), 18.
22. Rosen, *Hoover, Roosevelt, and the Brains Trust*, 196.
23. On the Commonwealth Club talk, see Davis W. Houck, "FDR's Commonwealth Club Address: Redefining Individualism, Adjudicating Greatness," *Rhetoric and Public Affairs* 7, no. 3 (2004): 259–82.
24. It was *Time* magazine that called *The Modern Corporation* the administration's "economic bible." See Hessen, "The Modern Corporation and Private Property," 279.
25. Moley writes of Berle and other campaign advisers who declined and delayed when offered appointments: "No Elizabeth Bennett ever dodged her Darcy more tantalizingly than some of the men asked to serve by Roosevelt put off their answers." Moley, *After Seven Years*, 123.
26. Arthur M. Schlesinger, *The Coming of the New Deal, The Age of Roosevelt, Volume II* (Boston: Houghton Mifflin, 1988), 432–33.

27. Krebs, "Adolf A. Berle Dies at 76," 40.
28. Lemann, *Transaction Man*, 22.
29. Moley, *After Seven Years*, 18.
30. Schlesinger, *The Crisis of the Old Order*, 10077.
31. Roosevelt quoted in Sebastian Edwards, "Gold, the Brains Trust, and Roosevelt," *History of Political Economy* 49, no. 1 (March 1, 2017): 12–13. Edwards notes not just the importance of experimentation to FDR, but also the centrality of the Brains Trust in implementing this vision.
32. Adolf A. Berle, *Navigating the Rapids*, 1st ed. (New York: Harcourt Brace Jovanovich, 1973), 32–59.
33. Ibid., 33.
34. Ibid., 58.
35. See, for instance, Berle's critique of the proposal from conservative Democrat Bernard Baruch, which focused on corporate bailouts. Baruch saw the role of the government in markets as much more limited beyond times of war than Berle did. To that end, Baruch proposed extensive budget cuts to reduce federal expenditure. For Berle, this would put individuals in a vulnerable position, and was therefore unacceptable. Ibid., 51.
36. On Congressional FDIC plans, see Ronnie J. Phillips, "The 'Chicago Plan' and New Deal Banking Reform" (June 1992), Jerome Levy Economics Institute Working Paper No. 76, ssrn.com.
37. Ibid., 47.
38. Dodd-Frank Wall Street Reform and Consumer Protection Act, 12 U.S.C. § IX.
39. S. 1482, S. 2343, 76th Congress (1939).
40. "Draper Suggests Federal Reserve Small Loans Unit," *Wall Street Journal*, June 3, 1939, 1.
41. "Reserve Advisory Council Opposes Terms of Mead Bill," *Wall Street Journal*, June 14, 1939, 2; "Democrats in Senate Attack Plan to Insure Small Business Loans: Berle's Proposal for New Public Works Finance Group Also Assailed," *Wall Street Journal*, May 31, 1939, 1.
42. Jesse Jones, "To Provide for the Insurance of Loans to Business. (Mead Bill Hearings)," 76th Congress (June 29, 1939), 408.
43. James Stuart Olson, *Saving Capitalism: The Reconstruction Finance Corporation and the New Deal, 1933–1940* (Princeton, NJ: Princeton University Press, 1988).
44. Elliot Rosen, *Roosevelt, The Great Depression and the Economics of Recovery* (Charlottesville: University of Virginia Press, 2005).
45. Turner Catledge, "President Pushes Congress to Enact Loan Program Now," *New York Times*, June 24, 1939; Self-Liquidating Projects Act of 1939, S. 2759 84th Congress (1939).
46. "Debt Deceit Seen by Republicans: Lending Program Denounced as

Device to Circumvent the 45 Billion Limit," *New York Times*, July 26, 1939; "An End of Pump-Priming," *New York Times*, August 6, 1939.

47. Representative Voorhis (CA), Congressional Record 83, 75th Congress (May 11, 1938), 6706.
48. Jerry Voorhis, *Confessions of a Congressman*, 1st ed. (Garden City, NY: Doubleday, 1947).
49. S. 3630, 75th Congress (1938).
50. "To Provide for the Insurance of Loans to Business (Mead Bill Hearings)," S. 3430 75th Congress (March 7, 1938), 433.
51. Voorhis, *Confessions of a Congressman*.
52. Marriner Eccles, "To Provide for the Insurance of Loans to Business (Mead Bill Hearings)," 76th Congress (June 5, 1939), 91. Eccles offered a creative accounting plan that used a surplus from dollar devaluations to ensure that the new corporation would involve "no additional appropriation of public funds and no increase in Budget outlay." Ibid., 93. The corporation was to use $25 million of these funds to insure short-term loans to small businesses. Remaining funds would be capital for the corporation either to make loans of up to $1 million or to insure or rediscount loans made by banks. Altogether, the plan seems to be a scaled-back version of a proposal generated from an earlier committee that included Henry Morgenthau Jr., Jones, Eccles, and Leo Crowley. That earlier plan would create a new industrial loan corporation that would operate completely independently of both the Fed and the RFC, but the Board of Governors rejected the proposal as neither "necessary [n]or desirable," given the existing RFC and Fed programs. Here we see that it was not just Berle who recycled and repurposed the many ideas for reform that circulated at the time. Report of Committee on Credit for Industry to the Interdepartmental Committee on Legislative Matters, *Diaries of Henry Morgenthau Jr, April 27, 1933–July 27, 1945*, 141:248.
53. Eccles, "To Provide for the Insurance of Loans to Business," 96.
54. Interdepartmental Banking Committee Meeting, *Diaries of Henry Morgenthau Jr* (April 13, 1939), 178:288.
55. Ibid., 280, 287.
56. Patricia Waiwood, "Recession of 1937–38" (2013), federalreservehistory.org/essays/recession-of-1937-38.
57. Hawley, *The New Deal and the Problem of Monopoly*, 408.
58. Ibid., 419.
59. Olson, *Saving Capitalism*, 216.
60. Jesse H. Jones and Edward Angly, *Fifty Billion Dollars: My Thirteen Years with the R.F.C. (1932–1945)* (New York: Da Capo Press, 1975), 183.
61. For more on Berle's vision for the state and credit, see Olson, *Saving*

Capitalism, 35–40, 86–91, 118–20; Jones and Angly, *Fifty Billion Dollars*, 183.

62. Olson, *Saving Capitalism*, 236.
63. The First New Deal included a push for a more European-style, corporatist, centralized planning through the National Industrial Recovery Act. That push for European-style planning failed spectacularly, undermined by internal divisions among New Dealers even before the Supreme Court ruled it unconstitutional in 1935. Ira Katznelson, *Fear Itself: The New Deal and the Origins of Our Time* (New York: Liveright Publishing Corporation, 2013); Hawley, *The New Deal and the Problem of Monopoly*; Schlesinger, *The Coming of the New Deal*.
64. Adolf A. Berle, "The Investigation of Business Organization and Practice," Berle Memorandum of Suggestions to the Temporary National Economic Committee, Kiplinger Washington Agency, Berle Papers, File: "708 TNEC Memorandum: 'A Banking System for Capital and Credit,'" FDR Presidential Library, 1938, 21; Berle, "A Banking System for Capital and Capital Credit," Hyde Park, NY, Berle Papers, File: "708 TNEC Memorandum: 'A Banking System for Capital and Credit,'" FDR Presidential Library, 1939.
65. Here Berle provides a somber warning against regulatory capture: "The possibility of perversion or recapture of an agency like the Securities and Exchange Commission, for example, gives pause for thought." Berle, "The Investigation of Business Organization and Practice," 21.
66. Ibid., 25.
67. Berle also notes, in what is perhaps a sly dig at the anti-monopolists, that if one wants to keep business small, simply take away limited liability. Ibid.
68. Ibid., 6.
69. Ibid., 25.
70. Ibid.
71. Ibid., 6.
72. Ibid., 10.
73. Berle, "A Banking System for Capital and Capital Credit."
74. Ibid., 10.
75. For a discussion of the economic viability of the work of Moulton and Berle, see Ronnie J. Phillips, "Bank Credit and Capital Formation: The Heretical View of Harold Moulton and Adolf Berle," working paper, Colorado State University, July 3, 1996, ssrn.com.
76. Berle, "A Banking System for Capital and Capital Credit," 7.
77. Ibid., 9.
78. Ibid., 26.
79. Ibid., 19.
80. Temporary National Economic Committee of the United States,

Investigation of Concentration of Economic Power (Washington, DC: US Government Printing Office, 1940).
81. Berle, "A Banking System for Capital and Capital Credit," 11.
82. Ibid., 13.
83. Ibid., 6.
84. Ibid., 5.
85. Ibid.
86. Ibid., 13.
87. Ibid., 19.
88. Ibid., 13.
89. Adolf Berle, "Investigation of Concentration of Economic Power (Temporary National Economic Committee)," Res. 113, 76th Congress (May 23, 1939), 3832.
90. Olson, *Saving Capitalism*.
91. Katznelson, *Fear Itself*.
92. Ben Protess, Jessica Silver-Greenberg, and Rachel Abrams, "How Private Equity Found Power and Profit in State Capitols," *New York Times*, July 14, 2016.
93. Chris Edwards, "Encouraging Private Infrastructure Investment," 2013, cato.org.
94. *A Study of Federal Credit Programs: Subcommittee on Domestic Finance, Committee on Banking and Currency, House of Representatives, 88th Congress, 2d Session, Volume 1* (Washington, DC: US Government Printing Office, 1964), 5.
95. John Zysman, *Governments, Markets, and Growth: Financial Systems and the Politics of Industrial Change*, Cornell Studies in Political Economy (Ithaca, NY: Cornell University Press, 1983), 76–77.
96. Kevin T. Leicht and J. Craig Jenkins, "Political Resources and Direct State Intervention: The Adoption of Public Venture Capital Programs in the American States, 1974–1990," *Social Forces* 76, no. 4 (1998): 1323–45.
97. United States Office of Management and Budget, *Analytical Perspectives, Budget of the United States Government, Fiscal Year 2020* (Washington, DC: Government Printing Office, 2019).
98. Office of the Special Inspector General for the Troubled Asset Relief Program, "Quarterly Report to Congress, October 26, 2016," sigtarp.gov. See also Jonathan G. Katz, "Who Benefited from the Bailout?," *Minnesota Law Review* 95, no. 5 (2011): 1568–613.
99. On the history and legacy of racial inequality in US credit markets, see especially Melvin L. Oliver and Thomas M. Shapiro, *Black Wealth, White Wealth: A New Perspective on Racial Inequality*, 10th anniversary ed. (New York: Routledge, 2006); Guy Stuart, *Discriminating Risk: The U.S. Mortgage Lending Industry in the Twentieth Century* (Ithaca: Cornell University Press, 2003); David

M. Freund, *Colored Property: State Policy and White Racial Politics in Suburban America* (Chicago: University of Chicago Press, 2007); Douglas S. Massey and Nancy A. Denton, *American Apartheid: Segregation and the Making of the Underclass* (Cambridge, MA: Harvard University Press, 1993); Devah Pager and Hana Shepherd, "The Sociology of Discrimination: Racial Discrimination in Employment, Housing, Credit, and Consumer Markets," *Annual Review of Sociology* 34, no. 1 (2008): 181–209.

100. Karen Kroll, "Kat Taylor: A Beneficial State of Mind," 2016, ababankmarketing.com.
101. During slack periods, the capital credit banks could move their lending more toward short-term and shovel-ready projects. In periods of full employment, lending would be biased toward longer-term development. Berle further proposes dynamically changing interest rates and payment schedules of existing loans during downturns, as a kind of socially managed approach to adjustable-rate loans that shifts risks away from families and onto the state. By providing flexible payment schedules, the banks could allow individuals, businesses, and budget-constrained municipalities to delay payments to maintain employment levels during slumps, which both shortens the slumps and provides stability to families.
102. "RFC Problems," in *CQ Almanac 1949* (Washington, DC: Congressional Quarterly, 1950); "RFC 'Influence' Investigation," in *CQ Almanac 1951* (Washington, DC: Congressional Quarterly, 1952). "Boyle, Gabrielson, and R.F.C.," in *CQ Almanac 1951* (Washington, DC: Congressional Quarterly, 1952).
103. Greta Krippner, *Capitalizing on Crisis: The Political Origins of the Rise of Finance* (Cambridge, MA: Harvard University Press, 2011).
104. Sarah Quinn, *American Bonds: How Credit Markets Shaped a Nation* (Princeton, NJ: Princeton University Press, 2019).

7 Democratizing Finance or Democratizing Money?

1. An earlier version of this paper was published as Mary Mellor, "Money for the People," Great Transition Initiative, Cambridge, MA, August 2017, greattransition.org.
2. Mary Mellor, *The Future of Money: From Financial Crisis to Public Resource* (London: Pluto Press, 2010).
3. Mary Mellor, *Money: Myths, Truths and Alternatives* (Bristol: Policy Press, 2019).
4. See, e.g., Geoffrey Ingham, *The Nature of Money* (Cambridge:

Polity Press, 2004); L. Randall Wray, *Modern Money Theory* (Basingstoke: Palgrave Macmillan 2012); Josef Huber, *Sovereign Money* (Basingstoke: Palgrave, 2017).
5. Michael McLeay, Amar Radia, and Ryland Thomas, "Money Creation in the Modern Economy," *Bank of England Quarterly Bulletin* Q1 (2014): 1–13; Jaromir Benes and Michael Kumhof, "The Chicago Plan Revisited," IMF Working Paper No. 12/202 (August 2012), papers.ssrn.com.
6. Josh Ryan-Collins, Tony Greenham, Richard Werner, and Andrew Jackson, *Where Does Money Come From?* (London: New Economics Foundation, 2011).
7. John Kenneth Galbraith, *Money: Whence It Came and Where It Went* (London: Penguin, 1975), 18–19.
8. Mary Mellor, *Debt or Democracy: Public Money for Sustainability and Social Justice* (London: Pluto Press, 2015).

8 Democratizing Investment

1. Federal Reserve distributional financial accounts, 2020, federalreserve.gov.
2. Though this chapter was written before its publication, this idea bears similarity to Thomas Piketty's proposal for a universal capital endowment in *Capital and Ideology* (Cambridge, MA: Harvard University Press, 2019).
3. Robert C. Hockett, "Finance without Financiers," this volume.
4. Chris Brummer, "Disruptive Technology and Securities Regulation," *Fordham Law Review* 84, no. 3 (2015): 977.
5. Erik Olin Wright, "Introduction to the Real Utopias Project on Democratizing Finance," Real Utopias Project Conference on Democratizing Finance, June 2017, Madison, WI.
6. Since some households own stock directly and indirectly, the two proportions add up to more than 50 percent. Edward Wolff, "Household Wealth Trends, 1962–2013," *RSF: The Russell Sage Foundation Journal of the Social Sciences* 2, no. 6 (October 2016): 24–43.
7. Ibid.
8. Jesse Bricker Michael, Joseph Briggs, Elizabeth Holmquist, Susan McIntosh, Kevin Moore, Eric Nielsen, Sarah Reber, Molly Shatto, Kamila Sommer, Tom Sweeney, and Alice Henriques Volz, *Introducing the Distributional Financial Accounts of the United States*, Finance and Economics Discussion Series 2019–017 (Washington, DC: Board of Governors of the Federal Reserve System, 2019).
9. Federal Reserve distributional financial accounts, 2020.

10. Edward Wolff, "The Decline of African-American and Hispanic Wealth since the Great Recession," NBER Working Paper No. 25198, October 2018.
11. "Accredited," meaning their net worth exceeds $1 million, or their income exceeds $200,000, with an expectation that such income will continue.
12. The definition of "accredited investor" has evolved over the decades. After the Supreme Court decided *Securities and Exchange Commission v. Ralston Purina* in 1953, private offerings were limited to those persons who had "no practical need for [the bill's] application." A private offering was defined as an "offering to those who are able to fend for themselves." Since this broad standard proved to be unworkable as private offerings expanded, the SEC enacted Rule 146 in 1974 to create an objective standard for private-offering investors. The issuer had to believe that the offeree was "sophisticated," which was determined by wealth or knowledge. The issuer also had to have a reasonable belief that the purchaser had assessed the offer and could bear the financial risk of the offer, and the offeree had to receive adequate disclosure about the company.
13. Adolf A. Berle and Gardiner C. Means, *The Modern Corporation and Private Property* (New York: Macmillan, 1932).
14. Julia Ott, *When Wall Street Met Main Street* (Cambridge, MA: Harvard University Press, 2011), 5.
15. Thomas Piketty, *Capital in the Twenty-First Century* (Cambridge, MA: Harvard University Press, 2014).
16. Elizabeth Parisian and Saqib Bhatti, "All That Glitters Is Not Gold," Roosevelt Institute, 2017.
17. Barbara Roper, "Whose Side Is the SEC On?," Consumer Federation of America, 2018.
18. Piketty, *Capital in the Twenty-First Century*.
19. Another available exemption that was improved under the JOBS Act is under Regulation A, which limits companies to raising no more than $5 million in a twelve-month period, but has no wealth litmus test on the type of investors allowed in. Another exemption is under Regulation D, which establishes two separate rules, Rule 504 and Rule 506. Under Rule 504, issuers can offer securities to an unlimited number of accredited investors and a small number of unaccredited investors. Though these new offerings create opportunities for new companies to raise capital, they do not change the structural dynamics of access to investment for the non-wealthy.
20. For a broader discussion of futurist versus incrementalist fintech, see Frank Pasquale, "Exploring the Fintech Landscape," written testimony before the United States Senate Committee on Banking, Housing and Urban Affairs, September 12, 2017.

21. Natascha van der Zwan, "Making Sense of Financialization," *Socio-Economic Review* 12, no. 1 (2014): 99–129.
22. Gordon Mills, Karen McCarthy, and Brayden McCarthy, "The State of Small Business Lending: Innovation and Technology and the Implications for Regulation," Harvard Business School Working Paper 17-042, 2016.
23. Piketty, *Capital in the Twenty-First Century*; see also Piketty, *Capital and Ideology*.
24. Mehrsa Baradaran, "It's Time for Postal Banking," *Harvard Law Review* 165 (February 2018): 165–75.
25. Darrick Hamilton, "Neoliberalism and Race," *Democracy Journal* 53 (2019), democracyjournal.org.
26. William Lazonick, "Profits without Prosperity," *Harvard Business Review* 92, no. 9 (September 2014): 46–55.
27. Lenore Palladino, "Small Business Fintech: The Need for Comprehensive Regulation," *Fordham Journal of Corporate and Financial Law* 24, no. 1 (2018): 77–103.
28. I use the term "Americans" rather than "citizens" deliberately; some mechanism should be used to allow undocumented Americans who are working in the country for some period access to the system.
29. This fund should in no way supplant adequate funding for retirement or Social Security.
30. Fred Block, "Financial Democratization and the Transition to Socialism," this volume.
31. Mark Paul and Thomas Herndon, "A Public Banking Option as a Mode of Regulation for Household Financial Services in the United States," Roosevelt Institute, 2018; Baradaran, "It's Time for Postal Banking."
32. Sabeel Rahman, "The New Utilities: Private Power, Social Infrastructure, and the Revival of the Public Utility Concept," *Cardozo Law Review* 39, no. 5 (2018): 1635.
33. Ibid., 1656.
34. Hockett, "Finance without Financiers."
35. Adam Levitin and Susan M. Wachter, "The Public Option in Housing Finance," Georgetown Law and Economics Research Paper No. 1966550, 2013.
36. Hockett, "Finance without Financiers."
37. Rahman, "The New Utilities."
38. Levitin and Wachter, "The Public Option in Housing Finance."
39. Platforms can look to the SBA loan programs' due diligence or the due diligence required by CDFIs, for example, as a starting point to evaluating the risks posed by any given small business.
40. The experience of, for example, the rollout of the website of the Affordable Care Act means it is not obvious that government can

actually build an effective platform, but the operational constraints should be considered separately from the theoretical constraints.
41. The question of how much wealth a household should be able to risk would be a critical design question in the establishment of the platform.
42. Darrick Hamilton and William "Sandy" Darity, "Can 'Baby Bonds' Eliminate the Racial Wealth Gap in Putative Post-racial America?," *Review of Black Political Economy* 37, no. 3–4 (2010): 207–16.
43. Maury Gittelman and Edward Wolff, "Racial Differences in Patterns of Wealth Accumulation," *Journal of Human Resources* 39, no. 1 (Winter 2004): 193–227.
44. One design question is whether individuals should receive whatever sum their account holds at retirement or if that sum should be adjusted to a longer-term average in order not to unfairly advantage account holders who happen to retire when the stock market is high or disadvantage those who happen to retire when the stock market is low.
45. Lenore Palladino, "Reality Check: Raising Revenue for Structural Reform and Large-Scale Public Investment," Roosevelt Institute, 2017.
46. Hockett, "Finance without Financiers."

Concluding Observations

1. Margaret Somers, "The Moral Economy of the Capitalist Crowd: Utopianism, the Reality of Society, and the Market as a Morally Instituted Process in Karl Polanyi's *The Great Transformation*," *Humanity* 11, no. 2 (Summer 2020): 227–34.
2. Thomas Philippon, *The Great Reversal* (Cambridge, MA: Harvard University Press, 2019).
3. Fred Block, "Beyond the Commodity: Toward a New Understanding of Political Economy," *American Affairs* 4, no. 3 (Fall 2020): 20–47. See also Block, *Capitalism: The Future of an Illusion* (Oakland: University of California Press, 2018), Chapter 2.
4. The advanced manufacturing institutes created by the Obama administration to accelerate new technologies such as 3D printing are an example of such persistence. They gained enough corporate and congressional support to survive the Trump administration's proposed budget cuts. On the institutes, see William B. Bonvillian and Peter L. Singer, *Advanced Manufacturing* (Cambridge, MA: MIT Press, 2017).

Notes for Pages 273 to 274

5. Moreover, once this transition had been completed, Mary Mellor's vision of democratized money could then be on the agenda.
6. Similarly, the Adolf Berle "tool kit" described in the chapter by Sarah Quinn, Mark Igra, and Selen Güler also involves a potentially dangerous level of centralization. In contrast, the proposal developed by Lenore Palladino would work in the direction of decentralizing financial power.
7. This was the theme of an earlier volume in the Real Utopia series. See Archon Fung and Erik Olin Wright, *Deepening Democracy* (London: Verso, 2003).

Name Index

Addams, Jane, 192

Balls, Ed, 154
Baradaran, Mehrsa, 168
Barkley, Alben, 199 Table 1, 202
Beard, Charles, 193
Berle, Adolf A., Jr., 19, 189–200, 202–22, 250
Berle, Adolf A., Sr., 191, 192
Binder, Sarah, 155–6
Bishop, Beatrice Bend, 192, 193, 195, 196
Block, Fred, 19, 24–5, 59, 65, 70, 74, 79, 119, 139, 144, 145, 151–2, 157, 159, 161–2, 165–9, 175, 180, 182, 190, 217–18, 221–2, 223
Borio, Claudio 148
Brandeis, Louis, 192, 194, 196
Braun, Benjamin, 148
Brown, Gordon, 154

Capra, Frank, 27
Caro, Robert, 131
Channing, Edward, 192
Chase, Stuart, 193
Christie, Chris, 125
Churchill, Winston, 2

Clinton, Bill, 44, 95
Coase, Ronald, 194
Commons, John R., 140
Corbyn, Jeremy, 154
Culpepper, Pepper D., 176

Darity, William "Sandy," 263
Deeg, Richard, 101
Douglas, C. H., 85
Draper, Ernest, 200
Drucker, Peter, 181–2

Eccles, Marriner, 199 Table 1, 200, 202–4
Eisenhower, Dwight D., 220

Fairbairn, Carolyn, 180
Faulkner, Louis, 197–8
Fisher, Irving, 49
Floyd, George, 8
Frank, Jerome, 200
Frankfurter, Felix, 206
Fried, Barbara, 140

Galbraith, John Kenneth, 193, 225
Gesell, Silvio, 85
Gilens, Martin, 184

NAME INDEX

Hacker, Jacob, 91
Hamilton, Alexander, 60, 69, 192
Hamilton, Darrick, 255, 263
Hansen, Alvin, 199 Table 1, 201
Hansmann, Henry, 121
Hawley, Ellis, 205
Henderson, Leon, 205
Herndon, Thomas, 168
Hindmoor, Andrew, 175
Hockett, Robert C., 6, 13, 17–19, 80, 92, 119, 138–40, 148, 155, 159, 165–6, 190, 217–18, 221–2, 223–5, 244, 258, 260, 273, 274
Hoover, Herbert, 69, 198
Hopkins, Harry, 200

Jensen, Nathan, 125
Jones, Jesse, 196, 200–6

Kalecki, M., 158
Keller, Matthew, 169
Keynes, John Maynard, 83, 85, 193, 210
Krippner, Greta, 220

La Guardia, Fiorello, 195
Lemann, Nicholas, 192
Lindblom, Charles, 175

Malesky, Edmund, 125
Marx, Karl, 269
Mazzucato, Mariana, 169
McCarthy, Michael A., 17, 19, 119, 218, 220, 271–4
McDonnell, John, 171, 183
McGeechan, Josh, 175
Mead, James, 199 Table 1, 200, 203–4
Means, Gardiner, 190, 193–5
Mellor, Mary, 20
Mendell, Margie, 101

Minsky, Hyman, 98
Mizruchi, Mark, 194
Moley, Raymond, 195, 196
Morgenthau, Henry, Jr., 202, 205
Moses, Robert, 131
Moulton, Harold, 210
Murphy, Liam, 141–3

Nagel, Thomas, 141–3
Nixon, Richard, 125, 151, 202–3

Obama, Barack, 5, 146, 147, 157
Offe, Claus, 121
Ott, Julia, 250

Page, Benjamin, 184
Palladino, Lenore, 20, 119
Paul, Mark, 168
Pepper, Claude, 199 Table 1, 203
Pierson, Paul, 176
Piketty, Thomas, 15, 81, 97, 254
Polanyi, Karl, 85, 140, 143, 156

Quinn, Sarah, 18, 19, 220

Reagan, Ronald, 94
Reinke, Raphael, 176
Rogoff, Kenneth, 153
Roosevelt, Franklin Delano (FDR), 2, 19, 69, 151, 191, 195, 197, 201–2, 205, 215, 250
Roosevelt, Theodore, 194

Sachs, Alexander, 201
Sanders, Bernie, 171, 177
Santelli, Rick, 147
Sargent, Thomas, 153
Schlesinger, Arthur, 193
Schneiberg, Marc, 101
Simmel, Georg, 138
Simon, William H., 18, 274

Name Index

Somers, Margaret, 269
Spindel, Mark, 155–6
Steagall, Henry, 197, 199 Table 1, 202, 211

Thatcher, Margaret, 11, 171
Tsuk, Delia, 194

Varoufakis, Yanis, 84, 155
Voorhis, Jerry, 199 Table 1, 202–3

Wald, Lillian, 192, 196
Wallace, Neil, 153
Weber, Max, 143
Wiesenthal, Helmut, 121
Wilson, Woodrow, 69
Woodruff, David M., 19, 268, 269
Wright, Erik Olin, 11–13, 86, 109, 167, 246, 273
Write, Augusta, 191

Zuckerberg, Mark, 269